The Life and Destruction of Olshan
(Gol'shany, Belarus)

Translation of *Lebn un umkum fun Olshan*

Original Yizkor Book Written and Edited by:

Former Residents of Olshan in Israel (*Irgun Yotzey Olshan*)

Published in Tel Aviv, 1965
(Hebrew, Yiddish and English)

This English Version was
Translated and Edited by Jack Leibman

Published by JewishGen

An Affiliate of the Museum of Jewish Heritage - A Living Memorial to the Holocaust
New York

The Life and Destruction of Olshan (Gol'shany, Belarus)
Translation of *Lebn un umkum fun Olshan*

Copyright © 2016 by JewishGen, Inc.
All rights reserved.
First Printing: December 2016, Kislev 5777
Second Printing: March 2019, Adar II 2019

Translator, Editor and Project Coordinator: Jack Leibman
Layout: Joel Alpert
Image Editor: Martha Forsyth
Cover Design and Olshan Map on page 5: Nina Schwartz
Publicity: Morris Whitcup
Indexed by Kathy Wallach

Published by JewishGen, Inc.
An Affiliate of the Museum of Jewish Heritage
A Living Memorial to the Holocaust
36 Battery Place, New York, NY 10280

The mission of the JewishGen organization is to produce a translation of the original work and we cannot verify the accuracy of statements or alter facts cited.

Printed in the United States of America by Lightning Source, Inc.
Library of Congress Control Number (LCCN): 2016956050
ISBN: 978-1-939561-46-6 (hard cover: 340 pages, alk. paper)

Front cover photos: A cornfield in modern Holszany. Inset: Three tiny dreidels found nearby. Photographs © 2016 by Ilay Halpern.
Back cover photos. Top: The Lemelman family in Olshan, circa 1919. Left to right, Motel, Yehuda, Elka, Golda, Chasha, Nachum, Chana Matla, and Dworja. Photo courtesy of Dayna Chalif, zoeys_mom@yahoo.com
Bottom: A destroyed gravestone is one of many in Holszany. Photo ©2016 by Ilay Halpern.

JewishGen and the Yizkor-Books-in-Print Project

This book has been published by the **Yizkor-Books-in-Print Project,** as part of the **Yizkor Book Project** of **JewishGen, Inc**.

JewishGen, Inc. is a non-profit organization founded in 1987 as a resource for Jewish genealogy. Its website [www.jewishgen.org] serves as an international clearinghouse and resource center to assist individuals who are researching the history of their Jewish families and the places where they lived. JewishGen provides databases, facilitates discussion groups, and coordinates projects relating to Jewish genealogy and the history of the Jewish people. In 2003, JewishGen became an affiliate of the **Museum of Jewish Heritage - A Living Memorial to the Holocaust** in New York.

The **JewishGen Yizkor Book Project** was organized to make more widely known the existence of Yizkor (Memorial) Books written by survivors and former residents of various Jewish communities throughout the world. Later, volunteers connected to the different destroyed communities began cooperating to have these books translated from the original language—usually Hebrew or Yiddish—into English, thus enabling a wider audience to have access to the valuable information contained within them. As each chapter of these books was translated, it was posted on the JewishGen website and made available to the general public.

The **Yizkor-Books-in-Print Project** began in 2011 as an initiative to print and publish Yizkor Books that had been fully translated, so that hard copies would be available for purchase by the descendants of these communities and also by scholars, universities, synagogues, libraries, and museums.

These Yizkor books have been produced almost entirely through the volunteer effort of researchers from around the world, assisted by donations from private individuals. The books are printed and sold at near cost, so as to make them as affordable as possible. Our goal is to make this important genre of Jewish literature and history available in English in book form, so that people can have the personal histories of their ancestral towns on their bookshelves for themselves and for their children and grandchildren.

A list of all published translated Yizkor Books in the project with prices and ordering information can be found at:

           http://www.jewishgen.org/Yizkor/ybip.html

Lance Ackerfeld, Yizkor Book Project Manager

Joel Alpert, Yizkor-Book-in-Print Project Coordinator

JewishGen
Yizkor Book Project

This book is presented by the
Yizkor Books in Print Project
Project Coordinator: Joel Alpert

Part of the
Yizkor Books Project of JewishGen, Inc.
Project Manager: Lance Ackerfeld

These books have been produced solely through volunteer effort
of individuals from around the world. The books are printed and
sold at near cost, so as to make them as affordable as possible.

Our goal is to make this history and important genre of Jewish
literature available in English in book form so that people can have
the near-personal histories of their ancestral towns on their bookshelves for themselves and for their children and grandchildren.

Any donations to the Yizkor Books Project are appreciated.

Please send donations to:
Yizkor Book Project
JewishGen
36 Battery Place
New York, NY 10280

JewishGen, Inc. is an affiliate of the
Museum of Jewish Heritage
A Living Memorial to the Holocaust

Introduction to This Translation

I am a retired physician, now (2016) 88, born in 1927 in Baltimore, living in San Francisco since 1951. I received my B.A. from Johns Hopkins U. in 1947, and my M.D. from U. of Maryland in 1951. Since then, I have been writing intermittently, initially in the scientific area, then more generally, mostly essays, reportage, memoirs, poetry, and a few translations from German.

I knew very little about my family background. But my son, who is much more interested in genealogy than I, had come up with some interesting new information about my father's origins, new to me. He had ferreted out copies of my father's naturalization certificate and his draft registration, which led to additional facts about the actual location of his village in Poland-I had always thought it was in Russia. My father had served in the Russian Army in World War I, and had been wounded. When he came to the US in 1923, he left behind a family, a wife and two sons. Somehow he, his mother and younger sister made their way to Copenhagen, and boarded a ship to America. And the outlines of his subsequent history were fairly clear. He had married my mother in 1926; she had come from a shtetl in Latvia, named Preili. But what about his earlier history in Poland? His shtetl was named Olshon or Olshan, near Lithuania, an area occupied by the Germans in WWI, then for three years by the Russians, interrupted by Cossack raids, then again by the Poles, the Russians, and finally by the Germans. During the Russian interval, my father had been drafted into the Russian army. Then came a momentous finding by my son. He had discovered, from an archive in the NY Public Library, a Yizkor book about Olshan. A Yizkor book is a remembrance volume, dedicated to the history of a town and its inhabitants, and there were many such volumes to honor each small town eradicated by the holocaust.

As I glanced at this volume on-line, I noted that the more Polish name of the town was Holshany, and that there were 580 pages, and it was almost all in Yiddish except for a Hebrew translation at the end. I had learned to read and understand Yiddish in my childhood, and with the aid of some fluency in German, a dictionary and a few consultants, I began to read. I found that I was able to translate most of the material, much of it written in a clear colloquial style, reminiscent of the sounds of my childhood. Of course I hoped to find some mention of my family name, and indeed I came across several brief references, in a list of land plot owners - a pair of brothers perhaps, dated 1929, most likely cousins. The Necrology contained two memorials for at least three with my family name, and also one picture I remembered as the husband of my aunt.

The history described daily life in the *shtetl* of Olshan, before, during and after World War I, the inter-war period and the Holocaust in great detail, enlivened by personal anecdotes about many of the more prominent town inhabitants, often enhanced by nicknames. A final section describes the remarkable odyssey of a young man's career as a partisan. As a result I became engrossed first by the challenge of the translation, then by the remarkable vignettes themselves, culminating in the exciting survival odyssey of a young partisan fighter.

I would like to acknowledge and thank Dr. Sheldon I. Clare for the translation of the Table of Contents, the Necrology and the chapter "The Jews of my Generation." The remainder of the book is my own comprehensive translation.

Jack Leibman

Dedication

Dedicated to the hallowed preservation and memory of the history and tragic end to the prototypic Yiddish *shtetl* of Olshan.

Acknowledgements

Thanks to Eric Leibman, who inspired this project, to The Jewish Community Library, to Yedida Kanfer at the San Francisco Jewish Holocaust Library and to Ken Blady, who assisted in translation.

Special thanks to the National Yiddish Book Center in Amherst, Massachusetts and the New York Public Library for supplying the high resolution images used in this book.

ESTONIA

LATVIA

RUSSIA

| 2012 Border |
| 1940 Border |

BELARUS

0 25 50   75   km

0   25   50   75 miles

LITHUANIA

RUSSIA

VILNIUS •

• **OLSHAN**

1940 Border

• MINSK

BELARUS

POLAND

UKRAINE

Olshan on Map of Belarus

Geopolitical Information:

Gol'shany, Belarus is located at 54°15' Latitude and 26°01' Longitude

Alternate names for the town are: Hal'shany [Belarussian], Gol'shany [Russian], Olshan [Yiddish], Holszany [Polish], Alšėnai [Lithuanian], Halšany, Holshan, Holshani, Olshani, Olszany

	Town	District	Province	Country
Before WWI (c. 1900):	Golshany	Oshmyany	Vilna	Russian Empire
Between the wars (c. 1930):	Holszany	Oszmiana	Wilno	Poland
After WWII (c. 1950):	Gol'shany			Soviet Union
Today (c. 2000):	Hal'shany			Belarus

Jewish Population in 1900: 1,049 (in 1897)

Belarusian: Гальшаны. Russian: Гольшаны. Yiddish: אָלשאַן. Hebrew: הולשאני

In NW Belarus, 12 miles SSE of Ashmyany (Oshmyany), 22 miles SW of Smarhon (Smorgon).

Nearby Jewish Communities:
   Traby 8 miles SSW
   Krevo 12 miles ENE
   Vishneva 12 miles SE
   Ashmyany 12 miles NNW
   Zhuprany 15 miles N
   Dieveniskes, Lithuania 17 miles WSW
   Soly 20 miles NNE
   Smarhon 22 miles NE
   Bakshty 23 miles SSE
   Lipnishki 24 miles SW
   Valozhyn 24 miles ESE
   Iwye 24 miles SSW
   Laibiskes, Lithuania 25 miles NW
   Astravyets 25 miles N
   Salcininkai, Lithuania 26 miles W
   Byenyakoni 26 miles W
   Zaskevichi 26 miles ENE
   Liebiedzieva 28 miles E
   Voranava 28 miles WSW

Notes to the Reader:

Within the text the reader will note "{34}" standing ahead of a paragraph. This indicates that the material translated below was on page 34 of the original book. However, when a paragraph was split between two pages in the original book, the marker is placed in this book after the end of the paragraph for ease of reading.

Also please note that all references within the text of the book to page numbers, refer to the page numbers of the original Yizkor Book.

The original book can be seen online at the NY Public Library site:

http://yizkor.nypl.org/index.php?id=2185

In order to obtain a list of all Shoah victims from Olshan, the reader should access the Yad Vashem web site listed below; one can also search for specific family names using family name option. These lists are continually updated by Yad Vashem, so it is worthwhile to periodically search these lists.

There is much valuable information available on this web site, including the Pages of Testimony, etc.

http://yvng.yadvashem.org

A list of this book and all books available in the Yizkor-Book-In-Print Project along with prices is available at:
http://www.jewishgen.org/Yizkor/ybip.html

The story of the dreidels pictured on the front page can be found at:

www.digitalhistory.uni-bremen.de/summerschool/wordpress/the-story-of-three-dreydls/

Local Administration Building in Golshany

Courtesy of the Center for Jewish Art at the Hebrew University of Jerusalem. Photo by Michael Heifetz, ©1993

Lemelman Family in Olshan circa 1919

From the left: Motel (Morris), Yehuda (Julius), Elka (Ella) married name Nass, Golda (Goldie) married name Alansky, mother Chasha (Ida) maiden name Rabinovitz, father Nochim (Norman), Chana Matla (Anna) married name Siegel and Dworja (Dora) married name Weisberg. The surname was changed to Land in America. Two older children, Natan Leib (Nathan) & Hinda (Helen) married name Schreibman had immigrated to America prior to the photo being taken.

(Photograph courtesy of Dayna Chalif <zoeys_mom@yahoo.com>)

Channa Lemelman with friends in Olshan in 1920

The girl on the bottom at left is the same daughter in the family photo on the previous page second from the right, Channa (Anna) Lemelman. This was likely the final photo taken with her girlfriends before she came to America in 1920.

(Photograph courtesy of Dayna Chalif <zoeys_mom@yahoo.com>)

Yiddish Title Page of Original Yizkor Book

לעבן און אומקום

פון

אָלשַאן

הוצא לאור על ידי ארגון יוצאי אולשאן בישראל

אויסגאבע פון אַלשאַנער לאַנדסמאנשאַפט אין ישראל

אייר תשכ״ה   ★   תל־אביב   ★   מאַי 1965

Translation of the Title Page of Original Yizkor Book

The Life and Destruction
of
Olshan

Published by the Former Residents of Olshan in Israel

_____

Iyar 5725   1965 Tel Aviv   May 1965

Table of Contents

Family Notes

[Page 2]

Book Committee
Executive Committee

Shabtai Kaplan, Ziml Abramovitz, Pesakh Gershonovitz, Shifra Kotin-Trabski and
Reuven Leond, Aharon Shuster

Members

Aharon Abramovitz, Arye Gershoni, Yitzhok Khodosh, Yakok Kozlovski,
Khaniya Yisraeli (Gurvitz), Moshe Ziskond

Editor of Hebrew Part

Meir Shli

[Page 3]

Reception by the Book Committee for Yakov and Batya Kaplan from America
Sitting from Left: **Ziml Abramovitz, Shabtai Kaplan, Batya Kaplan, Yakov Kaplan, Ayre Gershoni, Aharon Abramovitz**
Standing from left: **Khanya Yisraeli, Reuven Leond, Aharon Shuster, Shifra Kotin-Trabski, Yakov Kozlovski, Pesakh Gershonovitz, Moshe Ziskond, Yitzhok Khodosh**

Table of Contents – Page Numbers in

the Original Yiddish and Hebrew Yizkor Book

Types of People and Images

Olshaners in America

In the Years of the Jewish Extermination

אלשאן

Map of Olshan (Gol'shany, Belarus)
on the eve of the Second World War

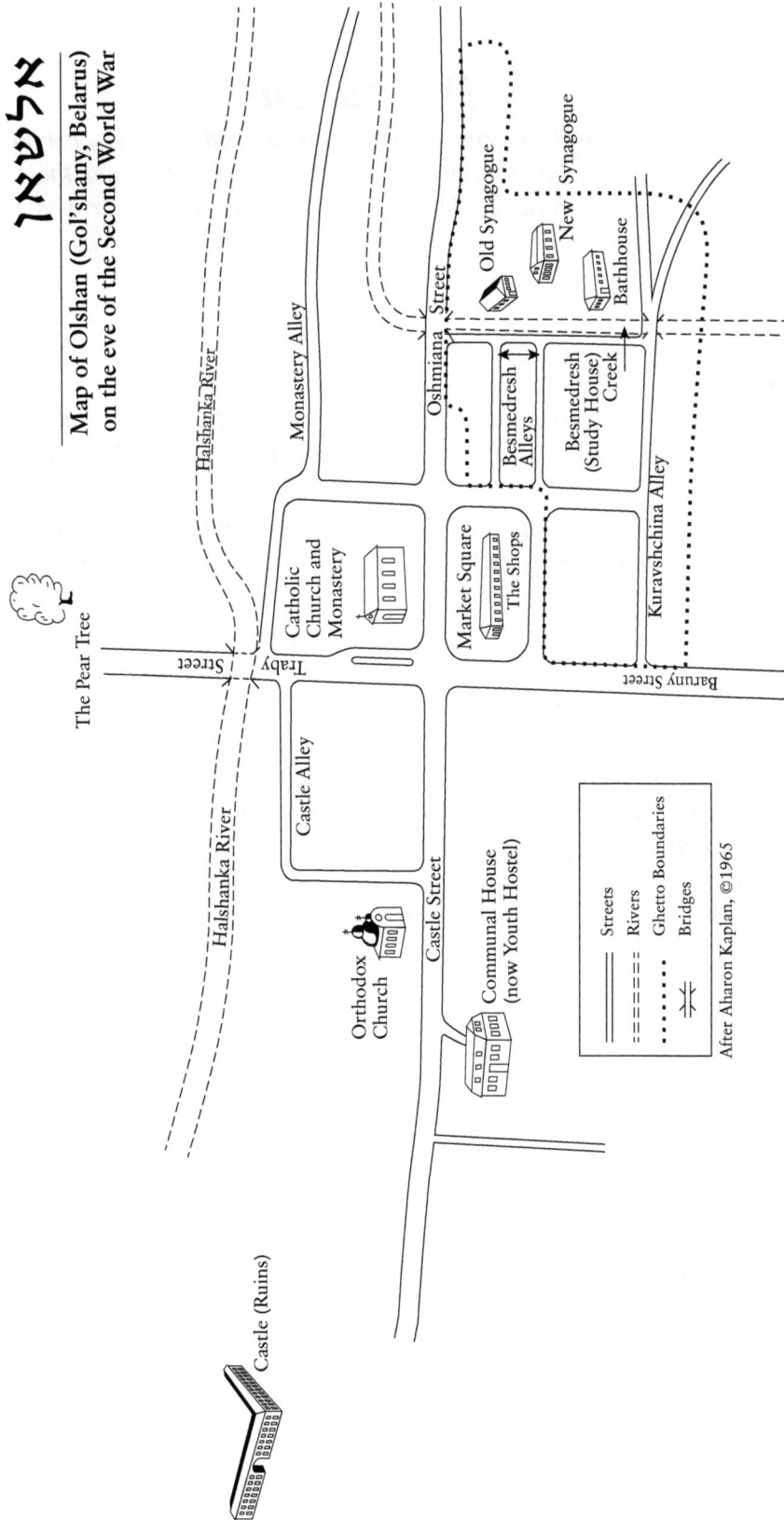

Halshanka River

Monastery Alley

Oshmiana Street

Old Synagogue

New Synagogue

Bathhouse

Besmedresh Alleys

Besmedresh (Study House) Creek

Kuravshchina Alley

Catholic Church and Monastery

Market Square
The Shops

Traby Street

The Pear Tree

Baruny Street

Castle Alley

Halshanka River

Orthodox Church

Castle Street

Communal House
(now Youth Hostel)

Streets
Rivers
Ghetto Boundaries
Bridges

After Aharon Kaplan, ©1965

Castle (Ruins)

[Page 13]

Dedication

Unhealed wounds, ceaseless grief, figures of dear souls-parents, brothers, sisters, women and children, who accompany the shadows by day and their dreams at night-the picture of a brotherly Jewish society which was destroyed by the Nazi murders-all this had inspired the tiny scattered remnants to create for Olshan a memorial book.

We know it is beyond our power to tell it all, despite our longing and memories of everything that's now gone. Could anyone really convey the unspeakable horrors they have seen? Is it possible to portray the reality of a Jewish shtetl in a foreign land where such a spirit was nurtured despite being an expelled people?

But is this possible, cry the survivors, that everything should remain erased, disappeared as if it never existed? Without a memorial, without a grave-stone?

Yet they came together, the few suffering exhausted remnants, heart-broken, each one weeping inside, on this hallowed mission which has become their duty. They won't forget, they can't forget, they will speak from their hearts, their tongues, they will speak to themselves, to their dead ones, their children-each will tell about their fates, especially to their children and to future generations. They do not wish only to lament what they have lost and will never recover or to pour out their bitter hearts, that can never be consoled. This narrative of their experiences is for their children, their children's children and the whole world, to those who have found a safe and peaceful home overseas and those who have found refuge in the free independent Jewish historic home.

May they all know their heritage, and remember that they are children of a people who could not be torn from their roots and their sacred national identity by thousands of years of hostile enmity. In their 3000 year history, including chapters of heroic struggle, chapters of God's grace, up to the last terrible fate, unique in world history, in which so many have perished at the hands of a fanatical enemy intent on their destruction.

And let the children in Israel know and understand that their parents' blood, crying out everywhere, just like their brothers' blood cries out from Israel's land-together these are the price paid for their physical and spiritual freedom, and will always remain as a memorial for the Jewish people.

[Page 17]

The Town of Olshan Until World War I

Historical Notes

The town of Olshan, previously known as *Holshany*, was mentioned as a community in documents from the 15th century. It belonged to Lithuanian Grand Prince Norgmund and Algemindov–Holshanski, thus the name Olshan. The *Algemindov* castle was constructed on a well–designed fortress near the town and was completely destroyed, but the fortress remained. The people called it *Horodishche*.

The local peasants related various legends about this fortress, where annual ceremonies were held. Farmers would dig up pieces of glass and faience and remains of the foundation, but they feared to move these remnants 'because the spirits of the dead princes were watching their property and taking anything might cause some disaster in the whole area.

In mid 15th century, the Holshany property, including the town of Holshany was involved in a quarrel between Sigmund–August and his daughter– in–law Anna, the wife of the Vilner Voyevada Bogdan Sofieh, who had inherited the Olshan property as well as the town of Oshan. Pavel, the son of Voyevada who was the Lithuanian vice chancellor, became the ruler of the Holshan region.

In the 18th century, ownership shifted from the Sofiehs to the Jobis and then to the Korsaks. In the last half of the 19th century the town was bought by Gorbunov. We have no documentation of when the Jews first settled in the old community of Olshan. They were probably there in the 18th century, because there was a significant Jewish population there in the 19th century, which numbered 336 by 1877. According to the census of 1897, there were 2183 inhabitants of Olshan, including 1049 Jews, 48.5% of the total.

"Polski Slovnik Geografitshne", volume 3, which appeared in 1882, describes Olshan at that time: Holshany, a town in Oshman province, near Lake Lusta or Dzhianka, 18 viersts from Oshman, 92.75 vierst from Vilna. The town includes a police station, a public school, a post–office which handles all correspondence, baggage, a Catholic church of St. John, and 2679 inhabitants, 1040 men and 1639 women. The Christians work on the farms or

make woolen goods, sacks or so–called Olshan '*shpenzers*'. The Jews, like everywhere, are busy trading or in brandy sales. The free–spending Olshaners sell more than 10,000 rubles worth of brandy annually. There is also a small brewery which employs five workers; four brewers who serve only Jewish families, one janitor and two loaders.

It is puzzling why the "*Polski Slovnik*" doesn't record the number of Jews, as it did for other towns. So we don't know how to estimate the real numbers of Jews at that time.

[Pages 19-39]

The Jews of My Generation
(memories and records)
by Yakov Kaplan

I belong to a generation which emigrated to America in 1906, at the beginning of this century. I had already had significant life experience. At 14, I had already studied in the *Yeshiva* and was firmly rooted in traditional Judaism, and then I broke away from the religious life, progressing to the broader world of Hebrew and Yiddish literature.

These were the popular names among the young people of the town. Not many of my generation remain. I will try to recall some episodes and vivid personalities and revive some images of Jewish life in Olshan.

The Exterior Appearance of Olshan

The town of Olshan lies between two hills, as if lost from God's attention. On one side, up to Drum–Tzu, flows a sluggish little stream [maybe it's cleaner now], flanked by weedy grasses since primeval time. One day along came Leib the miller, who hammered together some branches, created a channel and utilized the water power for the large mill, grinding out the flour for the local peasants.

On a summer *Shabbos* after dinner, the Jewish men, their wives and children strolled and filled up Trober Street, singing popular songs of the day. Like men with status, they paused in front of the mill. The wheel rotated and splashed against the setting sun and broke into sparkling rays. When it became darker, the younger folks gathered on the other side of the mill. There a group was singing, providing opportunity for enthusiasts to take off their caps and boots, and for enamored couples to flirt, out of the public eye. Only when the stars came out did they all get up– it was time for *Maariv* [evening prayers].

On weekdays, both young and old bathed in the river. They engaged in contests to see who could swim faster to the mill. The great cathedral was surrounded by many stalls; the vendors waited until Sunday, when the peasants from the nearby villages brought in their wares: flax, roof thatch, pig skin, chickens and eggs. On Sundays, the market was busy. Bearded Jews, women with scarves around their heads shop, examine the chickens, and bargain. The stalls are filled with wares. The church bells are ringing, horses are prancing, drunks are quarreling just like their fathers did. Merchandise is spread out on the tables: candles, graters and other metal wares made by Naftali the metal worker. At his place in the market Chatzkl the *shamesh* [synagogue warden] sells his torts, *taiglach*, [honey–dipped confection] honey cake and candies.

Next to the Olshan market was the place for the women peddlers. Sweating in summer they sat by their bundles and chatted. In winter, next to a pot over glowing coals, they wore old worn–out clothes, head wrapped in rags. They dealt mostly in greens or fruit recently harvested, so that their menfolk might sit in the shul studying Torah, getting ready for a seat in Paradise, if they survived for 120 years.

In Olshan the Jews made their living from the markets and small businesses. The local peasants brought produce into town, fruit, pigskin, housewares, etc. The merchants and shoppers bought these products or bartered in exchange for other products, and sent them to Vilna. The peasants also made their purchases at the Jewish stalls. There was one other profitable enterprise especially for women, namely selling geese. They tied them so they couldn't move much, then stuffed them so they'd get fat and sold them. An offshoot business was feather plucking. The children enjoyed the gravy. After preserving the schmaltz it was poured on the gravy for the children to enjoy.

In Olshan there were also craftsmen–shoemakers, tailors, most of whom worked alone. A few of these experts even employed apprentices, and they would work late into the night, especially when it was necessary to dress up for the holidays. There were also those who hunted in the forest for greater incomes. In my time, the youth of these professional craftsmen didn't have much status. A craftsman in the family was considered a necessity. Mothers wanted their talented children to become 'people', to become Torah lovers and scholars.

Torah and Daily Life

Like most Jewish towns in Lithuania and Poland, in those times, Olshan had traditional institutions including a *Beys Hamidrash*, several societies, a prayer group, a *Talmud Torah* for poor children who couldn't afford tuition, a public bath and a *Mikveh*.

In my day, Olshan featured great teachers, Kollel activists who were leaders in troubled times, who resisted the wild demands of the Tzarist Pristov, an enemy of Israel. Certain members of the community were punished by deposing a rabbi who was not allowed to read from his prayer book on Shabbos, until the state official compensated for the damage done to a Jew in Areman, and the congregation wouldn't agree to a fund to support orphans.

The shuls in Olshan were filled with enthusiasts, who prayed fervently. A big celebration was held whenever a new chapter was read from the Torah. Young and old danced in the streets when the new book was carried into the shul. In the same way, weddings were celebrated. Everyone was jubilant, because all the Jews in town were related.

Olshan Jews had their own special religious traditions, based on the 'Jerusalem' creed from Vilna. The small-town Jews, merchants or shoppers, thirsted for higher values, and the villagers consistently sought sons-in-law who were Torah scholars. When Avrohom Yedidias had accepted a son-in-law for his daughter Golda, it was rumored that he was a brilliant scholar. When he was called up to the Torah, he delivered a magnificent very impressive reading, which, it was said, was a masterpiece. He had combined Torah with knowledge. Isaac Hertz the tailor had gotten his son-in-law from the Voloshin Yeshiva. Of course, not all were scholars who could be acknowledged at this level. In those days, 60–70 years ago, there were wealthy, middle class and poor people in town.

So what was it like for the average Jew in Olshan? The home consisted of a large four-cornered room, with a dried earth floor. On holidays, this was decorated with yellow sand. A quarter of the dwelling was taken up by beds with straw mattresses. The adults and children slept in this bedroom, as in Avrohom Reisen's song, "*A Gezindel zalbe Acht*". Much of the room was taken up by a large stove. [In upper class homes, this was ringed by white benches.] Near the stove was a bench where ten people could sit, and at night it served as a bed. In winter it was comfortable and warm.

In the long winter evenings, parents, children and friends sat and told stories about the good Jews who had been rescued through prayer and fasting, and who had defied a decree. They also told worldly stories, of a girl who had been thrown out by her parents, because they objected to her intent to marry her beloved, so she killed herself. The demonic spirits who occupied the bathhouse near the Beys Hamidrash prayed during the night, and disappeared at dawn at the first rooster's crow– these were old traditions fostered by the average Olshan Jews.

Olshan also had many talented people. Chaim Gelkes, all skin and bones, had cut out a large crown decorated with leaves, to honor the coronation of the last Nicholas. My mother Liebe, the dyer, had sewn little colored tassels, woven by peasant women. She was outspoken in shul; on holidays she sang Zunser's songs. Her remarkable fantastic tales about saints who could separate the righteous from the devils and spirits, were famous in the town, stories retold for hundreds of years, now re-animated by her talents. Moshe the butcher, red-headed with a dignified face had been ordained as a rabbi, and settled in the shtetl Bal-Kicho to make a living. He was the father of the writer and co-editor of the New York 'Daily Morning Journal', and son-in-law of Shalom Aleichum–Ben Zion Goldberg.

The Tinkevitz Genius

I remember old Rabbi Moshe Shimcha Rabinovitz, called the Tinkevitz genius, bearded, a great advocate for good deeds, who knew nothing of worldly conflict. He was deeply religious, a great scholar. When he learned a page of Gemorah, he didn't use any reference, even Rashi. His fellow students imitated him, but didn't understand a single word. However in his comments, he thought they understood the same as he. He radiated benevolence and holiness. In the course of the year, he read only one sermon, on 'Shabbos tshuvah'. He didn't have a clear knowledge of the ritual, but he spoke out with special clarity words with religious content such as repentance, compassion, and the Holy Name. Most of his audience didn't really listen to him, but they spontaneously stood up to honor such a Talmud scholar, when he came off the pulpit.

On Friday nights, we had a minyan in the rabbi's house; we were cousins. After prayers, we talked about politics. In the Rabbi's house, the 'Hatzfirah' had already arrived, and he, the *Tzadik*, didn't see any conflict with his piety and faith.

Once a woman with a young child came to Olshan, and she locked themselves in the Beys Hamidrash. The little girl started squawking like a chicken. It was said she had been taken over by a Dybbuk. Some money was collected in the shtetl so that they might be helped bosom Jewish authority. When the old rabbi, Mordechai of Oshman, arrived at the shul, he saw how the child was being tortured by the Dybbuk. He told the mother to slap her hands and order her to stop being foolish.

When a notice was posted in the Olshan shul signed by r' Chaim Brisker, addressed to the whole congregation, warning against mounting any National collection boxes because that conflicted with the order of r' Meyerl Bel–Hanes , the Olshan rabbi tore down the notice, proclaiming, "Rev Chaim was in charge in Brisk, but I am in charge in Olshan."

It was rumored that the old rabbi had become a Zionist. When we Yeshiva boys told about this in our classrooms, everyone roared with laughter– it was unbelievable that such a great Tzadik could be a Zionist.

Holidays and Shabbos in the Shtetl

In Olshan on the eve of Pesach, the sun is warming. It is Spring, deep blotches appear on the snow. The bakers have already kashered their ovens. All the laborers are hard at work. Pious Jews on their carts are bearing sacks of flour to bake certified matzo. Near the clear little stream, young girls polish copper pots with cloths, then take them to the bathhouse, to have steaming hot embers thrown in the water to kasher everything for Pesach. On Seder night, the streets are empty. All Jewish families are sitting at their holiday tables. At the head sits the father in his elevated seat, wearing his tallis. The great epic drama of the Exodus from Egypt is related in the family circle. The singing of the Hagodah is heard from every home and echoes in all the streets and alleys of Olshan.

Every holiday is certainly observed. During Purim, the children, then the Yeshiva boys perform theater, presenting Mordechai with his long beard and Esther, 'the young girl from Shoshan'. On Shavuos, the young folks gather greenery, to decorate the homes with the beauty of the forest and field, since Shavuos is the feast of regeneration, when fruits ripen in Israel. On Shavuos night we youngsters go to shul to read Tikkun Shavuos. It is the festival of the giving of the Torah and we wait with eyes closed for the heavens to open to reveal the future.

My Home

As I write these memories I'm in a room where a TV stands in the corner, and on the screen I see the American cosmonaut flying into outer space. In the next room is a kitchen with a refrigerator, an electric oven, and another half–dozen electrical gadgets, to assist the American housewife. She has time to read books, relax, rest, and not work hard at cooking like her Bubbe in Olshan. Now I imagine how difficult it is to reflect on my life and experience during childhood in Olshan and bring out the Jewish experiences from those times and those Jews who will be immortalized by my remembrances in our memorial book.

I was born in Volovike, a little town near Olshan. In those days, the smell of the night lamps in a house meant you had arrived into a civilized place. In those days we still used a candle stuffed into a crack in the wooden wall of the house for our illumination. My duty as a 4 year old was to cut off the charred end of the candle so it wouldn't burn out. In the town there were two Jewish families, mine and Nachman, a nice family, supported by an inheritance. Nachman also dealt in horses. Our home was in the center of town, with a roof of straw. My mother was busy, and father helped make a living by sewing ' *bagdim*', skins for the peasants.

After the Tsar's edict decreed that Jews could not dwell in the towns, we were forced to leave Volovike. I recall how we gathered together our belongings, loaded them on to a wagon and rode into Olshan. I was five then, my mother held me by the hand. So, on foot, we walked into the shtetl on Oshman street, direct to the market. A new world opened up for me. The huge market place, on one side was surrounded by several two–story houses, and the stalls on the other side were laden with all sorts of goods.

My Mother the Family Support

My mother Feina Liebe supported the family. When we left Volovike for Olshan she went off to Vilna and learned how to dye garments. She became noted as 'Feina the Dyer Lady'. Peasants from the towns brought in their own woven materials to my mother and she transformed them into various vivid colors.

It was a hard life. Alone she had to drag the water from the fountain near the Rev's house, while father spent weeks away in the town. Mother also dragged the heavy barrels of water needed to warm on the oven.

Children Years and Cheder Learning

I became an Olshaner, and started cheder, taught by Elia the Borovik [in Olshan everyone had a nickname]. He was an angry teacher, who sometimes used the stick but also knew how to evoke a child's ambition to be first in class. He didn't promise the children any immediate benefits like a piece of candy but told them it was a *'Mitzvah'* to be first in class, and one would get eternal honor, as well as a piece of candy in the future for the top student.

We also benefited from the goat's products. Every morning, mother drove the goat to market, and that produced milk for the family. A shepherd with a stick and a whistle took the goat and led it out of town to the pasture. The blow of the stick, the melody of the whistle, the bleats of the goats and cows always distracted me so that I was late for class thus wasting part of my chance for fame.

The years passed, we studied in the cheder from dawn to night. When we went home at night, the stars were sparkling above, and we lit our way with lanterns made from materials with fantastic colors. When we learned *Chumash*, we experienced these biblical figures and their deeds. We felt we were with Eliezer Svita, wandering together with him to Arm Naharaim to find a bride for Isaac; we crawled in the water up to our necks until Moses parted the sea; at Mount Sinai we gratefully received the Torah.

At that time I was very religious and followed all the laws [mitzvahs]. I owned a little mirror, an important item in my childhood possessions. I had left it in my pocket while going from shul on Shabbos. After a struggle between good and evil I left it on the street, because on Shabbos one must not carry anything. But we also played like children of our age. The girls played at drawing in classes. We distinguished ourselves by hopping on one foot, and played with sticks. In this game, one lays a stick on two stones. With a cut off board, the stick is flipped into the air to be caught by one of the players.

Our greatest success was with the *Shli–Shlach* game, because here was a chance to show off skill and physical strength. Two armies opposed each other, and saying 'Shli–Shlach', declared war. The soldiers attacked in order to break through the ranks of the other side to win the battle.

Today, the Passover games are played with assorted nuts in a cap, the daily games with buttons of all forms. My brother became a 'button millionaire'. He won a collection of various sizes, forms and colors–red, green,yellow–worth a fortune!

When it was warm in the month of Tamuz, we all marched to the pond and jumped naked into the water, made waves and had fun chasing each other. In another game we imagined the little pond was a great ocean and we pretended to be creatures in its depths.

And that's the way the childhood years passed in Olshan. And now I was a Gemora student, learning from Moshe Elieh, the Gemora teacher. There were several levels; I was ambitious and quickly rose to the highest rank. Besides Gemora, Moshe Elieh taught other chapters from the Hebrew literature. To this day, the teaching of Moshe Elieh and his face remain in my memory, how he swayed his body, shaking the bench on which we sat. With a sweet sad *Niggun*, he sang the song of Joshua's rod,"Woe to all you sinners". And we actually visualized his tirade against the people.

In those days I became deeply rooted to the world of teachers, of yeshiva boys. It was a grand event for me when Reuben Katz came from the yeshiva and presented a beautiful *Pilpul Drash*, a talmudic discussion, much of which I didn't understand. There was joy that such a large group had come from Olshan; mothers who had sent their children to the yeshiva looked with happiness at this 18 year old dark skinned boy who had swum through the Talmudic sea with such skill. His father Simon Italas had also been a great teacher. Katz listened several times to my Gemora recital.

The Spiritual Change in My Life Later

When I was 19, I started to read books, which I used to buy from a dealer. He laid out his wares on a table at the shul, offering various holy books and also short novels and other writings of those times. The Dreyfus Affair was then going on in Paris and a paper had come out describing all the details of what had happened to Captain Dreyfus. We took all this in avidly. We went on to read Mendele Muter Sforim and one evening I read it for my mother until she fell asleep.

And that's how my life started to change. My friends and I started to think that besides *Tanach*, Talmud and *Midrash*, there was another side to being Jewish, a great and interesting world. We were more mature and started to get interested in social problems, and national Jewish history. We were also shocked by the Kishinev pogrom of 1903.

Bialek's "*Moshe Nemirov*" in which he exhorted Jewish youth to self-defense had not reached us yet. But we received a letter from Gitel Isaacs from New York, containing clippings from a Jewish newspaper [the *Forwards*?], with pictures showing how New York Jews reacted to these events. There were speeches by Jacob Schiff, the prominent Jewish banker, and quotations from other highly placed American officials angrily attacking the Tzar for having allowed this. Later there were mass demonstrations with signs "down with the Tzar and his pogroms".

In those days messengers started coming to Olshan who spoke about the newly arisen Zionist movement, about Herzl, and the first Zionist congress. The rabbi excused us from cheder and we went to the shul to hear a speaker from Vilna. He gave us the news about Hersh Lekertz shooting the governor of Wall, who had beaten and shamed the Jewish revolutionary youths who had organized the first united May Day demonstration.

And that's how the first spiritual changes occurred in the lives of the Jewish youth of Olshan.

A teacher, I think his name was Levinson, taught us Yeshiva boys about the new Hebrew literature. He set out for us 'Mshabbos Lshabbos', a weekly paper by Nachum Sokolov which had been printed in *Hatzfirah*. Our teacher was attracted to Sokolov's language virtuosity, in which the Mishna and Midrash were expressed in a modern newspaper style, which would perhaps clarify the daily events of politics and history and the new currents of modern European literature. We read the *Hatzfirah* with great interest, and books from the new Hebrew literature. The new books resounded together with the Gemora– we didn't feel as sharp a conflict with the traditional teachings as in other settings.

We were inspired by the modern Hebrew style of Reuben Brainen, became familiar with 'Al Parshas Drochim' by Achad–He, who was more interested in *Sholes Hay'hudas* than in *Shalos Hayehudim*. The greatest influence on us was Peretz Smolenski with his 'Hatueh Bdarchi Hachaim' which cleverly featured our yeshivah boys life. He influenced us to look within ourselves to develop some certain goals.

Avrohom Mapu, with his 'Ahavos Zion' inspired us with Tanach style, to become ambitious, and had awakened us to a love of Zion. We read the Hebrew press but at the same time we read "The Friend", a daily Jewish paper, published in Petersburg. The yeshiva boys took to reading Yiddish and were captivated by the new Yiddish creations, by the Yiddish and classic literature. Even mimeographed illegal sheets were brought in.

In Ramailah's Yeshiva in Vilna

After the holidays, the yeshiva boys scattered, to Radin, to Voloshin, Telz, and I went to Vilna. The cart driver sat me on top of his wagon, piled high with merchandise like on a house boat. It was a cold night, the sky was glittering with a million stars. My feet felt like pieces of ice. The driver wrapped them in a blanket, otherwise they would have frozen.

I arrived in Vilna at the Ramailah yeshiva. I spent a lot of time in the library, yeshiva, and studied Gemora, a little Russian, arithmetic, geography, history and other subjects. There my thirst for knowledge developed. I spent a lot of time in the library and read books too difficult for a 15 year old, like 'Conventional Lie' and 'Paradox' by Max Nordau in Hebrew translation. I became attached to the works of the German philosophers Kant and Schopenhauer and read about Spinoza and his philosophical heresy.

The yeshiva boys' lives began to change. Many of them started to work. They had gotten instructions on teaching Hebrew, others got jobs as student teachers, usually from rich neighbors, who wanted their children to know more about Jewishness than a little bit of Hebrew prayer. I took such a position with a rich merchant in the town, not far from Vershbalova and I taught his sons Chumash, Rashi and a little Hebrew.

"Bund" and Zionism

It wasn't easy for these yeshiva boys to adjust and we tried to find a way for ourselves in the ideas and arguments of those days, at the start of this century. The old ideas of our fathers had become remote, and the new ideas of the *Haskala* were a mish–mash of thoughts, violent words, nothing useful to put your hands on.

A girl from Vilna came to Olshan and told us about Hirsch Lekert who had fired on the Vilna governor because he had punished the demonstrators on 1 May. That led to talk of a workers union, and that's what arose in Olshan, the "Bund".which attracted a few of the yeshiva boys and the poor student teachers, who had experience working long hours in the cramped shops of the shoe–repairmen and the tailors. In those days I was a Zionist and sold shekels to the workmen. When I asked Lazar, who had been learning tailoring from Avrohom Isaac, to buy a shekel, he declined. He took out a book from his pack, "*A World with Planets*", and turned to me with the words, "Now I know everything about how the world was created. There is no god. We must throw off our chains of slavery". That's what he told his boss Avrahom Isaac. Lazar had fought against Avrohom Isaac's authority against his prayers. He wanted to throw all his past away.

Conspiratorial conferences were held in a house in a distant corner of the town. There were sharp discussions between the S.S. (soviet socialist), the Zionists and the 'Bund'. This is how these meetings took place. After sunset, all of us, Zionists and Bundists went immediately to the '*Zostzienik*', a meadow. A little path climbed up from the town. Both sides were surrounded by wild grasses and a little forest.. That's where the boys had their discussions, and also some flirting with the girls.That's how it started in my time. I closed my Gemora and became a revolutionary. In my house the 'arsenal' was hidden, mostly revolvers, while we waited for the next pogrom. I collected money from the bosses in town for self–defense. For this sacred task I dressed up in a jacket and on my hat was a ribbon. In demanding money, I didn't beg, only threatened. Later, they told my mother they hadn't expected that "your Yankl, so quiet and studious should become such a firebrand." At that time I belonged to the S.S., which held that Jews must find a place, a territory, not necessarily Eretz Israel. My assignment was to collect money to buy arms for the forest people.

The First Strike (*Zabastovke*) In Olshan

Eruv Pesach in Olshan. the shoe store and the tailor's place were cluttered with preparations. Really a big deal! Yom Tov Pesach, commemorates the exodus from Egypt. Everyone saves up scrupulously for new clothing for the children of the angels, and also for themselves.

Several apprentices were working at Bruch the tailor's. Some were advanced and were supposed to become masters; others were just beginning. Bruch the tailor was not rich; at his tailor shop; he developed other business. He dealt in cedar, and he bought cloth from the peasants to send to Vilna. He was also not such an expert. The tailor apprenticeship lasted three years. In the first year, the apprentice learned little of the trade, he weighed the material, he carried out the remnants, cared for the sod in the summer. Only in the second year was he allowed to handle the material and by the end of the third year he was a master apprentice. The trainees didn't know any limits on their work hours. Sometimes they worked all night.

Among the yeshiva boys who became revolutionaries, was the son of Bruch the tailor. He had just finished the Ramailah class and came to Olshan. He organized the first strike in Olshan, and it was in his father's washroom. There remains in my memory a picture.

It was 1 AM.The yeshiva boys who had come to Olshan to celebrate Pesach with their families were going to study all night. But some of them had with them their text books of Russian grammar, and the '*Bauer*' in German by Moshe Mendelson. The purpose was to learn the German language so they could be accepted into a Swiss university. In a corner the tailor's son. thinks and plans. He looks in his bag for a mimeographed sheet he had gotten in Vilna. He reads and whispers with his closest friend. They decide to close down Bruch's night shift. The two friends went to Bruch's washroom. On the way they met Freydel the cantor's daughter, a seamstress, a Bundist, who had just arrived from Vilna. It was rumored in the town that Bruch's talented son was almost ready to be ordained and had been walking around with the attractive cantor's daughter.

All three went to Bruch's laundry room and at 2 AM, they signaled the apprentices with a whistle, that they had to tear apart their work. They knew about this ahead of time so they were already outside and had left their work.. Bruch the tailor didn't understand what was happening. He ran outside without his coat, in his *talis–koton* and saw an unbelievable sight. His own son stood there, whistle in hand, and declared loudly " You workers are the makers of all this." Bruch exclaimed, "My god, what I see is that I won't be able to finish the work. God in heaven, my own child has destroyed my Holiday!"

Bruch woke his wife Esther, to see who was leading the apprentices astray. When Esther saw this, she fell into a faint, as one related later in the town. That dawn, when the drowsy Olshan Jews came to the market–place to open their stalls, they heard the news, that a strike had occurred at Bruch's tailor shop–and their new clothes could not be sewed for Pesach.

The young folks drove in from the big cities. That Pesach had been historic in Olshan. Police patroled the town. It had been a disrupted holiday; in Olshan had occurred the organization of the "General Jewish Worker Union, of Lithuania, Poland and Russia ".

The 1905 Revolution Against the Tzar's Rule

The revolution against the Tzar did not spare Olshan . The whole land was on strike and there was a demand for a constitution and a democratically elected parliament. I was then an activist in the S.S. organization. We had declared the way, an important beacon to affect the course of the revolution. We issued decrees; no one was to enter or leave Olshan, no one was to work, bake bread, conduct business until the revolutionary Tribunal, as we called it then, said the strike was over. I wrote up these points and posted them in the shul and the market place.. We locked down the Monopol, the state–run brandy store, organized a demonstration in the market, set up platforms where speakers could clarify the edicts. There were cries, *"Down with local government, Down with pogromists, Long live Free Russia"*. The speakers were surrounded by our *Bayevoi Otriad*, combat companies, that protected them from attacks by the police and their agents.

We argued a little, fought over the questions of "here" or "there", i.e. whether to uphold Jewish life here, or emigrate to Eretz Yisroel, to create a Jewish national home there. The Bundists maintained that Marxist principles did not justify a Jewish National Home outside of Russia. Since we already have a home, we need only fight for freedom. In my opinion we were influenced by Joshua and other heroes, and that we must defend the repressed and downtrodden. The yeshiva boys of Olshan had more common sense and followed the heroes rather than the Marxists whose works we hadn't read.

The Yeshiva Boys of That Time

These are the Yeshiva boys of those days, inscribed in my memory.: Old Reishke, tall and generous, a good student like the others. He had noted the negative aspects of our new laws and discussed the contrast in schoolboy style with the other boys. Pesach Chaim later became a fighter in Israel. Both died in N.Y. Lazar the sad shoe–maker's son, died in a yeshiva in 1904. Reuben Mshalas, a dandied –up, handsome lad, a boss's son chose to stand with us, the poor class.

From the yeshiva I remember Nashke Geles, a fine conversationalist; he knew how to gain entry, to establish a relationship and to win sympathy. Thanks to him we lived in a fine house, furnished by a rich Vilna Jew. He had left for a dacha for the whole summer. This became a camp for talented children who were imbued with Jewish ideals.

Avrahom Chaim, the cantor's son, was not inspired by the times. He had a fine voice and became a cantor somewhere in Lithuania.. Bruch Gershon had worldly interests, he became a professor and got married. When I departed for N.Y., I saw him, with tallis and tefillin in his arm, walk into the shul, with sure tread, just like a prosperous official in the town. We regarded him with some envy. Oshram, a brother of Motel from Ashman Street became an Olshan expert, settled in Minsk and was active in the social revolutionary movement. Together with the great Gershon, he was a sick man who came home to convalesce. During the short time he was in Olshan, he set up a camp for the perpetrators of the strike, who were penalized by being forced to whitewash the walls. He was an extraordinarily noble and ethical person. Chaim Leib (see below) also he helped us a lot and he died too young.

Toviah Isaacs had been renowned as a scholar. In 1904 he got ready with his family to join his father in NY. He suddenly became ill with typhus. I'll never forget his enthusiasm in the heat of summer, his fantastic willpower for his voyage to America. After the voyage over stormy seas, his father could hardly recognize him and brought him to a home in NY. There he learned a trade, later became a manufacturer, employing hundreds of trainees. He climbed higher and higher, became rich and famous. Everything that Toviah had imagined during the heat in Olshan came true. He eventually became a shirt manufacturer. He died young–he hadn't foreseen that, when he was delirious with fever.

I remember Moshe Yose Michles, when he was still a only a sentimental argumentative boy. He was a believer, but also a doubter. At age 9 he asked questions; whether the Tzadiks would wear their crowns on their heads in the Garden of Eden and teach Torah, how long would they sit, one year, 100 years, 1000 years–how long? When he was older he philosophized about the concept of 'Time'. He labored over this concept which the great thinkers had sought to define. He died in NY.

In conclusion, I am reminded of one of the chief leaders with whom I spent a day as a yeshiva boy: Moshe Elieh the Teacher he was called. I was 12 years old when I entered his house. It was the time when R. Isaac**Error! Bookmark not defined.** Reineses's yeshiva was founded in Lideh. There besides Talmud, one learned modern subjects. Moshe Elieh chatted with me about Torah principles and clarified the need for worldly subjects in the yeshiva. When the student learned about worldly subjects in the university, the professor would declare: Nature is like that–nobody can change it. But if you study science in the yeshiva, the religious teacher will conclude: "You see how complex and logical the world is constructed, how precisely and perfectly the planets orbit. All this harmony and synchrony is regulated by God." In 1911, I met Moshe Elieh in NY, but know nothing more about his fate.

Chaim Leib (Hyman) Sneider

Chaim Leib Avrahom Isaac (Hyman Sneider was my close friend since the age of four. He was charming, with rosy cheeks, a nice voice and a distinctive personality. We grew up together in a house which seemed like a ramshackle warehouse, the home of Avrahom Isaac, a son of Moshe the tailor. On Friday nights, when the lights had burned down and we came home from shul, the singing of 'Sholom aleichum Malachi Hashiros' could be heard through the open windows in all the streets of the town. That's how Avrahom Isaac and the children celebrated holy shabbos with singing. Chaim Leib's voice sounded the sweetest and strongest.

When we came from the yeshivas and filled the shul with the Gemora Nigguns, Chaim Leib's "Tanu Rvonin" filled the whole space with his sweet tenor. When we, his friends, were captivated by the new winds of Hebrew and Yiddish literature that blew through the streets, Chaim Leib was among the first of our group. He became close to the workers and Zionist organizations.

Here he is at 14, with sensitive face, proclaiming lofty ideas about freedom and tearing off the chains of slavery. He cited Karl Marx, but what did his tender vibrant soul have to do with 'capital', with 'gaining wealth'? It was simply a revolt of the Jewish youth against the old exhausted concepts.

Chaim Leib's strength was in his tender romantic soul, his dear countenance which inspired his audience. Before we looked around, took our eyes off him, he had snapped up the prettiest young girl in our circle, Rachel, the shochet's daughter. The boy's attention was diverted from us. When we used to meet him on the 'Zostienik', embracing Rachel, it seemed as if we had caught him stealing. In those days, the foremost principle was that the whole person belongs to the movement, it was not proletarian to be distracted by 'love'.

After the 1905 revolution, when the great emigration began, Chaim Leib moved to New York, where there were already compact Jewish communities and cultural life. He became part of a Jewish circle which determined to strengthen the new generation to maintain Jewish traditions and principles. That was the Shalom Aleichum Institute in which Chaim Leib had become rooted spiritually. In that circle he made friends and admirers.

As soon as he appeared, he became an object of interest, and when he settled in, one of his friends said,"Chaim Leib, sing something!". He started a sweet melody and the whole group was enlivened. He also had important duties in the formation and maintenance of the Olshan community organization before the first and second world wars. He helped create aid for the Olshan victims. I was present at a meeting of Olshaners where he presided. It was evident that he provided the spiritual strength that cemented and maintained the organization. And then Chaim Leib passed away. In the big city of New York, where most people are not noticed, when Chaim Leib died, in mid–week, hundreds of people came to the last rites. The Olshaners mourned–he had been their shield, their talented child. His friends who were enthralled by his personality, and I who had been together with him from the earliest youth–were inconsolable. In our Yizkor book, our Chaim Leib shall be remembered. We must tell our children about this man, this Jew from Olshan who lived, created, and brought joy to all. Gone, long before his time. Chaim Leib, we will always remember you.

[Pages 40-44]

What I Remember About the Shtetl Olshan
by B. Z. Goldberg

Our family lived in Olshan for about 12 years. We came and left for other places, and had no family in Olshan. Perhaps it might be of interest to Olshaners, how their town may have appeared in the eyes of a child like me. My father was from Denburg, which was re–named Dvinsk. He was the older of two sons of Itze Noteh, a teacher, a bitter opponent of the Chassidim of that town, and an intense scholar. My mother was the daughter of the Drevitz rabbi. Her family lived in Vilna. As soon as my father was ordained, he became the shochet in the little town of Barun, near Olshan, and soon after my birth he became shochet in Olshan.

By the time I was 10, my father had left for America, and the family was already looking for shipping routes to join him. In the few years that we were waiting I went to school at the Lider yeshiva, then for a while in Volozhin. I stayed with my grandfather in Dvinsk, and came to Olshan only at holiday times. So how much could I remember about Olshan in such a short time under these circumstances?

But now the Olshan families have created an eternal memorial for their shtetl and they gave me the great honor of asking to me to write about Olshan, to describe how the town appeared to a young boy, now fifty years later at the start of the 20th century.

I see Olshan at that time: a shtetl with four wide streets which intersect at the Market. A square where a beautiful large cathedral stood. The Jewish market stalls stood near the cathedral grounds. The other two sides of the market were taken up by various shops, with access to the market. Each of the four streets had two names. The first street, leading to the Market, was named Oshman Street, since that was the road to Oshman. On the other side of the Market, the street was named Schloss Street, because that was the road to the former Prince's castle. Another street, named Trober Street led to the town of Trob, while on the other side it was named Baruner Street, leading to the town of Barun. There were many little alleys branching off. I have seen enough cities and towns to conclude that Olshan was laid out nicely, if not quite modern.

In one such alley, near a lively lake, was the Beys Hamidrash, the shul and the public bath. These were the only public buildings in Olshan, if you don't count the Goyish places like the Post Office and the Police, the priest's enclave and private companies. The Jewish registry recorded births and deaths, and handled passport changes, valid or faked. And the rabbi's house to which one came not only for advice or Torah law, but also for salt and spices, which were the rabbi's monopoly. The rebbetzin handled those items, for which there was a fee.

I must say here that I have seen many instances where rabbis charged fees, even when the rabbi got his income from an atheist communist power. I think that the Olshan system of giving the rabbi a monopoly in such matters, was not so bad. Thus the rabbi was not dependent on the rich and powerful people in the town, as is the case even now in America. The religious leader didn't have to wait for contributions to be sent in, he only had to pray to God that the Jews should have enough to eat, and would have enough salt and spices. He didn't have to be concerned with every little part of his dominion. The rebbetzin was the only one to handle such transactions.

[Pages 45-48]

This Is What the Shtetl Looked Like
by Shepsl Kaplan

From 1920 to 1939, Olshan belonged to Poland. This area was called the Eastern district, the border lands. The Ziganke river streamed past the town, through gardens and orchards, surrounded by meadows and flowers, and was used for a watermill and to generate electricity. There were two smaller streams that flowed through the town; their clear waters arose from the hills near the fields. In summer, the flow was minimal, hardly evident. On Passover eve, when the snow was warmed in Spring, the current rose and overflowed its banks, spilling into the houses. Both streams emptied into the Ziganke.

The shtetl was surrounded by fragrant verdant forests, tended by gardeners and planters, giving rise to a beautiful fresh aroma. There the young Jewish folks used to enjoy themselves. From summer to late fall, The Ziganke was used by bathers, men, women, children, Jews and Christians from the neighboring towns. On the edge of Schloss Street, was the historic castle of Pavel Sapyeha, the great Lithuanian vice–chancellor.

Because of the course of events in Olshan between the wars, the shtetl's appearance changed. Instead of old wooden houses, brick walls and modern houses were built. The Jews lived in the center of town, and the Christians dwelt in the side streets and alleys. On one side of the market place, near the Catholic cathedral, stood a row of centuries–old wooden houses that belonged to Jews. The stalls were hated by the Catholic clergy, and in 1934 a mob of peasants, incited by the Catholic priests, inflicted a pogrom and damaged the roofs of some of the Jewish stalls and houses, which were then torn down by the Polish authorities. In their place they walled off two rows of stalls in the middle of the market place, dividing them among the Jewish merchants.

Market day was twice weekly. Peasants from nearby communities brought various products in to sell, such as eggs, butter, chickens, cows, horses, calves, sheep, flax, seeds, wood, straw, hay, apples. Everything they needed, they bought in the town stalls. There were two shuls in town, one new and one old. The Torah ark in the new shul was a work of art. There was also a Tarbos school and a *Kavshechne* school where many Jewish children attended. In order to get to a middle school, Jewish children had to go to Vilna, 70 kilometers distant. There was a Gymnasium in the area in Oshman, 20 km away, but Jewish children were not welcome there, especially in the last years before World War I.

On the edge of the shtetl, in the forests and meadows, the Olshan Jews with wives and children used to take walks every Shabbos afternoon or between Mincha and Maariv, to enjoy the beautiful luminous landscape surrounding the shtetl. The fragrant air was filled with sounds of children laughing and playing. Boys and girls used to go further into the woods and various spots along the river. Joyous shouts, Jewish and Russian songs filled the air.

Today, Olshan is 'Judenrein'. The Jewish houses are all occupied by Christians. There is no trace of our past. The two shuls and the bath have all been sold for wood. The Christians have destroyed the cemeteries, the trees all cut down. The more ornate grave stones have been taken down, smoothed and re–sold. The simpler stones were used as paths in the basements of buildings. And there where former generations had rested in eternal sleep, cows and horses graze.

The last Jewish families left Olshan in 1958. The hundred remaining survivors live mostly in Israel and America.

The Historic Relationship Between the Jews and Christians

Jewish Olshan was composed of varied occupations: farmers, horse stable operators, shoemakers, tailors and a certain number of dealers and merchants. The Jews got along well with the Polish and White Russian peasants. Hundreds of Christian laborers, men and women, were employed in harvesting, binding and pressing the flax for the farmers. The relationship between the Christian workers of those days, and the Jewish farmers was good. There were no conflicts. The Christian inhabitants of Olshan had become accustomed to their Jewish neighbors. And that's why the Olshan Jews reacted to any affront by the Poles and White Russians, to organize anti–Semitic policies in the town.

In Tsarist times there were instances when the bold Jewish youths beat off attacks by anti–Semitic hooligans, discouraging them from future anti–Jewish excesses. It is worth remembering the battle that took place on Pesach eve, 1906, when Tsarist agents organized a pogrom against the local Jews. The young Jewish men bravely repelled an attack, and defeated the ruffians. The pogrom had been organized in response to a demonstration by the Jewish youth against the Russian rule. The demonstrators had forced the leader of the opposition to surrender his horse, which was then led off, bearing a red flag.

[Pages 48-50]

The Jewish Workers Movement
by Moshe Baron

The revolutionary movement which stirred Tsarist Russia 1904–1905 also affected Olshan. The shtetl , which was in the Vilna district, was influenced by the revolutionary fervor there. Yaakov Kaplan has described the revolution's beginnings among the Jewish youth of Olshan . The next segment tells about some of the individuals who created and led the organizations of the Bund and the S.S.

The Founders of the Bund and S.S.

In 1904–05, our town had two parties, the Bund and the S.S. Both parties were founded by activists from Vilna. They had gathered in the young workers in the tailoring, weaving and shoe repair trades. Most of them belonged to the Bund. The S.S. attracted former yeshiva boys, who had dropped out to follow worldly Yiddish and Russian literature. Of these comrades, I remember: Chaim Leib, son of Isaac the tailor; Pesach Chaims, son of a tailor; Beilah, daughter of a teacher. I was then active in the S.S., which had been started by the teacher, Dolinski.

The comrades of the S.S. party formed a charity group, concerned with helping the poor and ill. They also organized a savings and loan bank, which was supported by various outside Jewish organizations, and provided low interest loans to merchants and farmers. Later, the head of the bank was Polanski.

During the pogroms of those days in Russia, Olshan was relatively quiet. There were only occasional attacks on Jews. Ruffians sometimes broke windows with stones. It could be that we avoided pogroms because the Christians knew that we had secret weapons. The head of the Bund at that time was the teacher, Comrade Samson, who had been sent from Vilna to energize the party. He had a strong effect on the town and the region, but one day he shot himself in the heart. The reason for his suicide was unknown. His funeral turned into a huge demonstration, comrades came from all over, to sing revolutionary songs, to accompany him to his grave. Other Vilna activists were a Tzerna woman and finally Dolinski.

The Discussions Between the Bund and the SS

In 1902–03, the Jewish organizations of socialist worker parties greatly increased. They called themselves S.S., which meant Zionist socialists [in Russian 'sionisti']. This organization was quite active, and sponsored lectures and discussions, with support from the Bund. We remember those discussions about the thoughts and ideas that influenced the Jewish youth of Olshan and what became of them. The activists from the Bund asserted that Russia was the home of Jews now, and they should not seek new territories. If the revolution would succeed in Russia, the Jews would be free, and there would no longer be a Jewish Question. The Jews would be liberated, equal, autonomy would be secured, with development of Jewish culture. That was the mantra of the Bundists.

The S.S. proponents argued that no revolution could fully solve the Jewish Problem; as long as Jews had no territorial center, they would not be able to develop their economic and national interests. This center didn't have to be in Palestine, but could be created in any land with scanty population. But how long should Jews have to struggle in Russia together with non–Jewish socialists to win a free democratic destiny? What would be most helpful in getting such a land?

One of the organizers of the Olshan S.S. party was Chaim Leib. His father, Isaac, was a tailor, who had given his son a strict religious upbringing. Chaim was a good student, and at the time of the 1905 revolution he left his studies and joined the S.S. He was an activist and a good speaker.

[Page 51]

The Period Between the World Wars

[Page 53]

In the Years of the First World War
by Shepsl Kaplan

The Front near Olshan, Cossacks Plunder the Jewish Farms

The outbreak of World War I was marked by conscription of Jewish and Christian reservists. From 1914–15, the people experienced little of the war. Only after there was a lull in the fighting, a band of Cossacks entered the town, and the Jews felt the brunt of the war. In the town there was much wailing when the Russians carried out an incendiary battle against the Germans on the town outskirts. The civilians were forced to evacuate to Russia. The Jews wept as they packed up their belongings on wagons and left the town to join neighboring Christians in an adjacent area to await the German attack on Olshan. Some of them fled to Minsk when the Cossacks appeared in town.

The front had changed. Cannon fire was heard and bombs fell near Olshan. The Cossacks pillaged the Jewish houses and farms, looting in one day 32 farms and a few houses. When the cannonade became heavier all the Jews left the town.

A number of them were sheltered with Christian neighbors in town. Most of them, with their baggage, fled to a field, between the thick walls of the historic castle on the edge of the town. As the artillery fire intensified the Jews abandoned their baggage and hid in the deep cellars under the castle.

As the cannonade continued, fires broke out in the town. Jews ran back, together with some Christians, to put out the burning houses ignited by the Cossacks before they left town. By dawn the cannonade stopped, the Germans entered, then left without further damage, and the Jews returned to their devastated homes.

[Page 54]

The Russo–German front had stalled at Lake Beresina, about 20 km from Olshan. The Germans remained there at the lake for three years. Olshan was restored in this period; Jews and Christians remained in their homes. Movement out of the town to other communities was forbidden and restricted. No one was allowed out between 8pm and 6am. Farmers were not allowed to bring products into the town. Hunger was widespread, especially among the poor.

The relationship between the Germans and the Jews was correct. For a time the Germans sold corn for bread for the Jews. However they cataloged everyone's possessions and every one was obligated to contribute as much milk and eggs as required.

In 1917, allotments of corn stopped, and hunger increased. The Germans had sent the youths off to work battalions in the forest and to dig ditches, make bricks. The best trees around Olshan were chopped down and sent to Germany. During these three years of occupation, the children of school age had not attended school. After the abdication of Kaiser Wilhelm, the Germans had fled for their lives and a new era of troubles had begun for the Jews of Olshan.

Cultural Activity During World War I

In 1916, while the town was occupied by the Germans, a theatrical circle was created, under new conditions. Those Jewish youths of Olshan, who had managed to avoid German forced labor conscriptions, were increasingly burdened with food deprivation consequent to more and more stringent rationing. They were cut off from their cultural center in Vilna. There was no newspaper, no books, no Jewish literature; they had nothing to do during the long winter nights. These young boys and girls decided to create a drama circle. A group of youngsters, advised by Shepsel Abramovitz, asked the German command for permission to stage plays, and this was quickly granted. And so the Drama Circle, under Abramovitz' direction, was founded.

[Page 55]

They began to rehearse Goldfaden's *Shulami,* inspired by Isaac Gershon, a cantor of Olshan. One of his boy students, who had aspired to become an independent cantor knew the name of this operetta, Shulamit. A significant number of youths had joined the Circle. All the members got official permission to go out at night for rehearsal, and return home. Otherwise strict control ensured that no one could open a door or window until dawn.

The German commander authorized two professional musicians, a 'foot–harmonist' and a fiddler, who were to accompany the hearty songs of 'Shulamit. Otherwise, they played at parties or entertainments at night. The performers: Shepsel Abramovitz, Herzl Katz, Roshe Kossvitzki, Shepsel Kaplan, Asher Levin, Hirsh Gurvitz, Reina Abramovitz, Kiva Kaplan, Isaac Kaplan, Herschel Kousevitzki, Natan Kousevitzki, Blume Chernivoski, Blume Gurevich, Ida Adamovitz.

The rehearsals lasted so long, they attracted attention, and the commander directed them to put on the show. The dress rehearsal was staged in the Grand Hall of Mottel Kozlovski, and was attended by the German officers. The commander was so pleased that he authorized construction of a wooden stage with traditional theater sets that would serve many productions.

But in the end, the Germans decided not to build the stage, for the temporary cease–fire had broken down in 1918 with the revolution against Wilhelm in Germany. The Germans lost their motivation.

[Page 56]

Origins of Polish Independence and the Revenge of the 'Halerchiks'

At the end of the war, the Poles took over the Olshan area. To represent the Polish authority, a detachment of soldiers from General Haler's army took over. The 'Halerchiks' established order and began to beat the Olshan Jews. It was enough that a person wasn't Christian and had a doubtful background; Jews had no standing. They were dragged to the market place, given 25 lashes. This didn't last long, because war started between the Poles and the Soviet Union. Shortly the town was overrun several times by the Russians and the Poles.

In 1920, after the Bolsheviks left, the Poles resumed civil power in Olshan. They started with a ghastly murder of a 20 year old Jewish woman, Esther Levin, who had been active in the Communist movement. The Olshan Poles got revenge: Babronitzki, Adamovich and the shoemaker Smalski betrayed the girl to the Polish authorities who murdered her and cut up her body. A trial resulted in the flight of the shoemaker, who was blamed by the other three, who were acquitted. For many years, the Olshan Jews mourned the terrible murder of this innocent girl, coinciding with the re–birth of Poland.

Gradually things became more normal in the town. Jews began to organize economically and culturally, and started businesses. They started a Peoples Bank, charity group, Hebrew school, shul and a theater group. A big library was created, of Jewish, Hebrew and Russian books. Youth organizations, Zionists and Communists also appeared.

[Page 57]

Cultural and Educational Activities

Even in Tsarist times, Olshan had supported a theater group featuring historic themes, such as *Bar Kochba, Mchiras* Joseph, and various Purim plays. The audience attended for social and charitable reasons. Those productions produced memorable roles, remembered as Gershon Abramovitz as Pharoah, King of Egypt, Beryl 'the Kaiser', Hershel the 'Turk', Chaim the 'Faskatz'. After World War I, cultural and educational groups, unaffiliated, flourished until the start of World War II in 1939. Included were Hershel Katz, Hirsh Horovitz, Moshe**Error! Bookmark not defined.** Yalek, Shepsel Kaplan, Joshua Potashnik, Blume Tzerniovski, Blume Gurvitz. Valuable books were saved from the pre–war era library and thousands of Jewish, Hebrew and Russian books were added–the best authors. In time, the Olshan library became famous, worthy of a big city. The drama group included: Baruch Hirsch Gurvitz, Moshe Yalek, Herzl Katz, Shepsel Kaplan, Leibl and Hersch Potashnik, Isaac and Kiva Kaplan, Leah and Ida Abramovitz, etc. Directors are also listed; a professional from Lodz, a gifted artist and singer, who married a local girl, and ended his life in an insane asylum in Vilna.

[Page 58]

The successful repertoire played to overflowing houses and included dramas and comedies of Sholem Aleichem, Peretz Hirshbein, Pinski, operettas of Goldfaden. Young and old attended, also from other towns, even intelligent Poles and Russians. The first productions were on a large wooden stage, donated by the woodworker Eliezer Kaplan. Then one of the Russian merchants of Olshan established a walled enclosure with 100 seats. A fire in 1935 consumed 1/3 of the houses in Olshan, including the theater. The Catholic diocese then provided a large space for us in the cloister, which we shared with them, thus providing us with our third theater space, now used for various shows in the town.

All the town's youth joined in the Cultural and Education Program. Lecturers in various fields appeared. Outdoor performances were often accompanied by an orchestra, and Olshan was blessed by such contacts. Lake Ziganka was used in summertime for swimming; Jews and Christians often had swimming contests.

[Page 59]

Directors pf Jewish cultural–Educational Council
Sitting, from right: **Bruch–Hirsh Gurvitz, Shia Potashnik, Sholom Kaplan**
Standing, from right: **Sandor Gurvitz Shepsl Kaplan,, A.A. Potashnik**Error!
Bookmark not defined.

'Literary Trial'
A 'Literary trial' of Esther Rozengold, heroine of the book 'Remembrance of souls' by David Rishman.
Attorneys, judges, collegium, counsels and guilty parties

[Page 60]

[Letter in Yiddish to family asking financial aid]

[Pages 61-63]

Child and Teenage Years
by Arye Gershoni

My mother was born in Olshan, my father in Kreve. After their marriage, they lived in Kreve. There my father was the mayor, and also managed several other towns. When I was five, we moved to Olshan, and I went to *cheder*. I don't have any good memories of my teachers there. Aleph–Beys I learned from a teacher who had a long beard. He beat us with 'noodles', which he made out of leather strips, which looked like broad noodles. My next teacher, Hershel the Turk was a tyrant and beat us with sticks, and he taught us Tanach. After my father died in 1913, we moved to Trov. Here I resumed cheder, learning Hebrew, *Tanach* and *Gemora*. My teacher had additional occupations–cantor, *mohel*, barber for the peasants who came to town. Often the student was taught in the same room where the teacher was cutting hair. But he saw every mistake the boys made, and the teacher–barber soon corrected them.

World War I

In Olshan, when the Russians were there, things were not so bad. After Rosh Hashonah 1915, the Russian forces started to evacuate and advised the people to flee to Russia. Meanwhile the retreating Russian soldiers plundered the Jewish farms, including ours. After the fighting subsided, after Yom Kippur, we returned to town for a look. Everything had been looted by the local Christians. We returned to the Castle to celebrate Succos; many Jews and Christians also stayed in the Castle, hiding in the cellars. Jews and Christians prayed, but the artillery fire increased. German troops directed everyone to return to their homes.

We returned to Olshan, amid great disorder. Families were separated, parents sought their children who had been sheltered by other families during the Russian period. Gradually things calmed down and order was restored. Life was difficult; the peasants were unable to supply food because the Germans had taken everything. Then a German manager, Schmidt, took over and created a good relationship with the Jews. During this time, the Germans behaved well. There was smuggling of goods as well as cultural activity. A *shul* was allowed to teach Hebrew, *Tanach* and Yiddish. German was the language of instruction. Olshan had a Jewish mayor, Dolinski. Germans had taken Jewish youths to labor camps, where they worked hard in the frost and cold but were not persecuted, as in World War II. After 1918, with peace, our war really began. The Germans left, the Poles came, then the Bolsheviks, then the Poles again, and the Jews were victims. The Poles set up a kangaroo court, resulting in the bestial murder of the young Jewish girl, and the Jewish community was terrified.

The Polish Pogrom in 1922

The Poles had established order in the Olshan region, and Jews resumed commerce and activity. But peace didn't last long. The Russo–Polish war brought the Red Army into Olshan for a short time and they seized everything. In October 1920, the Poles returned and re–asserted their authority. The Jews resumed their lives, opened shops–then came new troubles. The Catholic clergy was hostile to the Jewish vendors near the Cathedral in the market place. They incited the Polish authority to pressure the Jewish merchants to liquidate their stalls near the cathedral, claiming that Jews did not follow their own rules. A wave of anti–Semitism resulted in a pogrom.

Early winter 1922, on a Sunday, after mass, the peasants of the adjacent towns together with their priest and Polish officials attacked the Jewish merchants, and thus began the familiar pogrom scenes. Several days later, when things quieted down, a Jewish delegation complained about the riot and the damages to the stalls and their houses. An official investigation resulted in the granting to Jews of another location in the market to set up shop. So the Jews set up again. No damages were ever assessed against the mob responsible for the damage.

[Pages 64-65]

The Tragic Fate of Esther Levin Memories from 1918
by Shlomo Halevi–Levin

In 1918, the Poles returned to Olshan. My sister Esther had been allied with the Russian side, the Bolsheviks, opposing the Germans. One evening, she came home with a young Russian, who had induced her to flee the town, but she hadn't made it to Russia. With companions, they got to Oshman. She stayed there for a while, but remained in contact with home. Now in Olshan, the Polish goyim, who had previously served the Russians, were fervently supporting the Polish regime. They came to us and demanded to know where Esther was, acting as agents of the Polish police. They became threatening, bound my father's arms and legs and locked him and my mother in a room. The children were locked in a stable for several days. We endured the abuse and did not reveal Esther's location. We had expected that she and her friends would escape to Russia. But that didn't happen. Maybe she hoped the Soviets would return; she was also so closely bound to her father.

One evening, after the abuses had subsided, the mother prepared a supper. Suddenly Esther and her boyfriend entered, armed head to foot with guns and ammo. They cried "Help! Hide us, they're hunting us". We turned off the lights and hid them in the barn in a water tank; their weapons were buried under ground.

We all pretended to go to bed, to arouse no suspicion. But then an armed group of goyim broke in, shouting, demanding that we tell them where the fugitives were. Again we were all tied up, locked in a room, while the search went on, with wild cries. I can still see the scenes of that search; the house seemed like a pogrom again.

Later we learned that the Poles had searched several locations and were going to leave, when they detected a movement in the water barrel. They captured the fugitives and marched them off under gun–point. We sat in the locked room, trembling with fear. One of the band opened the door, unbound us, and we saw that the whole house was surrounded by an armed mob. No one was allowed to enter or leave the house. We didn't sleep the whole night. At dawn, the rabbi was allowed in and he told us how Esther was tortured.

The criminals dragged Esther into Pinchas Koslovski's house and tortured her all night. Then they tore off her clothes and drove her to the cathedral, where she was again tortured, killed, quartered and hung on a tree. On the appeal of the rabbi and the Jewish community, the remains were released and were brought to our house. The parents were kept from viewing the tortured body, to avert the horror. I pushed my way into the cemetery. Someone had unveiled the corpse; I'll never forget that sight.

[Pages 66-68]

Memories of Childhood
by Leah Bloch–Rudnick

As long as we were with our parents we were not aware of the war. After peace, my parents created a cheder in our house, along with selected children. A rabbi was employed to teach. The approach of war to our area greatly increased hardship and hunger. The students could no longer eat at our table and we couldn't observe the Sabbath rules. Actually, we weren't so badly off, but then our dear mother died, perhaps from hunger since she always gave her last food to the children. She died while my brother and father were away in Russia. They had intended to bring us there to provide food. But things got worse there than at home. The border was closed because of the war. The Germans took over, and my brother Moishele became our provider. He became a shul *shaliach*, and said kaddish three times a day, and we wept together. We two wretched children kept up this big house all alone. We parceled out our food, ate from one plate, and in fear, slept in one bed. We were often hungry, but told no one. That's the way we were brought up–not to ask for any help.

Unexpectedly, the 'Batushka', the priest, became interested in us and invited us to meals, but we declined because of kashrut. The priest understood, and gave us some flour. Moishele baked some bread, so we survived World War I. The tragic events after the Germans left have remained inscribed in my memory to this day. After the Russians came the Poles, the worst of all. The soldiers ran wild, plundered the houses and shops, and committed various atrocities.

There was a lot of gunfire near our garden on Castle Street. The Russians and Poles exchanged fire, so bullets whizzed through our house. Moishele and I hid under the bed, weeping silently, crying for our dead Mama. When the shooting stopped, we crept out from the floor into the kitchen, looking out into the garden. There we saw a terrible sight. Trenches were dug in the garden, and in one, two soldiers were fighting face–to–face. Suddenly one of them stabbed the other with his knife.

I heard loud shouting. In terror, I ran into another room. Through the window, I saw a lot of soldiers running past, heard their boots stomping, the wagons rolling madly past. Every house was shut tight, the shops were empty, and no one dared to stick their noses outside. The soldiers had been running for several kilometers, with their mouths gaping from thirst and exhaustion. A young Polish soldier, no more than a boy, collapsed in front of the house. Our housekeeper, Zippah, opened the door and gave him a drink of sour milk, risking her life. She thought to herself, "He is, after all, a mother's child".

Another episode has remained in my memory: Once at night we heard a troop of horses tramping outside. They stopped before our house; there was a knock on the door. We trembled in fear. I felt I had to open the door no matter what, as long as Moishele wouldn't be harmed. He opened the door himself. "Give us bread!" They were Bolsheviks, and my brother gave these hungry Russian soldiers our last crumbs.

All this horror and terror from World War I seemed like a game compared to the fate of the Jews in World War II. But my brother learned a trade– he became a barber. He replaced the town barber who emigrated to America. Moishele then became a scribe, married a teacher from Smorgen, and had a normal life until it was torn apart for him, his wife and child by the horrors of the German persecution.

[Pages 69-72]

Teachers, Cheders and Modern Schools
by Shepsl Kaplan

My first teacher was my older brother, Isaac Jacob, now in America. He'd open a book, show me an aleph, then turned a page, bade me find one. I was rewarded each time with a kopeck, 'dropped from heaven by an angel'. I continued to receive kopecks for additional learning.

My first rabbi was Chaim Boron, who taught me Hebrew and '*davening*', with individual techniques, much love, a pat on the back, a pinch of the cheek. The children loved him and learned quickly.

Reb Note Kaplan wasn't a professional teacher; he was badly educated. He had a wife and three daughters, who read the books of Moses and assisted at weddings. When they got older, Nathan became a teacher of Talmud and *Tanach*. Previously he had been a woods–forager and guardian, posted at the gate of the old walled synagogue in the center of town. Reb Nathan was a *Kohen*, with snow–white beard, who was not allowed access to children. Therefore he couldn't supervise the students. Instead he read *Chumash* and *Tanach* with his 13 and 8 year–old children.

In winter, when the soft snow tempted the children to go play in the streets, he locked the door and refused their requests. After he punished one resistant student, the classmates got together and broke all the window panes in the school. In the morning, the fathers of the students and the Reb had to re–install the windows and made peace, but no real teacher appeared.

Reb Moshe–Elia, the Gemorah Teacher

My teacher of *Chumash* and *Gemorah*, Moshe–Elia was a watchman at a home with a large garden. Reb Moshe was one of the best teachers in town– there wasn't a better one. The students were like his children. Those who could afford paid only 15 rubles per student. As a sign of his piety, he did not discriminate–he only required that his students should understand and think about what they learned, so that his efforts were not in vain. He didn't spank the students. Instead of spanking he gave them difficult assignments which were more painful than spanking.

I remember a few of these exchanges. When a student would mistakenly translate a Gemorah statement, he would say, 'Sara Iron mouth, you have blundered like a blind horse in a ditch–like leading geese with a whip, you'll be no better than Michael, the shabbos goy. Better herd geese, I wouldn't take your father's money in vain.'

No great scholars came from Reb Nathan's school, but his students didn't become like Michael. The kids learned their Talmud and Chumash. But some were punished, e.g. for carving their desks with a knife, which was every student's dream. He would hold them by the ears, set them on the bench in the rear until his wife or daughter would take them away.

The stormy revolution of 1905 caught up the older students of all the cheders. A group formed into a 'Little Bund' and conflicted with a group of Zionist sympathizers, resulting in a 'war'. This was conducted with snow balls in winter, and stones, sand and dirt in summer. The cheder which had dislodged the opposition was the victor.

Cheder 'Mtukn' and Dolinski's Russian–Jewish School

In 1907, a cheder was founded, with a famous teacher, Wiskind, who set up a modern school. He taught Hebrew, and after each lecture, he commented, wrote opinions, conducted tests, and published a weekly children's journal, which the kids read with bated breath. At the same time, Dolinski, a student from Vilna, a nephew of Goldinski, founded a second school, using Russian as the language, serving both Jewish and Christian children, boys and girls. Dolinski's school was in a large sunny room that he had specially built. For the first time Olshan children sat on comfortable modern school benches, four to a bench, with ink wells especially for the students.

Opposite the benches stood the teacher's desk, where the student would be asked to solve mathematical problems. In Dolinski's school, for a while, the teacher Boron [now in US] gave lectures in Jewish history. The school lasted about 10 years until World War I, teaching and enlightening Jewish youth.

[Page 73]

The 'Tarbos' School and its Educational Activity
by Pesakh Gershonovitz

About 1920, it was decided to build a new Jewish school in Olshan, to provide national Jewish and worldly education. It wasn't easy for the community leaders to support such a school, since their children had had conventional educations. So a combination school was devised with a wall between the old–fashioned class and the advanced modern class. In later years the school became the best in the Vilna region. Teaching was in Hebrew, with Polish classes, with consent of the Polish authority. Teachers came from Vilna. The school was affiliated with the Vilna school, and legalized by the Poles, with seven classes. Religious classes included Chumash, Tanach, Gemorah, Rashi. When they incurred a deficit, the Talmud–Torah provided help. Despite the difficulties, all Olshan children had an education. The Poles were not fond of this system and imposed restrictions, which threatened the closure of the school. Thanks to financial help from some Olshan emigrants in the US, the deficits were covered.

The curriculum was carried out in the spirit of Zionism, together with the ideal of 'Return to Israel'. The development of the school was associated with formation of youth organizations, cadres of potential farming collectives, dedicated to all Zionistic causes. The teachers Moshe Yalek and Abraham Soladecha were killed in World War II.

[Page 74]

The 'Tarbos' School – the Light of the Town
by Shifra Kotin–Trobski

Most of the Jewish kids of Olshan had their education in this old wooden building–Hebrew as well as Polish language. It had a strong presence in the town. Children flocked there from all the streets and alleys, happy with their books on their backs. In the school was a children's library in Hebrew, also a drama group and a chorus, and the children used to give productions all over town. All the Jewish holidays were celebrated. On *Lag B'Omer*, the children would march through the town and forest and sing Hebrew songs. The teachers included Abraham Itcha, Velvel Chernovski. The school was the light of the town. Despite the financial strictures, the school survived until the disaster.

[Pages 75-77]

Report of a Letter to Friends in America

We write to you as friends who are interested in our school's existence. You have published in an American newspaper an appeal signed by some Olshaners about our difficult time here, and how you might help us in a material and spiritual way.

The religious situation: Our elementary school is attended by 90 children, boys and girls, divided in five classes. There are four teachers, just enough for the total. The school is national–religious, i.e. all classes are taught in Hebrew, while in the lower classes the transition to Hebrew is gradual. Polish is also taught. A special place is devoted in every class for the holy books–the Torah, Tanach, Gemorah, prayer, which are taught by a special teacher. Details of this program are related. There are also a childrens' journal and a library, assisted by the teachers. The rabbi totally supports our program.

The article in 'Der Tag' stating that the rabbi wanted to change the character of the school is inaccurate. We are in great financial need because times are so hard in Poland, the parents are unable to pay for the children, we can't pay the teachers and we don't get any subsidies from the state. Parents are concerned about the gradual loss of Jewish identity. People are no longer able to make a living. A lot of Polish farmers and cooperatives have settled in Olshan. Despite the crisis, we are paying unbearably higher taxes. Things are getting worse and worse. We teachers are getting squeezed little by little, and we don't get paid regularly. The rabbi and a few elders at times have helped out to cover a part of the deficit. Unfortunately, no one has been able to relieve the poverty of the people of the town.

Without a remedy, we decided to appeal to our Olshaners in America. Please get involved with the welfare of our shul and help us so that our children are not left without a Jewish education. The fate of our children lies in your hands.

signatures–A.M. Cahn, Zerniski, Potashnik, Solodocha

Teachers from the Tarbos School
From right: Sandor gurvitz, Bineh Pietuchovski, Kagan, A.I. Solodukha,
Drozdovski (Polish teacher)

Teachers from the Tarbos School: M. Yold, Pietuchovski, Bineh Pietuchovski

Teibele Bukatman from Vvilna, Yiddish teacher in the Olshan community School, died in Vilna

Financial Reports of the Olshan Hebrew School

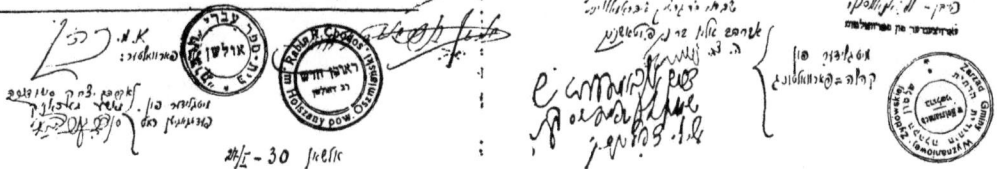

Financial Reports of the Olshan Hebrew School

Yiddish Community School in World War I (On the right stands A.I. Solodukha)

Yiddish Public School in 1917
School house built before 1917 by Shultan Hagormany

Hebrew School "Tarbos" after World War I

Yiddish Public School after World War I

Tarbos School 1929-30

Hebrew school Tarbos

Jewish students at the Polish public school with their teachers of Jewish religious studies in 1935

[Page 86]

The Religious Life

Rabbi Reuben Khodesh
by Shepsl Kaplan

Rabbi Reuben Khodesh was one of the most involved and attractive figures among the Olshan rabbis. He was the religious and spiritual leader of the Olshan community, and was chosen from many candidates for the position. Other towns had sought him but he remained devoted to Olshan. He quickly became popular in the whole Vilna region. Although other congregations sought him, he remained dedicated to the old–fashioned good Jews of Olshan, to whom he devoted his body and soul. He was much admired and loved by young and old, religious and unaffiliated, all admired his religious–worldly outlook. He was also gifted with unusual speaking talent. His speeches were always clear, logical and comprehensible to all. His words were deeply inscribed into their hearts.

Cantors, Singers and Prayer Leaders

There were two large synagogues in Olshan which always had good singers and cantors.–Elihu Gurvitz, (wonderful tenor), Gershon Abramovitz, brother of the famous cantor Lazar Abramovitz of Smorgen, Simon Segalovitz, Isaac Gershon, Chaim Gurevitz, Herschel the Teacher, also called 'The Turk'. For many years Olshan Jews enjoyed the heart–felt prayers of Cantor Yitchok Gershon. With the assembled choirs, they sang the complicated liturgical compositions, also those locally composed. At holiday times, the synagogue was packed, even Christians came to hear the music of the cantor and his choir.

[Pages 87-90]

The Synagogues
by Pesakh Gershonovitz

Near the flowing 'Jewish stream', as it was called, which never dried up, stood both the old Beys Hamidrash and the new one. They were always filled with people united in prayer. Rabbi Khodesh fulfilled his good works, supporting on his shoulders the poorest Olshaners. He sought help from his congregation for philanthropy, including the poverty stricken brides who had been overburdened by the expenses of their weddings. There was never any lack of needy persons.

When a traveler's horse fell, a room was found for the family, funds were collected within a week to buy a second horse, and the wheels continued to roll. R' Issar Polanski, after years in Olshan, became the chief rabbi in Vilna. Others ended in Vishniev and Novogrodsk.

R' Issar Polanski z"l

Other distinguished rabbis are described, performing remarkable and moving prayer rituals at Rosh Hashonah, Kol Nidrei, Yom Kippur. Cantor Shpira used to move the congregation to tears with his singing. R. Khodesh stood wrapped in his white robe and taliis at Kol Nidrei, and it seemed as if the heavens would part. Gershon**Error! Bookmark not defined.** Abramovitz, Moshe Yosef Soleducha and Avrohom Yitzchok Soleducha always assisted.

At Mincha and Maariv, the Jews sat at a long table, and listened to Meyer Gurvitz recite a verse from 'Chai Odom'. Suddenly this was interrupted by a loud bang on the table– Lasar Abramovitz had called out "It's *Maariv* prayer time!" After Maariv, the scholars sat studying Gemorah until late in the night. On Friday nights of course, all were greeted by "Gut Shabbos, Gut Shabbos". On Shabbos morning, old and young, rich and poor, prayed for a better week. During the Torah reading, there was some chatter of world politics or business matters, but then the shamesh called , "Enough!", all became silent, and listened to the rabbi's teaching about the Torah portion.

The synagogue was thoroughly painted beautifully by the artist–painter Avrohom Shlomo Varonovski. The old Beys Hamidrash was divided –one section for services, the larger one for the school. Olshan always emanated Jewishness. No matter how difficult, the whole congregation had preserved what was precious and holy.

Reb Moshe Soleducha– taught us, in summer *Pirkei Ovos*, in winter *Borchi Nafshi*. His calm manner, his neat beard, his whole person elicited deep respect; he seemed the image of Reb Herzl. We treasured his every word. He died too young, in America.

[Pages 90-93]

Erev Shabbos in Shtetl
by A.A. Potashnik

Erev Shabbos started on Thursday when the housewives come to market to buy meat. Names of the merchants are listed. Friday noon, housewives are busy with baking, cooking, house cleaning, washing the children's hair. The air is laden with the baking aromas. In the mild afternoon, a fiddler plays *nigunim*. A wedding *chuppah* is erected in the afternoon, customary in Olshan. Bride and groom are ushered into the shul, with music by *klezmorim*, usually from Oshman. Later comes Beryl, the 'Kaiser', a revolutionary of 1905, who proclaims that Shabbos is about to begin. "Jews, go to shul!", and he reminds the shopkeepers to close their shops.

Dina Potashnik was concerned with collecting money, challah for the needy. After she was finished for the week, she wore her Shabbos dress with a pearl string around her neck.

Friday evening all the business has ceased, shops are closed, market cleaned. From all the streets and alleys the Jews, with solemn tread, enter the shul to be greeted by the rabbi with his luminous face and proud stance. Friday night, everyone has come home from shul, they make *kiddush*, the Shabbos candles are lit for the table, and shine on the street. The house lights gradually dim. Most of the elders go to sleep, the youngsters go walking in the street, gather in their particular groups, discuss the news, amusements, sing the latest Eretz Israel songs. Their singing fills the streets with joy and hope. Groups are strolling on the sidewalk near the cathedral, and there's some flirting between the boys and girls. Such is a typical summer Friday in Olshan.

ŻARZĄD GMINY
WYZNANIOWEJ ŻYDOWSKIEJ
w Holszanach,

Dnia 21/III 19 29 r.

№ 23/29

שלמון הקהלה
היהודית בהולשני

פארוואלטונג
פון דער יידישער קהלה
אין האלשאן

A Letter from the Olshan Community to the Relief Committee in America 1929

Workers Union Leaders in 1921 with American delegates from the Oshman Relief Society in New York at an adult camp

Sitting- Gershon Kislovski, Smuel-Leib Dulinski, Nachamia Perski, Alter Krump Bruch Abramovitz, Herzl Katz, A. I.Soldukha, Shmuel Shlomo Ziskin
Standing- Shmuel Gersonovitz,Leib Putchnik, Chaim Leib Chernyovski, Bruch-Hirsh Gurevitz, Moshe Yulik, Sandor Potashnik, Yehuda Gershonovitz, Motl Kavalovski, Weinstein

[Page 95]

The Economic Life

The Jewish Peasants in Their Land Plots
by Pesakh Gershonovitz

Jews were very attached to their land, they wouldn't sell the least amount of it, even though working it gave such minimal incomes. The Christian peasants produced pigs, a much greater source of income. The Jewish farmers had in their inventories 2–3 cows, a few calves, a horse and mule. The land was farmed primitively, with horse, plow, and scythe for threshing, installed by the Jewish blacksmith. A stall and. stable were behind the shed. A small part of the land was for pasture for the cows and to dry hay. Into the stalls was brought the fragrant hay, and in summer the fresh vegetables–corn, barley, oats, wheat. A special place was used for the fodder for cows. In autumn, the cellars were filled with potatoes, radishes, red beets, carrots, cabbage. Flax was also grown, which had usually been reaped a little later. Flax required more work in the field, it had to be reworked in order to get a decent harvest. The fields were fertilized by manure from the cows and horses. For this the stalls were furnished with straw. The manure treatment could suffice for 4–5 years, and that was supplemented by additional fertilizer.

It was not easy to pasture the cows in the summer months. It wasn't worthwhile for every farmer to keep a pasture for his cows. There was a communal pasture in the town, a large communal meadow, ten or more hectares. In fact it belonged to all the farmers who owned property or a house. But the Christian farmers and town merchants didn't allow the Jewish farmers to use it and blocked the way, though they made some exceptions. After much confusion and dispute, an agreement was reached so the Jews could use some of the pasture, and relations were normalized. Every morning a herdsman took the 'Jewish' cows to pasture. It wasn't easy for the Jewish peasants to make a living, so most of them had an extra job.

The following names are listed among the peasants of Olshan, either bought or inherited:

Kaplan– 100 hectares.; David and Elihu Leibman–3 hectares.; Koslovski 3, Lidski 4, Gurvich 3 , Levin 15. Koslovski 4, Gershonovitz 6, Gershonovitz 3, Lieb 3; Dolinski 6, Shuster 10, Berkman 5.

When the Russians were there in World War II, they did not interfere with the Jewish peasants, who were allowed to do their work as usual, pay their taxes. In June 1941, when the Germans occupied White Russia, they also didn't ignore the Jewish peasants. They were driven off their land and persecuted. Whatever was left was sold off to investors. The land was given or transferred to a Christian, who was supposed to give it back later. Anything that wasn't sold, was held in common by the Christians, under German supervision.

[Pages 97-99]

Gardening
by Shepsl Kaplan

For centuries many Jewish families in Olshan were busy in the fields planting. They worked and lived off the land which had been theirs from the beginning throughout all political changes until the German expulsions. The Jewish plots were situated between the Christian fields and were divided into narrow long sections up to two km long. Together with Christians, the Jews farmed, sowed and harvested their crops. The Jews worked their land in order to maintain their families, without regard to the illegality. Despite the Tsarist law, the Jews continued to buy land from the Christians, understanding that they would eventually be able to affix their own names. In this way a capable and ambitious forester, Lazer Kaplan bought 100 hectares in the name of his neighbor Bashevski, and got it back under his own name after World War I. Lazer moved out of the town with his family, built a nice house on his own land, and together with his five sons worked the land. In a few years he accumulated 100 hectares.

It wasn't only the professional gardeners, but also ordinary folks who did it for their own use. Almost every Olshan family had a garden behind its house. They all tilled their gardens, raised potatoes, beets, carrots, cabbage for their own use. From 0.5 to 1.0 hectares, families such as Velvel Liand, Avrohom Koslovski, Israel Kaplan, Shmuel Elihu Shmukler had their own gardens. The professional gardeners, besides their own gardens, grew a variety of products for sale. The gardener bosses would haul wagonloads of sacks for sale to the markets of neighboring towns. Most of the buyers of the beets and cabbage were the needy peasants who had to stock up for winter by salting.

After World War I, Baruch Abramovitz, the head of the Citizens Bank, combined with a company that helped to restore the economies of the ruined farmers, enabling them, under easy conditions, to buy agricultural equipment and horses. Agronomists and instructors were also sent to teach the peasants how to farm in a more modern way, to produce greater harvests. They also began to plant fruit trees.

The Jewish farmers didn't have their own fruit trees, but bought fruit still on the trees, even when over–ripe. They used to buy a certain number of trees, or the whole orchard, after an evaluation of the yield. The trees were the property of the land–owners until the fruit was taken down. If the pears weren't ripe, the Jews had to hide them in special places so they wouldn't be stolen. Ripe fruits were packed up and sent to the larger Russian cities in Tsarist times, but not exported. Between the wars, the fruit was shipped to the larger Polish centers. Shepsel Abramovitz supervised and was trusted to record the yields from every tree as well as the total yield. The accuracy of his estimates was well known in the Olshan area.

[Pages 99-100]

Weaving and Housekeeping

Until World War I, Olshan had been a weaving center, producing shirts and wool scarfs. Knitting was a secondary source of income produced by the women, girls and older folks, as well as Christians. Two energetic Jewish ladies, Kusha Ziskind and Zifa Nomiot and their families really created an industry. The shirts were made for Russian soldiers. Three styles were produced: one finger, two fingers or five fingers thick. These women became masters of speed, handling the five spools of thread. The raw wool was washed in a machine, and the whole job of spinning, sewing, etc. was all done by hand. Once a week, after *Havdala*, Kusha and Zifa took their finished wares, and in the street, cried *"nessita tovor!"*. That was a signal for the Christians that it was now OK to buy their wares, and a group gathered around their houses. Women with packs of gloves pushed, eager to sell their wares faster, count their earnings and buy fresh wool. This industry vanished after World War I. After Polish independence, Ben–Zion Rudnick and his children revived this defunct industry on a loftier scale by bringing in sewing machines for the women and girls. The finished products–shirts, sweaters, scarves–were sold to Polish soldiers, up to World War II.

In March 1942, Rudnick and his family were moved from Olshan to the Volozhiner ghetto. He brought his machines with him thinking they might work for the Germans, but they all perished in May 1942. One of his sons, Michael lives in America.

[Page 101]

Charity Organizations
by Shepsl Kaplan

With aid of Olshaners in the US, charity organizations were founded in 1922 to help the needy, and were based in the community room of the new Beys Hamidrash. David Segalovitz, a flax dealer was the head of this organization; the bookkeeping was handled by Chanye Gurvitz, now in Israel. The efficiency of this system resulted in an increase in the capital of the bank, gaining the trust of the people of Olshan, as well as additional funding from America. The attack of Hitler's Germany in 1939, brought it all to an end.

[Pages 101-104]

Cooperative People's Bank

Founded in 1925 by Bruch Abramovitz, the bank was very helpful during the worst times, to all in the town, home owners, farmers, professionals, merchants. Credit was very hard to get, not available for many. Those who got credit got 50–1000 zlotys, to be repaid at the lowest rates. The operations of the bank are described–all Olshan Jews were eligible for a small fee. The bank was associated with the Central Jewish Co–op People's Bank of Vilna. The bank had about 350 members. Open 2–7, Fridays 11–2. Market days were especially busy, Monday and Friday. Friday was the 'Little Market', when the Christians came to town for their needs. Most of the business in Olshan was carried out on credit and bills. Every account had to be paid two days after due unless there was a dispute.

In the last years before the war, the bank financed land transactions, commercial and garden developments, strengthen existing businesses and to develop fruit orchards. With great effort in hard times, deficits were avoided. Interest rate was 9% a year. Recommendations were made to improve productivity. The management of the bank always was intent on the welfare of the Jewish community, which had been oppressed by the Germans. Listed are the officers of the bank, headed by Baruch Abramovitz, and the bank employees are also listed. I met Yuri Klianskin personally in the Vilna ghetto in 1942. It was difficult to speak with him because of his exhaustion. Survivors of the bank administration are also listed.

[Page 104]

Linat Hatzedek
by Pesach Abramovitz

This society played an important role in helping the poor and the ill. The majority of the work was done by volunteers, women, girls, and boys who devoted a part of their time to help families in time of illness. The institution handled referrals by the most needy, paid doctors to visit, and donated medicine and food to the needy [eggs, butter, sugar]. Some visited the ill nightly, to console their isolation, to raise their morale, get them healthy again.

[Pages 105-106]

STOWARZYSZENIE DOBROCZYNNE „GEMIŁUS-CHESED"

w _Holszanach_

גמילות־חסד אין האלשאן

SPRAWOZDANIE MIESIĘCZNE — דין וחשבון

za miesiąc _Luty_ 1931 פאר דעם חודש _פעברואר_

OBRÓT MIESIĘCZNY — אומזאץ פארן חודש				PASYWA — פאסיוון
Pozostało na dn. 1 _Marca_ 1931 געבליבן אין גמ"ח צום 1-טן _מערץ_ 19 Zł. — זל.	Rozchod miesięczny אַרויסגענונגען פון גמ"ח פארן חודש _פעברואר_ 19 Zł. — זל.	Przychód miesięczny אַרײנגענומען אין גמ"ח פארן חודש _פעברואר_ 19 Zł. — זל.	Pozostało na dn 1 _Lutego_ 1931 געבליבן אין גמ"ח אויפן 1-טן _פעברואר_ 19 Zł. — זל.	Skład kapitału „Gemiłus-Chesed": וויפל געלט האט דער גמ"ח און וואו האט ער עס גענומען:
598.35	—	50.—	548.35	Składka członkowska מיטגלידס־געלט
196.45	—	16.75	179.70	Różne ofiary פארשיידענע נדבות
3.657.55	—	—	3.657.55	Dochód z różnych פארשיידענע הכנסות
423.01	—	—	423.01	Kapitał גרונט־קאפיטאל
3.650.—	—	—	3.650.—	Pożyczka od kom. pomocy „Ekoro" הלואה פון „עקאפא"
—	—	—	—	Wkłady bezprocentowe אומפראצענטיקע פקדונות
8.525.36		66.75	8.458.61	BILANS באַלאַנס ס"ה
				AKTYWA — אקטיוון
155.—			155.—	Inwentarz אינוונטאר
7.421.15	3.600.—	3.286.—	7.107.—	Wydano pożyczki członkom ארויסגעגעבן הלואות מיטגלידער
				Wydatki administracyjne: אדמיניסטראַטיווע הוצאות:
166.65	21.50	—	145.15	Pensja (1 שכירות
—	—	—	—	Opał i światło (2 באַהייצונג און באַלייכטונג
—	—	—	—	Koszty lokalu (3 דירה
324.55	—	—	324.55	Wydatki różne פארשיידענע הוצאות
458.01	268.75	—	726.76	Gotówka w kasie מזומן אין קאסע
8.525.36	3.890.25	3.286.—	8.458.61	BILANS באַלאַנס ס"ה

BUCHALTER — בוכהאַלטער _____ PREZES — פאָרזיצער _____

SEKRETARZ — סעקרעטאַר _____

RAZEM צוזאמען	Innych zawodów אנדערע בא־ שעפסיקונגען	Wolnych zawodów פרייע פראפעסיעס	Rolników קרי-ארבעטער	Drobn. handl. קליינ־ הענדלער	Rzemieślni-ków האנטווערקער	Ruch członków באַוועגונג פון די מיטגלידער
141	18	2	19	67	35	Na początku miesiąca było צום אָנהויב חודש איז געווען
1				1		W miesiącu sprawozdawczym przybył אין חודש איז צוגעקומען
						W miesiącu sprawozdawczym ubyło אין חודש אַרויסגעגאַנגען
142	18	2	19	68	35	Pozostało w dniu 1-go געבליבן צום 1-טן

Ilość i suma wydanych pożyczek:
די צאָל און גרויס פון די אַרויסגעגעבענע הלואות:

za miesiąc Luty 1931 פאַרן חודש

Razem צוזאמען	Zł. זלאטעס	pożyczki הלואות צו	wydano אַרויסגעגעבן
600.—	150.—	4	
3.000.—	100.—	30	

Zł. **3.600.—** na sumę אויף pożyczki הלואות **34** wydano Razem בסך־הכל אַרויסגעגעבן

OD POCZĄTKU ROKU — פון אנהויב יאר

Razem צוזאמען	Zł. זלאטעס	pożyczki הלואות צו	wydano אַרויסגעגעבן
7.500.—	150.—	50	
135.—	135.—	1	
130	130.—	1	
29.600	100.—	296	
2.960	80.—	37	
70	70.—	1	
7.200	50.—	144	
45	45.—	1	
60		2	
100	25.—	4	

Zł. **47.860** na sumę אויף pożyczki הלואות **538** wydan Razem בסך־הכל אַרויסגעגעבן

Account balances 1921

[Page 107]

The Fire Department in Tsarist Times, and in the First Ten Years of the Polish Rule
by Shepsl Kaplan

The town Jews formed a brass band and bought new fire extinguishing equipment. Next to the new shul, on the shore of a little lake, in a locked shed were stored hoses, pumps, a few wheeled barrels full of water, ladders, rope tied to a curved iron with four teeth, dubbed "cat", additional equipment and rope. In the 30s, the Polish administration took over both Jews and Christians, bought mechanized pumps and other equipment. The department was headed by a Polish reserve officer, Matovski.

Fires were frequent in Olshan, mostly at night. The first observer shouted "pozhar", and men appeared promptly, half–dressed, in their assigned roles, shouting *"pozhar"*. The cathedral bell rang, the firemen ran to the fire, often breaking the lock because no one knew where the key was. Instead of a horse, the men hauled the water barrels towards the fire. There were many instances of houses burned after help was summoned. In 1935, in mid–day, a spark from a forge set off a fire which consumed almost the whole town. Firemen came from all nearby communities, but the wind spread the fire and the firemen were helpless. Such catastrophes happened a lot before World War I, but the dates of fires were especially memorable, along with weddings, deaths and other civic events, related by parents to their children.

[Pages 108-109]

Zionist Activity, Hakashra and my Zionist Involvement

My mother died in 1920. I was an orphan at 14. I attended Zionist meetings, where funds and support were sought for return to Israel. I decided to collect money for the return of Jews to Israel. All Jews in Olshan supported this, including my family. I asked to be sent to Israel, but I was told I was too young. At 16, I joined *Khalutz* and was sent to a camp near Vilna which was the center of Zionist activity then, an arm of the Polish Zion Party. The camp was part of a farming community which had belonged to a Prince, and that resulted in an interesting history.

The Prince was known as an anti–Semite. But in World War I when the Germans occupied the Vilna area, some peasants accused him of allegiance to the Russians. Dr. Vigodski, of Vilna, who was tortured by the Germans in World War II, was favored by the Germans during World War I–he stood up for the Prince and rescued him. The children of the Prince, after his death, were pro–Jewish out of gratitude for the defense of their father, so they donated the land for the Zionist group.

I was in the group for a year, and learned a lot about farm work. I was busy with cows, and knew that all these tasks had to be mastered because they were necessary in Eretz Yisroel. I decided that there, in our land I'd be a *shomer* [guard], in order to protect Jewish land.

In the *Hachshara*, you had to sign up for two years to determine whether the youths were suitable for *Aliyah* or not. After two years, the secretariat of the *khalutz*, based in Vilna, decided whether to accept the candidate. It wasn't easy after approval to keep going, because you needed money to cover all your expenses. Besides, the Polish government was especially harsh on the youths, because they were supposed to serve in the army.

After two years, in 1925, I was accepted by the khalutz for Aliyah. But by the time I was ready to go, the British had barred entry to our land, so I finally left Poland in 1929, and embarked on an old ship, arriving there just at the time of the Arab attack on the Jews. I was assigned to the Kibbutz 'Eilat Hashochar', volunteered as a *shomer* with others to protect the colonies, which had been established with such great effort.

[Pages 109-110]

Activity of the Khalutz
by Ariah Gershoni

In 1923, we founded the *Khalutz*. The founders were Yaakov Namiot, Moshe Yalek and I. Back then my name was Shklioronok, but now my name is Reuben ben Aharon.

The Khalutz concentrated on cultural activity, especially learning Hebrew and knowledge about Eretz Yisroel, and promoted Aliyah. Because I had worked in the forest I led a group of boys who worked for me. The girls had lighter tasks, such as baking matzos for Pesach–the goal was that all the comrades should get accustomed to all kinds of work. Money went into the general fund. We were connected with the Khalutz center in Vilna, and the comrades from Merchuz visited us several times. Rivka Berkman was the first to make Aliyah, followed by Saul Abramovitz, the teacher Biaritz, Rivka Ziskind, then me. I was supposed to be first, but I was directed to stay and continue training.

Reuven Ben Aharon

[Page 110]

Organization
and Cultural Activity Beys–R
by Shifra Kotrin–Trobski

Olshan had a strong *Beys–R* organization and youth membership, engaged in dedicated Zionist activity. Several good leaders are listed, [Motel Segalovitz, Shefa Dolinski, Hinda Lidski]one of whom got to Israel before the war. The organization enlivened the youth with singing, and dancing the horas, lectures, readings. People came from the nearby towns to meet. Everyone's morale was lifted, and the people lived in hope of going to Israel.

My sister as a young girl was active, my brother also trained as a guard and tried to reform the excessive restrictions which divided the organization. They both perished in the Holocaust. My sister died in the Shtuthof camp. My brother, the family star, graduated in medicine in Paris, practiced at the Rothschild Hospital and died in France– no one knows where.

[Page 111]

Raising Money
by Pesakh Gershonovitz

Many Zionist organizations raised money; the comrades spread the word at all levels and solicited from all Jewish families for the creation of Israel. Special collections came at celebrations of historic memorial days–such as Lag B'Omer, Shavuoth, Yizkor, Chanukah, weddings, births. The most active leaders are listed. The young were especially inspired to work at the annual bazaars; many worked all night. The townspeople gave generously, especially the people from Vilna.

Opening day at the bazaar was a holiday. Families all had fun together. It lasted two days, and all parts of the town participated. Contributions of as much as 1000 zlotys were made–a significant amount for Olshan's Jews.

Zionist fund raising group

וזכען פביר
און פביך-פביר-בשן
1935 אוליאן פביר

Activists at the fund-raising annual bazaar

Members of the 'Hechalutz' Zionist group

'Hechalutz' members

Hechalutz group

A group of Hechalutz members, on the departure of Yehoshua Liand for Eretz Yisroel

Zionist group

A group of youths from Olshan and Oshman celebrating

Celebrating departure of Moshe Kosluvski for Eretz YIsroel

Friends of Moshe Kosluvski

Group of leaders of Betar

Group of Youth of Betar

No Caption

Pioneer youth in training

A social group in Olshan

A group of youths near the lake in Olshan

At Lake Zhiganka

At the Olshan Lake

Chana Gurvitz in the Tzarist army

[Page 121]

Types of People and Images

Daily Life of the Olshan Jews
by Shepsl Kaplan

I see Olshan before my eyes, every house, young and old, their daily lives during the week, Jewish Olshan was lively on Shabbos and holidays. I remember, and it speaks to my heart–a neighborhood, an atmosphere. My memories are filled with uplift and love.

A summer evening in Olshan: Parents sit on their steps, the youngsters are out walking behind the town in the woods, around the lake and in other nice spots, blessed by Nature. Even in winter, the town was lively. Snow and ice didn't keep people from walking in the streets. Friends would meet in the library, in the theater group, even dance to the music of an orchestra.

Olshan was like a little town in White Russia, which had belonged to Poland until WW II. It was a rural life, which started in summer early in the AM, still dark. The cows were let out to pasture, daily work was performed, after a few crumbs for breakfast, then some feed for the cows. In winter they processed cabbage, neighbors helped each other. They rendered goose fat and made *gribenes*; in the copper pot was boiled *sagonchik* and onions, and that's the way it was for generations until the German invasion.

Jewish life pervaded all the streets and alleys, ending at the Market Square. Four straight streets and six crooked alleys led to the lake, which from beginning of spring to late autumn was filled with bathers, Jews and Christians, young and old. Cultural life was concentrated in the shuls and the library where there were periodic performances by traveling theater ensembles.

The market place, with its two Jewish farms, was empty all week. Only on Sunday and market days was it lively. It seemed entirely different near Shabbos. The Jews went in the afternoon from Mincha to Maariv, to walk, stand on the bridge for a while near the water mill, chat a bit with Aaron the miller, and go further beyond the town to the fields. One might rest under the leafy pear tree, to get some fresh air, then go to pray *Mincha*. Here I bring a few personalities who personify the life style of Jewish Olshan:

Bruch the Pharmacist

Bruch Abramovitz was revered in the town because of his conviviality and energy, which he had inherited from his grandfather and father. In the first years of liberated Poland, he was chosen to be a councilman, and he protected the interests of the Jews, downtrodden after WW I, and demanded that they be treated as equal citizens, like the Poles. After the Russo–Polish war, he put his energy into forming a cooperative People's Bank, in order to serve the poorest in the town. Thanks to his enterprise, the bank rapidly developed significant credit for the Olshaners to revive their town.

Bruch was a brilliant speaker. His words in the council were heeded by both Jews and Christians. His oldest son finished chemistry in Vilna University in 1939. His younger son had shown unusual talent as a painter. As a child of five, he had drawn with pencil the portraits of Joseph Pilsudski and President Moshchitzki; he received thank you letters from the Polish leaders. Bruch's wife and four children suffered in various camps, and Bruch was shot by the Germans in the first weeks of the bloody conquest.

Samuel Leib Dolinski and his Community Activity

The Olshan intelligentsia included the family of attorney Dolinski. He was born and raised in Vilna. His parents, intelligent ordinary people, provided a university education. He came to Olshan in 1905, sent by the central Zionist–Socialist movement of Vilna to promote the organization. As a brilliant speaker and organizer, Dolinski rapidly won the hearts of the Olshan youth, which had already been organized into the ranks of the revolutionary Bund groups which dominated Olshan. The gifted Dolinski, with his propaganda, successfully tore away some members of the strong and well–organized Bund party, and won them over to the Zionist–Socialist movement.

Olshan youth was already poised for a revolutionary movement. In those days, a large library had been created of Jewish, Russian and Hebrew books, nurtured by Mishkol Nachum Leib Abeliovich. Soon after his arrival, Dolinski worked as secretary to the Jewish mayor Goldanski. The young student met Goldanski's daughter Cherna, and later they married. After the wedding, Dolinski founded a modern Russian–Jewish shul. In independent Poland, between the wars, Dolinski practiced law. His five sons received higher education and were raised in the national–progressive Jewish spirit. The family had a special attraction to agriculture. Therefore Dolinski bought five hectares of land which his five sons, in their free time, learned how to cultivate. For this purpose Dolinski built a large barn next to his house, where his sons would load the crops of wheat, corn, barley, oats, and helped thresh the grains.. And that's the way it was until Olshan was occupied by Hitler and his murderous army.

Gershon Abramovitz and his Building

Gershon was called 'pharaoh', because he had played that role, king of Egypt. For many years, Gershon was busy building a new beys hamidrash, at the same time as a *chevra kadusha*. He was at the head of his congregation, which was several hundred years old. Gershon was also a good *bal tfiloh*, with a distinctive voice. With his lyric tenor voice, he improvised on the most famous cantors. His final high note, with which he used to end the service, was memorable. Only one of his six daughters survived, Chana, who had made it to Israel before the war. She died there in 1964.

The Olshan Shokhet Mordechai–Noteh and his Peasant Background

One of the most distinctive characters in Olshan was the shokhet, Mordechai Noteh. His father was a gardener and a farmer, and from Mordechai's childhood, he was uncommonly fascinated by farming. He didn't change his mind later, but fullfilled his dream.

His best years were spent in the yeshivahs of Voloshin, Mirre, and Slobodka. Everywhere he was a top student, and he was ordained at 25. Then he returned to his father's home and helped him to earn a living. Only after his parents died did he take on the position as shokhet in Olshan. Shortly thereafter, he realized his dream of returning to the land. He had bought ten hectares, farmed it with his own hands and the aid of his family. He sowed, reaped , threshed, tended cows, calves, horses and donkeys. He acquired a barn, an irrigator, a scythe, and established himself as an agricultural innovator.

In spite of his hard work and long hours, he continued to attend shul three times a day, and to study a little Gemorah. He also found time to console, also assist the oppressed and the poor.

This honest pious peasant family suffered the same fate as all the Olshan Jews. In 1942, the Voloshin ghetto Jews were slaughtered, including his daughter, her husband and two children. Also in 1942, his mother along with 400 Jews was killed in an *aktion*, carried out by the Germans with the aid of the ghetto police in Ashman ghetto.

After their disastrous fates in the ghettos and camps, the remnants of the family were herded to Klage in Estonia. Two days before liberation by the Soviet army, the rest of them were incinerated, except for the miraculous survival of Aharon, his youngest son, now in Israel. His oldest son Elye perished in Panor.

Reb Shimon Segalovitz the Bal–Tfiloh

He was one of the most prominent leaders in the town. He was a student and a flour merchant, with three sons, David, Bruch**Error! Bookmark not defined.**-Shmuel, Kalman, in the flax business. They were the founders and directors of the charity organization up to the last moment. A daughter perished in Zelianka. The only remnant of this far flung family is his son Bruch's wife Rivkah, now living in America.

Rev Yudel the 'Rufah' and his Wife the 'Heyvn' [Midwife]

He was an army medic, but because of his scholarly appearance, he was called the *Rufa*. His well–tended smoothly combed white beard, his elegant presence, black cane with silver handle made him look like a professor.

Most of the medicines used by R. Yudel to heal his patients, Jewish or Christian, were selected from: leeches, *piovket*, *rizinoil*, and *molinas* for sweating. If a poor patient didn't have any money to buy *molinas*, Yudel didn't charge him. Yudel's wife, dear Yenta, brought molinas and other confections to stimulate the heart. Yudel never wrote out any prescriptions. He personally went to the pharmacist to deliver them. Many patients felt that this was a benefit, that the medic himself helped to prepare the prescription for them.

There was another medic in town, a Pole, Krukovski, who was not as popular as Yudel. At Yudel's place, handsome ornate wagons and carriages often stayed waiting for him, the 'noble Yudel', and carried him off at a gallop to tend to a wealthy or noble client. After returning from a trip, Yudel first went to the pharmacist, ordered the medicines, and only then returned to his office, which was always full of patients.

Yudel's wife Liba Yenta was a midwife, who delivered children for the Jewish women of the town. Though childless herself, she loved the infants she delivered, calling them her grandchildren, often kissing and hugging them, and brought gifts. Liba Yenta was also the leader on Shabbos and Yomtov, in the 'ezras nishim', the women's section. Often she would gather contributions to divide among the needy. She and Yudel were much beloved in the shtetl. Every Shabbos at their table there were many unexpected guests.

Liba Yenta died just before World War I, and that ended Yudel's career. During the German occupation, Yudel lost his practice, became poor and depressed. In the town at that time there was a field hospital with German doctors who also provided civilian care. Impoverished, Yudel died after World War I.

Reb Itsche the Shamesh and Teacher

His slender income as shamesh in the new shul, and as a teacher often left him unoccupied by the end of the week. But he was a Jew with a lot of spirit, generous and cheerful, so he did everything for free. Because he was so short, his students crowned him as '*tal umtor*', and that stuck with him for the rest of his life. But they loved him and were attentive. The free time after teaching was spent in the Beys Hamidrash, where he cleaned and swept, took care of the books. In winter, he heated the stoves–he thought this was all holy work. He really loved children, compared to other shameshes, who used to exclude the poor orphans from the shul. Reb Itsche welcomed them, sat them down by the warm stove in winter and told them stories about the good Jews; this always charmed the children.

The town dignitaries admired him for the care he took of the shul, as did the needy ones, who had a warm place to sit on wintry frosty nights.

Reb Yunah Gdalye the Timber Merchant

Yunah was the youngest of four brothers. He was a rich Jew, a timber merchant who created a big business with an excellent clientele. He himself dressed elegantly, aristocratically, and had a smooth mastery of Russian and Polish. He was respected and admired by the Jews, as well as the Russians and Poles. He was aloof from the affairs of the congregation. Stiff and formal, he looked down from his reserved seat in the new shul, thus reinforcing their respect and admiration for him.

His wife Bella died in Olshan when the Germans came. Their son and daughter, Motel and Mirke, suffered in the camps. One daughter, Chana–Tsipa got to Israel before the war. The youngest son stayed in Russia, and lives now in Israel.

Bunya Kaplan and Reb Eliah Schwartz

Bunya Kaplan was one of the most respected figures in Olshan. His house was always open to needy Jews and Christians, no one went away empty handed. He was a symbol of cordiality, always surrounded by friends and women activists, who also provided help for poor Jewish families. Bunya felt strongly that he must always be receptive. Either alone or with his children, every Erev Shabbos, they had to deliver challah and meat, and also a few zlotys.

Always a scholar, Bunya honored his religious parents and grandparents. His grandfather, a leather artisan in Ashman, had experienced the death of Bunya's young father. The grandfather imbued his grandchildren with traditional religious spirit and implanted in them good will, honesty, love of the Jewish people and the urge to help the poor and oppressed. Reb Elia Hirsch made it his mission to marry off poor girls to men, to whom he gave money for the dowry. With his grandchildren, he hosted the guests until dawn. Bunya, the dearest of his grandchildren, had a fine voice, and took his grandfather along to sing joyously with the guests.

Two weeks after Reb Elia arranged a wedding for his only daughter Sarah, Bunya's mother, a remarkable event occurred. Just at that time, a groom of a poor bride, arranged by Reb Elia, stubbornly refused to enter the khupa, because the bride's dowry did not include any winter fodder. Immediately Reb Elia went to his daughter and told her about it. She brought her own dowry provision and gave it to her father, who kissed her thankfully, took the fodder back to the bride. The satisfied groom then entered the khupa, and they all had a big party.

Twice daily, winter or summer, Reb Elia rode his horse and wagon from the edge of town to the Beys Hamidrash to pray. Often he returned without his coat or hat which he had given away to someone with tattered or torn clothes. Elia's death was grieved by all. The funeral took place on a market day. Out of respect, all the farmers closed their stalls, and accompanied the procession. From the table where he had taught, a plaque was made in his memory, and was placed in his grave. The youngest most beloved grandchildren of Reb Elia, Bunya and Mayer, were murdered by the Germans.

Beryl the Kaiser

Beryl was called 'Kaiser' by both Jews and goyim. He was an expert cobbler, a good brother to all. And when he was especially happy he kissed everybody. He was also able to break the bones of any hooligan who tried to make fun of him. As well as being a very talented cobbler, Beryl had a special duty: At dawn, he wakened the Jews to prayer on Shabbos and called them into shul.

On a severe winter morning, under the influence of too many drinks, Beryl crawled under the window of a Christian neighbor, and awoke him by singing, "Get up! Get up! you holy Jews. Get up for services!" The goy just continued to sleep and wasn't even angry at Beryl. The name 'Kaiser' stuck to him because of a role he had played in a theater once.

Dudka the Blacksmith

Dudka was born in Biuchiska, a town 7 km away. His forebears had lived there for generations, farming, like all the peasants. Dudka's father had taken on the fiery profession of being a blacksmith. He serviced the horses and wagons of the town's peasants, and thus supported a large family. At 17, he came to Olshan and worked as an assistant to the blacksmith David Koslovski, who has been noted earlier.

Children used to run to the smithy to watch the sparks fly and to admire Dudka's skill. Dudka would grasp the heavy hammer by the end of its wooden handle in his muscular hand and swing it. He demonstrated other difficult feats working with iron. They called him Samson; no one could approach his skill and strength with the giant hammer.

Dudka's performance, his incredibly strong hands were admired not only by the Jews, but also by the goyim. They all feared his strength. Any ruffian who tried to match him would certainly avoid any further contact.

In his youth, Dudka was a good–natured quiet boy, steady and cheerful, always smiling, with blue eyes and blond hair. He loved children and enjoyed playing with them. When any Jews were threatened, Dudka was soon there. Often he didn't bother to take off his work clothes. He would approach the group of hooligans and immediately attack the group leader. At the first blow, these ruffians would flee. Woe to any who would try to fight Dudka who would overcome them with his strong hands. They would run off, like frightened mice. Dudka, contented and cheerful would return to his job as if nothing had happened.

A few years before World War II, Dudka married a girl from a nearby town. His fate after the German invasion is not known. His only sister Golda, the youngest in the family, and her husband were put into the Olshan ghetto. When the ghetto was liquidated, Golda ran back to her town and was sheltered by some Christian neighbors. But the same Christian friends murdered her a few days before the arrival of Soviet forces.

Joshua the Blacksmith

A cheerful care–free type, Joshua**Error! Bookmark not defined.** always greeted people with a good word or a joke. On Friday nights, he was always the last to leave the shul, in order to take home anyone who was poor. Even in the middle of the week, he would never dine without a needy guest. In his shop, because of his diligence and punctuality, he was respected and esteemed by everyone..

From his father, Joshua inherited the profession of healing by incantations. He had lots of patients, and he never took any payment. When asked if he really believed in his remedies, he answered, "That's not important, it's whatever the sick person believes, otherwise he wouldn't have come to me. His belief in my talking cure helps him."

The Pinchukes

Olshan was always distinguished by its remarkably healthy strong Jews, ordinary men who feared no one. The Kozlovskis belonged to such a family. They were called 'Pinchukes', a dynastic name from a great great grandfather, Pinye. For generations, they were blacksmiths and iron mongers. Under all circumstances, they would react with their iron fists to protect Jewish property.

Olshan had its ruffians and alcoholics, like other towns. Fairly often, on market days, a drunken city or town hooligan would quarrel with a Jewish vendor. It was enough however, if one of the Pinchukes was present, the ruffians would flee like mice. No matter how drunk they were, they knew the strength of a Pinchuk.

In Tsarist times and later in independent Poland, annually, in autumn, there were groups of recruits for the militia passing through town. For two months, the Pinchukes stood ready on call, to defend the Jews against ruffians' attacks. After the recruits passed through Olshan, the excited rabble hiding in the adjacent woods came back to Olshan and Oshman, and quarreled with the remaining Jews, farmers and the poor market vendors. But soon the Pinchukes showed up with their iron weapons and dispersed the mob of hundreds, who fled like rabbits, with bloody scalps and broken ribs, abandoning their horses and wagons. The police were pleased to see the hoodlums beaten, and they helped to remove the horses and wagons.

Peshe the Baker

Peshe was known as the *Bagdanoverin*. She was left as a widow with seven small children. With remarkable energy, she triumphed over her misfortune, and opened a modern bakery for bread and pastry. When the children were a little older, Peshe opened a restaurant, an impressive undertaking. She married off her first four daughters, got ready for the next two, and made plans for her son.

But fate turned out otherwise. Peshe and her children were moved along with the other Jews to ghettos and camps. On the eve of liberation, she was killed. In the German *Aktion* of children extermination, all the grandchildren were taken. Peshe's six daughters and her son survived; five of them with their brother now live in Israel.

Blume Berkman

Blume Berkman was known in town as an upright woman. She had been left as a young widow with six children, but this misfortune did not deter her. She raised her family, raised crops from her little farm, and gave her children a good Jewish education. She sent them to public school, which didn't charge tuition.

Two daughters were sent by Blume to Israel before World War II. A son and daughter remained in Poland and survived the horrors of the ghetto, and now live in Israel.

Shmuel Boyarski

When Shmuel Boyarski, a famous Yeshiva boy, married the daughter of Reb Shlomo Potashnik, all the mothers of eligible daughters looked at Reb Shlomo and his wife Dinah, and said, "when you are rich, you have luck". Friends tried to console those who begrudged the union–this prize package might still not work out.

In reality, Reb Shlomo and Dinah had no regrets. Quickly, their yeshiva boy became an aggressive developer. His tiny farm became a big business. Shmuel became an active participant in all the religious and social institutions, and was respected by all.

Shmuel and his wife Chasya suffered the same fate as all the Olshan Jews. They starved in ghettos and camps, experienced overwhelming misfortunes, persecution and terror. Shmuel succumbed in January 1944 in a camp. His wife Chasya died in another camp. Their son Simon, a daughter Rachel and a son Abraham now live in America. Their youngest son died tragically when he was run over by a fire engine, on the way to combat an all-too-common fire in Olshan.

Reb Leib the Butcher

Reb Leib considered he was in a blessed condition; "to bring a piece of meat from his store into the house was a sign of success", said the women. It was a special privilege for the Jews of his shul, when Reb Leib led Shabbos prayers. People said that one understood perfectly every passage.. Leib and his wife Rivke had six sons and one daughter. His house was always light, neat and cheerful. All the children were well-educated. The older ones helped the younger ones. Bruch Hersh helped his younger brother to finish medicine, and he planned to emigrate. Chaim, who lives in America, helped to found a music school in Vilna. The only survivor is Yossel Gurevitz, who lives in Canada.

Hirschl Rudnick

Hirschl was a noted yeshiva scholar, who moved to Volozhin. He felt comfortable in the outside world, and was familiar with Hebrew and Jewish literature. He was quickly married off in Olshan, then became a teacher of religion in the shul. However his remuneration as a teacher was not enough to support the burden of caring for his family of six and he had to resort to the generosity of his sister-in-law Sara, who had an old inheritance.

This turn of events was heartbreaking for Herschl. He had tried to make a decent living, but his spirit was broken. He sickened and died young. He had planned to send his two older children, Rishke and Isaac, to America. The younger ones, Avke and Schlomke returned to Olshan, and are now in America. His wife Rachel died in Zhelianka.

The Varonovski Family

The brothers Herschl and Reuben Varonovski were well known in Olshan. They had a business of their own in the market place making soda water and other drinks. Their lives ended tragically like most of the Jews of the town. Herschl and his wife Golde Teibe were killed in Zhelianka. Their older son Avrohom Shlomo, a gifted painter, died in a death camp. Their younger son Aaron, a lawyer, returned to the ghetto from Volozhin with his bride Liusa.

They were captured and murdered by the White Russian police of Vishneva. Reuben Varonovski was tortured in a death camp; his only daughter Peitche, survived and lives in Israel.

The Gurvitz Family

Reb Elihu and his wife Chaya Rocha were highly respected. Reb Elihu was very lively, good–humored –he was a wood gatherer. He was also very active in the religious community as a scholar, a prayer leader and was an excellent tenor singer. He organized and participated in all the religious and social functions in the town, and continued to appear on the stage as singer and actor. He also sang in the Beys Hamidrash choir, conducted by Cantor Isaac Gershon. Unfortunately he died at an early age during World War I. The whole burden of supporting the family fell on the frail Chaya Rocha. She maintained the tradition of helping the oppressed and needy. Despite her crooked spine, she sheltered in her home two orphans of a younger sister, and raised them along with her own two orphans. One of them, Blume, successfully made it to Israel before World War II.

Because of Chaya Rocha's poor health, her young daughter Shaina Blume was forced to take over, and from her little farm, she made enough to support her young brother Chanye in Vilna, where he was going to school.

Shaina Blume, despite her difficult work, continued her cultural activity. She found time to read Yiddish, Russian, Polish, and took part in the burgeoning youth culture. Her home was a meeting place for Olshan youths and their theater circle. For fifteen years, she was in the theater group, playing lead roles and singing as a soloist in operettas.

Chaya Rocha died on the eve of World War II. Her daughter perished in Zhezhmir in Lithuania and her husband Isaac was killed in Kovno. The youngest and sole survivor Chanye was drafted into the Polish army in September 1939. He suffered imprisonment by the Germans but managed to escape to Israel in 1942.

Reb Mayer the 'Agent'

Mayer Rudnick was not called by his family name, but by his business–as an 'agent'. Reb Mayer had distinguished himself among the town's residents by his wealth and his elegant life style. His wooden home in the center of town was noted for its comfort and beauty both inside and out. The path from his house to the sidewalk was lined by a blue–white fence, planted with colorful fragrant flowers which attracted all passersby. The glass veranda on entry and the blue–white doors framed by branches, the fruit orchard behind the house, caught everyone's attention.

In Tsarist times, before World War I, Reb Mayer arranged travel to America for both Jews and Christians, who had material or political motives to leave

Olshan. Such emigrants came to Reb Mayer, the 'agent', agreed on a price, and were then taken to Vilna, to the Hotel Venezia, owned by his brother Moshe. This was close to the Exchange. Reb Moshe took care of all the passengers' needs until they boarded ship.

From his easy work, Rudnick constructed his palatial home, and also gave major donations to the Tsarist police and other officials, as well as to the needy oppressed Jews of Olshan.

Reb Mayer spent World War I in Russia. After Polish independence, he returned to Olshan, but his business was gone, and he had no other trade. As matters grew worse for him, he sold his property and emigrated, not to America where he had sent so many others, but to Israel, where he lives in Jerusalem.

[Page 139]

Alikum Litski and his Love of Farming

[Memories of childhood]

by Mina Zhalovski–Litzki

My father's house was built after the Partition. Next to our house were humble peasants' shacks with roofs of straw. Behind our house sprouted a greens–garden, a grassy field. In summer it was full of wheat and corn. I recall such summer days. Part of the harvest was already cut and tied into sheaves, while the rest awaited reaping. A big pile rested in the barn full of bundles of straw and ears of corn, which had to be shucked. The cows waited to be milked.

My father Alikum Litski led a quiet peaceful life as an ordinary peasant. He pursued his business industriously and lived a traditional Jewish life in the shtetl. He worked the earth with his magic hands, he tilled, plowed, sowed and reaped. We children really enjoyed working with him, helping to reap and bind the sheaves. It was a special privilege to sit on the wagon atop the harvested crops and ride into the barn, where we had to lower our heads to clear the entry.

After the work was done, when we returned from the field covered with dust and straw, the whole family washed up, then had lunch, which consisted of a bowl of unpeeled boiled potatoes, beet borscht or sauerkraut, some barley kasha with lima beans or some rice pudding with milk, and to end the meal, a glass of milk. It was a heartwarming atmosphere at home. After saying prayers, we rested for a while before returning to work refreshed.

On Shabbos and holidays, we children all went to shul with our father, sat next to him and prayed. When we came home, our goyish neighbors bowed their heads, to acknowledge the Shabbos tradition of our father, and greeted us amicably. They recognized my father as one of them, who worked hard and sweated to earn his daily bread from the earth. My father believed that we all lived in the lap of nature, the basis of our entire lives. Nature was the love of his life in this small town setting. Our Christian neighbors often remarked that they should be inspired by our example.

And so the years passed. His life would have followed its natural course, but was then disrupted by the hellish German onslaught, which uprooted the entire Jewish community, including my father. He was driven off his land to which he had devoted his life, and would never see it again. [Minna Zholovski–Litzki]

[Page 140]

The Worker Families of Oshman Street
by Shifra Kutin–Trobski

Oshman Street extended from the Market to the bridge by the pond. The last house in the street belonged to Lokem, who worked on the land and had a little wooden shack. He worked hard for his family of small children. Despite his hard work he was always good–natured and friendly.

On the same block lived Benjamin the blacksmith, his wife Hinde and their three daughters. The oldest daughter Teibele, a student in the Oshman high school, was killed in the Volozhin ghetto.

Near the bridge by the pond, lived Michl the glazier and his two daughters. He worked hard all his life, going from house to house replacing windows. When he became old and sick, his older daughter Chaya Sara took over his business. I often saw her carrying a wooden chest containing sheets of glass seeking work. She was the wage earner for the family. Her sister Rache was weak and sickly, unable to work. Their little old cabin was always neat and clean.

My cousins lived in the next house near the pond, Afrim and his wife Mume Chashe. Their daughters Basye and Rachel Leah were quiet and modest. Afrim was a tall healthy man, who used to drive his horse and wagon to Vilna in the hot rainy summer and freezing winters, transporting farm produce. He was always generous and very accommodating. Mume Chashe managed an efficient household, and also helped with the income. On market day, one could always get a good lunch at her place. In spring, she sold compost to the gardeners. The young boys and girls of the town–friends of Rachel and Basye– used to gather together at Chashe's house.. At night, the house was filled with laughter and song. The kids used to pass the time away with innocent games.

Next door lived a widow, Devorale, with her children. She operated a bakery selling bread and rolls, cookies with poppy seeds. Naturally, in the bakery, no one slept at night, so that fresh bread might be ready early in the morning. My second cousin, Yankel, his wife Mume Frume and their children operated a cafe, and were very competent. He was always good–natured, a smile on his face. Tsimach their son died in childhood. His wife Hennye and her daughter Chana died in the German attack.

In 1943, Yankel and Mume escaped from Zhezhmir camp to Olshan, and hid in the forest. It was winter, they lit a fire, and a peasant reported it to the Germans, who shot the mother and daughter. The son, Bentzia, died in Kovno, Their two little children died in a children's *Aktion*. Bentzia's wife Perl lives in America. Yankel's daughter Grunya is the only family member to survive, in America.

Life in My Family

Our family name was Trovski. There were seven children, four daughters and three sons. Asher, the father, worked his whole life in the forest. I remember, when I was a child, he used to go to Danzig to bring home toys for the children, and he'd tell us about the big city. I used to boast and exaggerate to my friends about this German city.

We lived in two big houses with beautiful spacious rooms. The walls were covered with multi–colored tapestries. A path led to a hill near the house, entered by a high wooden gate. Behind the house was a cultivated garden, where every year the whole family worked to plant all sorts of greenery and potatoes.

Under the house was a large walled cellar. In autumn it was filled with vegetables and potatoes for the whole year. The mother, a tall beautiful Jewess, was a good housekeeper, who took good care of the children. She was cheerful, loved to sing, to tell little jokes. She concerned herself not only for her children but also for the neighbors. I remember how my mother in winter, used to throw dry wood over the fence for the neighbors. She never had to clean up our sweat though we used to sleep two in a bed. Our house was open to all.

My father was handsome, with a little pointed beard, always neatly dressed. His whole life was dedicated to the children. His work was not difficult, but it was essential that the children must learn. He told us, "I do everything to give you an education, that's the most important thing in life." In every free moment he was reading a newspaper or book–he was interested in everything. We children had in him a friend. I told him everything, and he always gave me a reliable explanation. He implanted in us our love for people and work.

In winter father spent the evenings playing chess with cousin Yankel. They talked about politics and the future of the Jews in Poland. In the last years before the war, the situation became progressively worse, while anti–Semitism increased.

[Page 143]

Dinah Potashnik
by Eliezer Potashnik

Our mother Dinah's life was filled with extraordinary love of Torah and with charitable behavior. On holidays, she was busy at home but always found time to help the needy, with heartfelt dedication. The women always contributed to her monthly or weekly collections. She herself went collecting, then was brought home by others. During World War I, when food was scarce, she always had a piece of bread for the needy.

She was so happy when she was able to have a prayer service at home on Shabbos, or on a weekday. She was dedicated to learning Torah. She was a saintly person, determined that her children would lead an observant life; she sent her son to a Yeshiva.

In spite of being such an extraordinarily devoted mother, during the stormy days of the war, she sent her son away from home to learn Torah. How remarkable, to send her son away during those times. Against all odds, she was determined that her children must become Torah scholars. When she came to Israel, she immediately devoted herself to charity work, until she passed away. Survivors include my brother Herschl, in Israel. His wife and five children were killed in Panor.

[Page 144]

The Liand Family
[A memorial for my parents]

by Reuben Liand

Velvel Liand was born into a religious family, living in Olshan for generations. As a *harepashnik* he became a revolutionary activist in 1905, a comrade in the workers movement. However he remained faithful to his Jewish identity.

Our grandfather Israel Liand, was one of the recognized leaders in the town. He assumed responsibility for the Beys Hamidrash, and he was also an advisor to Prince Yogmen, who owned Olshan. As such he would bring necessities to the congregation.

Our grandmother Shima, a good honest lady, took on responsibility for assisting the poor, a Jewish tradition. When her son, my father Ben Yichid, joined the workers movement, her health declined and she died at an early age.

In their later years, my parents sold their farm, which had been inherited from the grandfather, and was no longer productive. My father worked transporting passengers to the train station in Bogdanov. Our mother Rachel, a sensitive considerate woman, took in guests whom our father brought home from shul. No hungry or needy person could leave her home without sharing our meal at least once a week.

My older sister Zipporah and my brother Simon belonged to the Zionist movement. Our parents didn't understand the need for this. When the time came to emigrate to Israel, there were no funds, so the farm was sold, thus enabling the children to go to Israel.

Our dear parents perished in a death camp in Zhelianka in the second Aktion in the Ashman ghetto, managed with the active participation of the Vilna Jewish Ghetto Police.

[Page 145]

The Abramovitz Family

[A memorial to the parents and children of this wide–spread family, victims of the third Jewish destruction]

by Zeydl Bagdanovski

The Abramovitz family was noted as one of the most deeply rooted ancient families in Olshan. In the village they were known affectionately as the 'Zimchukes', based on an ancestor's family name 'Zimel'

Zimel was a tall handsome man with dark eyes and long broad beard, clever and folksy, friendly and cheerful, a singer– he was a unifying force, and he waited around for occasional opportunities. Zimel had time to sit a little longer in the shul, to study, and sometimes picked up some business. His wife Rivka also earned a little. She was an energetic little woman who would sit all day in the market place to sell fruits and greens. They lived together with their son Gershon in a large elegant house, a stable and a vegetable garden.

Gershon inherited his father's values, and became a merchant in fruits and flax. In summer, he bought up all the fruit from the neighboring Christian farmers, filling his barn so that the fragrance pervaded the whole street. In winter, the barn was transformed into a flax factory, where the workers cleaned up, assorted and packed the flax for export.

Gershon's home was open and drew in people from far and wide. The warm atmosphere of the house was created by his wife, Rikle [Bogdanovski], who bore and raised twelve children, six daughters and six sons. At her Shabbos table, there were always 16 house guests, besides 4–5 family guests and visitors as well as those brought home by Gershon from shul. Gershon labored long to create a new shul. He was much beloved, but died suddenly of a heart attack.

Gershon's oldest son, Eliezer Zelig, was a romantic type, who wrote well and with deep feeling for the theater and for art. He was quite active in cultural matters. With an amateur troupe of the town youth, he staged Goldfaden's The *Khishufmacherin*, 'the romantic melodrama *Shulamit*, the folk saga *Bar Kochba*, and others.' He was a distinguished and famous balladeer.

In World War I, 1915–18, he served as a soldier on the front, then found out that his wife had died. With his four children, he moved to Kharkov in the Ukraine. There, together with his second wife, he was killed at the hands of

White Russian pogromists, during the civil war in Russia 1919. Three of his four children, Saul, Aaron, Genisie, now live in Israel.

Some of his brothers and sisters emigrated to America, later bringing over his mother Rikle and all the children, except two brothers, who remained in Olshan, maintaining the family tradition.

Bruch had an extraordinary personality, concentrating all the good traits of his family. His intelligence was reflected in his dedication to intensive social activities. As the only pharmacist in the area, he also found time to become an advisor to the town council. There he proudly defended the interests of the Jews of the town, and fought against any discrimination. He founded a People's Bank, where he was a permanent director. He was a fine speaker and was loved by the Christians as well as the Jews. During the Soviet occupation, he was honored and respected. Consequently, he was Olshan's first victim of the Nazis. He was arrested and tortured in Oshman. His wife Dinah and all four of his children, died later in various death camps.

His brother Shepsel was another remarkable man, multi–talented with his own strengths. After his father's death, he took over the management of the large family, acted as a father to his younger brothers and sisters, until they emigrated to America. Step by step, he achieved unusual success in the flax business, and in social activities.

With his wife Gutl , Isaac Kozlovski's daughter, he enlarged and beautified the large house that he had inherited from his father. He established a factory to process and pack flax, which employed over a hundred workers, supporting many families. He soon became renowned as one of the largest exporters in the flax business, and later founded two more flax processing plants in Vilna. During the Soviet period, Shepsel worked as a chief flax distributor.

Shepsel suffered like all the ghetto inhabitants of Olshan and Vilna, and perished in a death camp in 1943 in Estonia. His wife Gitl died in Panor in 1942. Their two older sons Isaac and Gershon died in the Shemberger death camp. [cf. the article "The Shemberger Hell"]. Their daughter Rivka, her husband Leib, after their 3 1/2 year old son was killed in a *Kinder Aktion*, escaped from the Vilna ghetto and now live in America. Their youngest son Ziml escaped to a Soviet unit, studied in Kiev and volunteered in the Soviet army. He was active in the battle against the fascist murderers, became an officer, was severely wounded, but got several citations and medals, and now lives in Israel. [Zeydel Bogdanovski]

[Page 148]

The Kozlovski Family

In memory of Aaron Voronovski and the many branches of the family

Aaron descended from a much honored family deeply rooted in Olshan for generations. His grandfathers, Avrohom Kozlovski and Avrohom Yididihes were renowned as wealthy, respected and dedicated to Torah. Of Abraham's children, was a spiritual type, a scholar, clever and capable, but not so good at business. When his little farm plot was insufficient to support his family, he left it to his wife, Chaya Grunye, to manage, and he left for America. Though he was a hard worker, he wasn't able to put down any roots in the half–Jewish American milieu, and he returned home in a few years, to his little farm and his Beys Hamidrash. To this family were born Aaron and Golde Taibe.

Times had changed, but not the Jewish tradition. Aaron was blessed with extraordinary ability and energy, but was poor and had to contend with an oppressive anti–Semitic atmosphere. Yet he managed to find a way to the University in Vilna where he began to study law. After two years, with good recommendations, he was accepted to the university in Warsaw. And there he met a man named Pilsudski. He studied under him and finished with a gold medal, the only Jew that year. While he was searching for a practice opportunity, difficult for Jews, the clouds of World War II were darkening. In 1939, he wrote to his cousin Shlomo in America:

Dear Shlomo– I'm sending you copies of my documents, because there is so much unrest in Central Europe near us, and one can't know what the next day brings. So I'm thinking ahead, remembering World War I, and if such a cataclysm might happen again, so that's why I'm being so careful about the copies of my diploma and other documents. I may be overreacting, but it doesn't hurt. I am of military age, and if there is a crisis, there's no predicting. I hope things calm down, but in any case we must be careful. Please don't worry about me. In the last minute before total destruction of war fever, people of good will will find a peaceful way out, to thwart the forces of evil.

What blindness! To find a refuge for his papers, but not for himself. He had not imagined, along with millions of his brethren, how dark the future was from the murderous forces to be unleashed on the peaceful world. And how weak and few among the men of good will. This was evident on the day of the slaughter in the Volozhin ghetto, where he got lost in the confused chaotic flight, tried to save himself in the last minute, and was killed while fleeing. His older brother Avrohom–Shlomo, an artist, was killed in a second camp. His parents died during the second Aktion in the Oshman ghetto in Zielanke

[Page 150]

The Potashnik Family
by An Olshaner

Reb Nachum Potashnik came from Volozhin and was the first of his family in Olshan. He was much honored and beloved. He appeared patriarchal, with a long white beard and sharp eyes. His main business was dealing in 'tvuah'. He was quite busy and proud of his occupation. He was a symbol of honesty and truth.

But his greatest interest was in the Beys Hamidrash. Before dawn, in rain or snow he was always there studying the scriptures. He distanced himself from the congregation, which honored him. He was always ready for any special occasion, especially on *Simchas Torah*, when he was given the Aliyah, carried the Torah, and on Pesach, when he read the Omer.

When he died, his son Avrohom and his wife Rachel, carried on his work and traditions. They were known to both Christians and Jews as upright citizens. For years they were supporters of the Beys Hamidrash. Avrohom was killed by the Nazis.

Reb Nachum's youngest son Asher was considered among the prominent men in the town. Everyone respected and trusted him. He was a religious Jew, and was tolerant of all. His generosity influenced his whole family. His family were all well educated. He distributed charity freely. Asher was killed in the Kovno ghetto in 1943. The Olshan community had asked him to stay there until the war was over, but he refused. He didn't want to be separated from his family and the Jews of his ghetto.

Asher's wife, Chane Sarah, daughter of Joshua Landsman, from Trav, was truly generous. With her intelligence and deep understanding, she fostered in her home a warm atmosphere, and her children were very close. She used to send out a pot of food daily for poor strangers, and supplied everything possible for the local poor. She died in Zhelianka in 1942. Asher and Chana had eight sons–Beryl, Sender, Leib, Leizer, Shaia, Avrohom Elia, Yossel and Max.

Beryl and Sender married in Oshman, lived comfortably and were respected in the town. Beryl, his wife Rachel, and son Chaim were killed; their daughter Minna was rescued and lives in Israel.

Leib Potashnik moved to America after World War I. On his initiative, with his wife Basye Abramovitz, a union for Olshan emigres was formed, which sent aid to Olshan. Leib and Basye became the address for all Olshaners who needed help. In 1929, after the great pogrom, they organized an assistance program for the victims. They uncovered the graves and contributed significant sums for re–building the burned institutions.

Lazer Potashnik studied in a Yeshivah in Russia before World War I. On the way home he contracted typhus and died in Cherkask at age 20. Shaia Potashnik and his wife Rosa Cohen lived in Sventzian, and had a cultural life. Up to the time of his marriage, Shaia was quite active in Olshan. He died in Dachau in 1944.

Yosef experienced the same persecution as all the Olshaners in the ghettos and camps. He survived, made it to Israel, married, lived in peace, until he suddenly died in 1958, leaving behind his wife Ida Kulier, of Oshman, with two sons.

Avrohom survived the hell of Dachau, and now lives in New York. Max, the youngest, was drafted into the Polish army after the German attack. When the Olshan ghetto was liquidated, the Jews were moved to Oshman. Max, some other boys and his future wife Anye fled into the forest, and joined the Belski partisan brigade. After the Soviets re–took Olshan, Max and Anye returned, then emigrated to Baltimore.

R' Nachum Potasknik

Leib Kaplan and his family 60 years ago

Family of Leib Gurvitz

Families of Efraim Afroimovitz and Yaacov-Ber and Asher Trobski

Family and friends of Moshe Koslovski near the Olshan castle

Family and friends of Gershon Abramovitz

A group of Olshaners after World War I

The Koslovski Family
Upper: Avrohom and his wife Rivka
Middle Isaac, brother of Avrohom and his wife Chaya Grunyeh
Lower Isaac's daughters, Gutl, Nachama, Malka, Fruma-Sarah

Upper- R: Devorah Ziskind and family L: Chana and Shmuel-Leib Levin and family

Lower- L: Reb Itcheh the Shamesh and teacher with his wife and daughter
R: Bruch the pharmacist with his children

**Upper- L: Meir Rudnick (the agent) and his family
R: Feiga-Libe Kaplan (the fabric dyer)**

**Lower- L: Naftali (the painter) and family R: Libe and Alikim Litski and
family**

At the Olshan Cemetery

[Page 160]

Olshaners in America

Emigration and Nostalgia
by Leib Potashnik

The first emigrants from Olshan arrived in New York before World War I. Their organizational efforts in World War I were started by Shlomo Zalman Koslovski, Moshe Baron [son of Chaim the teacher], Yekusiel Koslovski [son of Keseler Antshelikes]. They founded the Olshan 'Relief Committee' and this was active until 1921. I arrived in NY August 1922, nostalgic for my family in Olshan, so I sought out my countrymen from Olshan. This wasn't difficult. At the same time, my niece Rikleh Abramovitz came with her children. Their home swiftly became a meeting point not only for Olshaners but also from Oshman, Vishniev, Trov and others.

Among the first ones I mentioned were also Chaim Leib Shneider, his wife Rachel, sister of Ben–Zion Goldberg [now editor of the Morning Journal], Kalman Brudni, Meyer Nissn, Gdalia Berman. I was told that an Olshan organization no longer existed, only a Hebrew school. Avrohom Abramovitz was president of the school, which was named Olshaner, but all the Olshaners had moved out. They had gradually become part of the New York Jewish community and had become Americanized members of their local schools and temples.

I always felt that there should be a relationship between the Olshaners in America and the community in Poland, which needed help, so I convened a meeting of those I have mentioned, a volunteer's evening of our countrymen. I acted as secretary, and thus created the Olshan Organization of America. The response was extraordinary. Our meeting was attended by our countrymen from far and wide, a warm heartfelt reunion for many after long years apart. At our second meeting, I produced a one–act play, "The Crazy Man in the Hospital". Ben–Zion Goldberg was the director and Chaim Leib Shneider was the reader. I continued as secretary.

The purpose of our committee was to support our countrymen's institutions in Olshan, the Hebrew schools, Tarbos school, refurbish the Bays Hamidrash, modernize the baths, restore the grounds around the cemetery, increase the capital of the savings and loan bank, found an interest –free charitable lending bank, and help our Olshan people in all their needs. Our Olshaners in America used all our talents.. The chairman of all the committees was Mayor Nissn Berman, associated with A.L.Gershonovitz

My correspondence with the Olshan community was through Reb Khodesh. In 1929, telegrams from my parents and Reb Khodesh brought sad news of the pogrom in Olshan, and then came a second pogrom. Our American supporters did their duty, and renewed our efforts to help the victims. Throughout, we devoted our efforts to support community organizations as well as to help re–unite families. Our activities cemented warm close connections among our countrymen in America, eliminating all class divisions. We all felt like one family with one purpose, to preserve our connection with our Jewish roots in the shtetl.

In 1945, at the end of the war, we got a letter from my brother Max in Olshan, and I had it published in a Jewish newspaper, with an appeal to revive the Olshan relief organization, to mobilize aid for the victims. I arose from my sick–bed to call on my countrymen , who responded, doing much to assist the survivors of the Holocaust.

Members of certain relief committees in America
Upper Moshe Baron and Shlomo Zalman Kozlovski
Lower Chaim Leib Shneider and I. Leib Potashnik

Upper Marta Leutinger and Yehuda Levin
Lower- Reb Moshe-Yosef Solodukha

Olshan Emigrants

The history of Olshan emigrants to America goes back 100 years. In the last half of the 19th century, young people from Olshan traveled to the *Medina* [golden land]. Among them was a 12 year old boy, Chaim Sholom Kaplan. His voyage to America involved a dramatic story. Chaim Sholom had asked his poor parents to allow him to travel to America with his sister Eshke, to join their sister Libe Disye. The parents refused, so the boy ran on foot to Vilna to follow his sister Eshke and brother Leib, who had accompanied her on the way. When he met them in the train station, he declared to them that he would never return to Olshan, and if they wouldn't let him go with his sister to America, he would throw himself on the train tracks. The brother and sister knew from this boy's firm character that this was no idle threat. So his brother paid for his trip, and he departed with his sister to the United States.

At the time of the Russo–Japanese war, a few Jews from Olshan came to America. After the collapse of the 1905 revolution, many Olshaners fled because they feared arrest and exile in Siberia. And that's how many of them were implanted and spread widely in the U.S. After World War I, the Olshaners in America organized a committee to help the starving people of the town, and to get them back on their feet. They're–built and repainted the Beys Hamidrash, and sent substantial funds to found a Free Loan Society. In those days, the work was supported by a surtax supervised by Moshe Baron, assisted by Shlomo Zalman Koslovski, Marta Lutinger, Chaim Gurvitz, Leib Potashnik, Moshe Yosef Soladeka, Yidel ben Moshe Mordechai Levin.

[Page 166]

Loyalty and Pride

Shlomo Koslovski was a remarkable personality, outstanding in all respects. He had a burning thirst for education, was generous, honest and dedicated. But all this was concealed hidden behind the walls of the Jewish ghetto in Tsarist Russia, on one side, and the paternal socialism, fanatically exclusive, on the other side. His best years were spent in the Yeshiva and in civil duties. The only way out was America.

Like many emigrants from before World War I, he had to work as a tailor and presser in small Jewish shops, under the most difficult primitive conditions. But unlike many others he escaped his confinement. Something bothered him; the 'something' was that he became a soldier in the American army in World War I. Post–war, he dedicated himself unstintingly to founding and supporting Olshan social organizations. Despite his fervent loyalty, strength and pride, money and education were lacking. Then came the terrible destruction of World War II. There were no survivors of his dear family, for whom he had lived and suffered. The catastrophe was too much for him, despite his strength. Broken and bewildered he remained entirely alone. If he had only known how admired and beloved he was by all who knew him.

[Page 169]

In the Years of the Jewish Extermination

The Outbreak of World War II
by Shepsl Kaplan

On the eve of World War II there were 200 Jewish families in Olshan. On September 1, 1939 the town shivered when the Germans attacked Poland. The effect of the news on the town was overwhelming. Many men were drafted into the Polish army. The houses from which the conscripts had left were scenes of lamentation. Women and children were weeping in the streets. Near the houses with radios, people stood listening to the news from the front. The prospects were uniformly dismal. On the first day of the war, it was known that many cities and towns in Poland had been severely damaged by bombs, and the death toll was great. In the second week, the news came to us that the high commanders of the Polish army had fled, abandoning their disorganized forces in the face of the terrifying German attack. Kartchevski, the Olshan deputy, was panicked, had run out of the police station, and announced, "The bolsheviks had crossed the Polish border; the police and the civil authorities had been ordered to leave Olshan. The town has no authority left. You must organize a civilian defense group until a new power takes over."

At the Market place, the frightened Jews watched the police abandoning the town. A self–defense group was formed, of Poles, Jews and White Russians, including some darker elements. But the news of the Soviet advance toward Vilna left mixed feelings while the town had no government. But no acts of violence occurred.

The Red Army Marches In

On the 15th day of the German attack, the Red Army marched into Olshan, without incident. The mood in the town calmed down. everyone talked about Molotov's speech on the radio, stating that the Polish government had collapsed, leaving chaotic conditions. The Germans were taking over all of

Poland, and in order to save the people from the White Russians and east Ukrainians, the Red Army was liberating these areas.

For now, the entry of the Red Army had ended the war for the Jews of Olshan, Jewish life had been saved, Jews were relieved and breathed more freely. The Soviet regime had radically changed the town's organization. The young and middle–aged adjusted well to the new order. Feeling themselves fairly treated, the older generation, willing or not, accustomed themselves gradually to the new system. Professionals returned to their offices. The richer farmers had lost their possessions, but their lives were safe and they started to look for employment. The civil authority was augmented from the general population. The head of office was a 20 year old Jewish boy, Misha Koslovski, an active Communist. Landless peasants, Christians and Jews were given land and were satisfied. The peasants who were dissatisfied had to submit.

Germans Occupy Olshan

Large Soviet detachments were stationed in Olshan. The Jews had settled down and felt they would remain safe. They resumed praying in the Bays Hamidrash, the children attended Hebrew school. Then on June 21, 1941 the radio news announced that the Germans had renounced their agreement with the Soviets, to the consternation of the town. Before anyone could make any plans, German planes flew over, sowing death and destruction. The connection with the outside world had been broken.

Establishment of the Jewish Council

In the first few days of the occupation, the Germans started to force the Jews to work. They did this brutally, by grabbing the Jews in the street, from their houses and wherever they could be found. They would beat them without mercy, and together with the Polish police, they herded 300 young men 30 km from Olshan, and day after day forced them to break rocks into small pieces.

Seniors, the sick, children, and pregnant women were forced to trim branches off trees and to dig up potatoes. The situation was unbearable, and this led to the effort to organize this intolerable chaotic system. R'Khodesh and a few others in the community tried unsuccessfully to lighten the load. At that time, the commandant Jurovski informed the rabbi that the Jews must leave their homes and assemble in a ghetto, and choose a *Judenrat*, which would be responsible for carrying out all the demands of the Germans, and to regulate the ghetto.

At a meeting in the Bays Hamidrash, R' Khodesh announced the order of the commandant. Then he assessed the situation, and explained that the German goal was to exterminate the Jews. He advised them not to be confused, but to be aware of any possibility of lessening or avoiding this horrible fate. Despite this, the Olshan Jews decided to appoint a Judenrat. The Germans had confirmed their understanding with R' Khodesh as the most senior Jew and demanded that they be responsible for carrying out the orders of the Germans and the civilian authority. The heavy load for the performance of the Judenrat fell on R' Khodesh. After a further detailed order from the civilian authority, the Jews had to impose their own regimen and organized the Jewish ghetto police. Young men and boys were transformed into brutal oppressors of the tortured Jews. Into the shtetl, groups of Lithuanian Jews were brought, who had to be housed and maintained, and this was extremely difficult because the ghetto was so overcrowded. During the night, about 100 more victims were crammed in, an impossible burden. The Olshan Jews had the dilemma of integrating them or perishing with them.

The Judenrat managed to handle these additional victims, and to provide workers for the Germans and the Polish authorities, with the condition that no sick person would be sent to work. The workers had to go where directed, to work as hard as possible. The Judenrat must carry out the orders exactly. They thought that the 'beast' would thus be restrained. The seizures on the street had indeed lessened, but then an additional penalty was inflicted. The Germans demanded that 200 youngsters down to age 12 be sent to work, and these were then sent to Zhezhmir, a concentration camp in Lithuania.

We know now that the German intent was to denigrate, torture, break the morale and destroy the Jews. Knowing this, there seemed no solution. Resisting was out of the question, against the heavily armed Germans, and there was nowhere to flee. There were no partisans yet in the forest. On the roads and towns, all sorts of bandits lurked, ready to kill and rob any Jews. Besides, any fugitive from the ghetto faced a more certain fate from hunger and cold, his family also was under threat of death, as was the whole community in the ghetto. The police forces always relished the Jewish burdens. No one wanted to endanger his family by fleeing the ghetto.

Looting of Jewish Possessions

Looting was also systematized. Instead of the police entering houses to steal, the Jews had to bring in their belongings themselves. Furthermore, all officials demanded that the Jews bring in at an appointed hour all soap, leather, clothing and any other valuable articles. There were no exceptions, and the penalty for non–compliance was death. All Jewish homes were emptied and poverty was universal. The Jews were terrified and confused. At the sight of any German vehicles, they thought they were doomed, for they had nothing left to give. To satisfy the German demands, the Judenrat purchased items from Christian dealers, to give to their persecutors.

Thanks to R'Khodesh's tactics, no mass slaughter occurred. His dedication helped the ghetto Jews, while the German beasts sowed death and destruction. He also remained in contact with the Catholic priest Khomski, one of the righteous few, who warned the Christians in his sermons in the cathedral not to participate in the persecution and violent acts against the Jews. The encouragement and support from R' Khodesh to the suffering Jews, strengthened their resolve and helped them to refrain from irresponsible behavior. A few months before the deportation of the Olshan Jews to the Oshman ghetto, R' Khodesh and a number of the Olshan Jews were taken away to the Volozhin ghetto, and within two months they were all executed.

Saved From Olshan Slaughter For Disaster in Volozhin

At end of 1941, Olshan and a number of other towns in the White Russian sector were assigned to the Lithuanian area by the Germans. At that time the Olshan ghetto had supported over 100 victims from Lithuania and from Vilna who had survived the slaughter inflicted by the Letts in the small towns of Lithuania in the first days of the German occupation.. Among them were many wounded, who had crawled out of the graves of the mass shootings during the night, and fled to Olshan. Being in the White Russian sector, no mass slaughters had occurred yet in Olshan, as compared to Lithuania. The Olshan Jews had integrated the fugitives. In Olshan, there was no German commandant. The Civilian authority, with few exceptions, was exercised by the Polish officials of the area. At first, relatively, accommodations were not too difficult, though dozens of Jews had been killed. Suddenly the Olshaners and the refugees found that Olshan would no longer be a 'Garden of Eden' in White Russia, but would become a Lithuanian town.

Panicked by the prospect of falling into the hands of the Lithuanian murderers, the fugitives began to flee further into White Russia, where mass slaughters had not yet occurred. Panic also spread among the Olshaners who were also seeking to escape from the impending Lithuanian take–over. The Olshan Judenrat had considered various stratagems to salvage as many Jews as possible. As we know now, the moving of the Jews was part of the German extermination plan, to concentrate the Jews in one place in order to carry out a mass slaughter. So the German authority in Oshman authorized the Judenrat, led by R' Khodesh, to move the refugees, along with 150 Olshaners to Volozhin, accompanied by White Russian police.

Two months later, in May 1942, a mass execution occurred in Volozhin, lasting three hours. Virtually all the Jews were killed, 8–10 survived. Thirty Jews reserved by the killers, along with the few survivors were forced to bury their own mothers, fathers, brothers and sisters in a mass grave in the Volozhin cemetery.

Some of the survivors eventually got back to Olshan. Those still living include Yitzchok Ziskand [in Israel], Michal Rudnik [in America]. Malech Dervatzki was killed in a town near Olshan. Aaron and Lusia Varanovski were killed on the way from Volozhin to Olshan. The Rebbetsin Deicha and her daughter Milye were tortured in Klage. Her daughter Hadassah, five years old was buried alive together with the Christians who were taking her home from Volozhin.

[Page 179]

The Great Slaughter in Volozhin
by Isaac Ziskind, recorded by S. Kaplan

In August 1941, the ghetto was founded in Volozhin. In about 50 houses resided about 3500 Jews, along with various other groups from Vishniev, Olshan, Oshman and Vilna. On May 10, 1942 at 5 AM, the ghetto was surrounded by S.S. and police, who broke in and shot two Jewish police, Yochanon Klein and Isaac Nuresevitz, then shot many others. Then they drove the Jews into a smithy, where 800 people were jammed together tightly. The wailing of the children was indescribable. The S.S. kept shooting into this crowd to quiet them and wounded many. R' Khodesh urged the men to tear off the oven doors, or take stones, tear down the gates, attack the S.S., and flee. But the elder from the Volozhin Judenrat, Israel Lunin, said that they were still alive and they should not flee.

In the Volozhin Ghetto - The Fate of Reb Khodesh

On May 9, 1942, the Volozhin Jews who had been working outside the ghetto were brought back to the ghetto at midnight and surrounded by Germans, Letts and White Russians. They were warned not to flee. The Jews were panicked and started to hide in the *melinas*, shelters which had been prepared in the houses. At 4 AM, the drunken mob unleashed a barrage of gunfire on the Jews, and gathered them all together in a large shed, part of a smithy. Then the Jews were led in sections to the cemetery to be shot. Anyone too sick, old or weak was shot on the spot. All the streets on the way to the cemetery were strewn with corpses of men, women and children.

In one house where five families lived, a hiding place had been constructed under a wood pile, which was accessed by a ladder which could be pulled up and hidden. In this critical night, the Jews hid in this shelter, and among them was R' Khodesh, and the narrator of these events. At dawn, the house was stormed by the drunken mob, and they found no one. They emerged to seek the hidden Jews, they noticed the path which led to the wood pile. Two Germans put up a ladder and uncovered our hiding place, and forced the Jews to climb down, under threat of setting fire. I and two others held back, until another German climbed up and forced us out. However, I jumped on to a roof on the other side, then down to the ground and ran off, and the other two also jumped down. The Germans were shooting at us and I was wounded in the shoulder. After about 50 meters I felt faint, and noticed some women in a nearby house. I struggled in and asked for some water. The terrified women helped me to flee, and declared that the *Aktion* was only directed at men. Outside I noted a cellar door, so I hid inside, but didn't lock the door.

Not far from the cellar was the group of re–captured Jews, and they were being taken in groups to the cemetery. From my hiding place, I could see Wileiker, the district commissar, who directed the process of murdering the Jews. Among a group of Jews being marched off, I could clearly see the Olshan Rabbi, R' Khodesh with a bloody hand; he approached the commissar and asked him to spare his life. The commissar knew R' Khodesh well, he had had many dealings with him in confiscating valuable items including two kilograms of gold. He was unmoved, and sent him off with the group to be shot. Thirty men, including Beryl Kogan and Joshua Glik, along with a group of laborers who had worked in the smithy, were selected and told to bring along their wives and children. Joshua Glik, a boy, was joined by two women, a pharmacist from Podvrodzh, and a woman with a child from Volozhin. The woman with the child was taken away, and the pharmacist remained, to pair with Joshua.

By Sunday noon, the mass Aktion was finished. The mobs milling around dispersed. I could still hear shooting from other parts of the ghetto. The White Russian police hunted down the *melinas* to find any more hidden Jews. Boys accompanied the police to help search the houses and uncover the hiding places. Any Jews found were immediately shot down.

When it was dark, I left the cellar and slipped into a nearby house and hid in the basement, where I stayed until Monday. At dawn I ventured out, but heard the noise made by the White Russian police and their boy companions, who had been in the building. So I crawled back into hiding until Monday night, when I decided I had to find some house to replace my filthy clothes and also to get some dressing for my wounded shoulder which had been very painful. I heard some noise, several gunshots and a a call in Russian, "Two Jews killed." As I later learned they were, Perski and his son–in–law, a brother of Zisl Perski of Olshan; they had been the ones who had escaped with me from the shelter. I went back into hiding. Tuesday morning I heard a voice at the top of the ladder into the basement; a child's voice shouted that there was nobody there. At noon I heard the two bodies being carried off. Occasional gunfire was audible. In the evening, I went up into the house and found a piece of bread, two baked potatoes, some horse radish, and also a *sefer torah*. I put the bread and potatoes in my bag, and with a flask of water returned to the basement. I didn't have the strength to dig into my hiding place, so just lay there. I wasn't able to swallow the bread and potatoes. I lay there exhausted for two more days. On Thursday i was unable to get up from the floor. The pain from my shoulder was excruciating. On Friday I dragged myself to the basement window and saw a familiar Jewish woman. I wanted to call her, but couldn't utter a word. With my last strength I knocked on the window, and suddenly I saw Michal Rudnik from Olshan. I was so excited, I fainted and lay on the ground unconscious. When I recovered, I heard Jewish voices, crept to the window and saw how the door from the house to the street had been boarded up. I shouted, "Here is a Jew! Open the door!" The boards were torn off and I was taken away to the house occupied by the thirty selected men. There I met Michal Rudnick and others who had survived from their shelters undetected.

Michal told me how he had survived. He was among those selected by the Germans to clean up the ghetto. They were ordered to collect all the hundreds of bodies now rotting in the streets and houses. Among the bodies, he found his parents, brother, sister and children. I asked if there was a doctor in the group and Michal Polaks operated on me with a sharp knife, removed the bullet from my shoulder and bandaged me. On Thursday, May 14, the Polish woman Dobrolovitz, from a town near Olshan, was sent by the Olshan Judenrat, to find what had happened in Volozhin. She said that everything in Olshan was the same and she took back a letter for the Judenrat.

On Saturday May 16, Michal and I decided to return to Olshan together with Ziske, from Volozhin. We left Volozhin late at night and by dawn were over the Zabrezher bridge, and all day Sunday we hid in the woods near Lasto. At night, after the peasants had left the cathedral, we sneaked through to the train station. I knew the peasants on the other side of the bridge. Nevertheless we avoided meeting any of the locals by using side trails, and we reached the Olshan ghetto by dawn.

In the Vishniever Ghetto
by Gdalia Dudman

On August 30, 1942, all the Jews in the ghetto were told to stand next to their homes, with their luggage, to be taken to another 'place'. Soon armed Germans went house to house and ordered everyone to assemble at the Bays Hamidrash. There they were ordered to lay face down on the ground, and threatened to shoot anyone who looked up. Then they took groups of 100 through the tower of the ghetto. The Germans ran alongside and beat the Jews on their heads with cudgels. The moaning and screaming increased, the weeping of the women and children rose to heaven. Later, they were transported by auto to speed things up. The trucks drove up to the Bays Hamidrash and the victims were forced to get in, and they drove through Krever Street.

When Zarak's building was packed with Jews, the Germans set it on fire. Anyone who tried to get out was shot. Dr. Padzelever was burned, standing at the window, with his face covered.

The Christians begged the Germans to spare Padzelever, the only doctor in the area, to no avail. After the building had burned, autos arrived packed with more Jews. They were herded into a field and killed by machine guns. The dead bodies were thrown into the fire. Bashke Podverezeki shouted, "Brothers, save yourselves!", and she tried to flee, but was shot down. Many others also tried to flee, but the Germans gunned them all down. All of Krever Street was littered with bodies. Even after the war, remains of the victims could be found.

I had run off after getting out of the truck and zigzagged through the alleys, then jumped into a ditch and hid. I could see the mounted police chasing down the Jews, shooting them. All night Saturday until Sunday, the town of Vishniev was patrolled by Polish police. On August 30, 1942, the Germans finished their slaughter. They had murdered all the Jews in Vishniev. I decided to flee into the forest, together with any survivors from Vishniev, to organize a brigade of partisans, to procure weapons and take revenge on the peasants who had helped the Germans to kill the Jews. Using a Christian friend, I had sent a letter to Olshan to Shepsl Abramovitz, telling of the disaster and of how many Jews remained alive. I also wrote to the Oshman ghetto, to Leib Bakin and Poliak Slodunski who helped to mobilize 31 persons in the ghetto, including Dr. Dolinski from Olshan, attorney Mazurek from Warsaw, Max Potashnik from Olshan and his wife Anna, Yosel Potashnik from Volozhin, Rabinovitz and others.

We should also note here the Christians who helped us during these times. Albert, Yulia and Stefan Slodunski helped us to flee on the day of the slaughter. Selevon, his wife and daughter from Dolknievitz took us in like their own children. Selevon gave me a rifle and a revolver, and we fled into the forest. With a weapon, it was easier to get food and more guns for six of our men. Our armed partisan group was based near Vishniev and the train stations in Bogdanov and Vaigon, and we revenged ourselves on the local peasants who knew all about the fates of the Vishniev Jews.

[Page 186]

THE SYSTEMATIC MASS-EXTERMINATION OF JEWS IN THE OLSHAN REGION

In Spring 1942 the Germans began the systematic massacres of Jews in White Russia. Dozens of towns were destroyed in a short time. Soon after the slaughter in Voloshin, the Jews of Vishniev, 18 km from Olshan, were also killed. The Nazi murderers herded all the the Jews from the ghettos into the market place, forced them all to lie face down, under the threat of death. In groups of 50, they were led into a shed. On the corner of Kreve Street, some of them were shot. The rest of them, men, women and children, were all incinerated, together with any remaining corpses.

The hostile residents of the towns in the Olshan area attacked all the Jews in the region, and it was obvious that all the Jews were to be killed. There was no resistance. The Germans forced all the youths of Olshan into their prison camps. It was possible to run away from the ghetto, but there was nowhere to go. The roads and countryside offered only death from cold or hunger, as well as attacks from Polish and White Russian mobs of Jew haters. Rarely was anyone willing to run off and desert wife and children, so they sat and waited for death. It was impossible to comprehend the despair and hopelessness in the ghetto, awaiting the imminent disaster.

RESETTLING OLSHANERS IN THE OSHMAN GHETTO

In October 1942, the few survivors from Olshan were taken to the Oshman ghetto.. At the same time, the ghettos of Kreve, Smorgen, Sol were liquidated, and those Jews were brought to Oshman, which belonged to the Vilna district. The Oshman Judenrat and his officers carried out the orders issued by Gens, the most senior Jew of the Vilna ghetto.

After all the Jews had been collected in Oshman, Desler came from Vilna with a group of Jewish ghetto police. They selected 400 Jews, who were taken to Zhelanke, 10 km from Oshman, and shot by a band of Lithuanian ruffians.

By early 1943, almost all the Jews of White Russia had all been murdered. Some Jews from a few smaller ghettos remained in the Vilna-Lithuanian district [Svir, Michalishok, Varnian, Oshman] and survived by an inexplicable fortunate circumstance. Since these towns were now across the border in Lithuania where the edict for destruction of the Jews had ended, these Jews were consigned to labor camps.

The German Authority in the Vilna- Kovne area decided that the remnants from the smaller ghettos should be merged with the larger ones, with the goal of giving the Jews a "free choice", to leave the Vilna ghettos for the camps in Zhezhmir and Vevye, where they would work on finishing the road from Vilna to Kovne. Many of the Jews, obeying the Germans, left the Kovne ghetto and boarded the train, bearing many Jews from other ghettos. A few survivors from the train later reported that there were 1600 Jews supposed to go to Kovne, but 1000 of them were taken instead to Panor and shot.

About 1000 people from Olshan, Kreve and Smorgen, chose to go to Zhezhmir, to be united with their children, who had been taken there earlier. When they got there, the German 'Death' squad, led everyone into camp, at the same station with many women, to meet their fate in Vevye.

[Page 188]

The Death of Rabbi Moshe Aharon Feldman

Rabbi Feldman was a distinguished Torah scholar, the son–in–law of Kushe Ziskand of Olshan. Often Reb Feldman conducted a Saturday afternoon *Drash* which was extremely popular. A few years before World War II, Reb Feldman became the much loved rabbi in the town of Kurenitz.

He became a victim of the German bestial tortures, and this history was written by Feige Alperovitz in *The Kurenitz Megila*, in Hebrew.

On the False Document Period

In Olshan a few Jews were hidden under false documents, by Christian neighbors. Only one of these survived, Velvel Tchepelunski. The others were killed by those same neighbors, or betrayed to their murderers.

In spring 1943, when the Olshan ghetto was liquidated, Velvel Tchepelunski fled, to a Christian friend in the town of Akolitsa, 6 km away. He stayed with an acquaintance Solatize from Moskutch. When the Germans seemed to be on his trail, he got away in time and at night wandered through the towns of his Christian neighbors, but found no refuge. He quickly realized that he must beware of these neighbors no less than the Germans. Hungry and cold, he trod through fields and woods, staying in a different place every night, in fear of death. Pursued by the Germans and without any friends, he wondered why he fled the ghetto and didn't stay with the rest of the Jews, but now there was no ghetto.

On a frosty night in winter 1944, Velvel, sick, discouraged and exhausted, dragged himself to the supervisor of his old employer Solatize, and knocked on the door. He was admitted to the house, not knowing that it was being watched by the Germans, and was put in the warm stable with the cows. At dawn, when Joseph Solatize, as usual, went to feed his cows, he noticed a group of Germans heading toward his farm. He had hidden Velvel in a pile of straw, and he wheeled his wagon into the barn, covering him with more straw. He opened wide the gate to his barn and returned to his cows. Shortly the Germans arrived and he came out to meet them. To the question of whether Solatize lived there, he directed them to another farm house 0.5 km away, where there also lived a Solatize. The Germans searched the premises thoroughly, but found nothing besides some hidden bacon. Content with their find, the Germans returned, searched the open barn where Velvel was hidden, then left. And that's how Velvel Tchepelunski was saved.

The Good Neighbor Promised Bread and Brought Death Instead

In winter 1943, while the Oshman ghetto was being liquidated, Bentsch Gernovitz of Olshan, together with his wife and 6 year old daughter fled from the Zhezhmir camp, to a Christian neighbor Lutkovski in the Kurovschtshiner forest, 2 km from Olshan.. They weren't able to stay there, so had to wander in the woods. All of the peasants in the area were determined anti–semites, who were actively engaged every night in killing Jews and Soviet prisoners who had been working for the peasants. They were awakened by a neighbor from Olshan, a Christian Pinkovski , who came seeking his pack that he had left by the fire while roasting a pig. Bentsch was glad to see him, because he was supposed to bring him some bread and other things that they had left with his neighbor before leaving the Oshman ghetto. Instead of bread, some police rushed in and led Bentsch and his family to the police station, and a few days later they were all shot.

Pinkovski accepted his prize, awarded for capturing Jews: several kilos of sugar and soap.

[Page 191]

From Volozhin Back to Olshan
by Hana Lev–Tcherniovski

When the Germans attacked the Soviet Union, the Olshan youths fled deeper into Russia, my brother Velvel among them. But he returned soon, all the roads were blocked and the Germans were everywhere. I ran away to a Christian neighbor, and left our possessions with them, hoping that they would keep them for us. They welcomed us and promised to hide us. When the Germans created a ghetto in Olshan, closely guarded, the goyim became quite fearful about hiding Jews.

We found a place in a field used for planting flax, to hide my brother. When I was able to leave the ghetto, I brought him some food. After things got quieter, he would come home at night and sleep in our house. In the middle of the night, someone pounded on our door. Velvel jumped out through the window. Two White Russians and some Germans had come to search our house. They looked everywhere "Is this your entire family?" asked the policeman –"where is your brother"?. I answered, "There's a war on, I don't know where he is". A few weeks later after things were quiet again, Velvel returned to sleep at home again, but again there was a knock on the door.

"Where is your brother?". He had a revolver with him. But Velvel had again escaped to the forest. The police sought Velvel almost every night. It was decided that he should go to Volozhin; we didn't want the whole family to go. Reb Khodesh and the Dolinski family advised that Velvel should go and save himself. I went to Volozhin with him–maybe I could help save him again. It was very confused and chaotic on the road. I asked if we could go together with Peshke and his whole family.

After arriving in Volozhin, we all reported to the authority, and were all given badges, to work outside the ghetto. I didn't want to stay in Volozhin, so I wrote home. Kole Pinkovski from Castle Street came after me. To my room also came Reb Khodesh and other Olshaners who asked me to send them news when I reached home. And so I set off.

After a few km, I said to Kole,"You know, if anyone asks who I am, you shouldn't say that I'm Jewish, just say that you are bringing your wife home from the hospital. If you tell them I'm Jewish, we'll both be shot." We kept on, but it wasn't long before we were stopped by the police and were told to drive back to the police station. What could I do? I had enough money. I told Kole, "Tell them I am sick, the children are waiting for us." I myself asked them to let us go. I gave them money, which they reluctantly accepted. We were stopped again by the police. I started weeping and gave them my last money, and we were able to drive on.

I knocked on the door, and Feigele cried, "Mama, our Khanke is here!" We all wept for joy.

In just a few minutes, the Lithuanian and White Russian police arrived, arrested me to take me to the police station. On the way, the Litvak left, so I said to the Russian, "What good would it do you if I am killed? If I live, I could give you gifts, money, other things." The policeman said, " Go home to your sick mother, but don't sleep at your home." I ran off immediately, then sent a message for Velvel to come home. But he had already left Volozhin. And so I was separated forever from my dear brother. Broken, sick, ailing, we were still alive.

[Page 193]

Zhelanke– Mass Grave of 400 Jews
by Haya Kzura–Katz

After liquidating all the smaller ghettos, the Germans gathered the remaining Jews still able to work in Oshman. It was very crowded– this concentration of the Jews was part of the German plan for the Final Solution, to kill all of us.

Our enemies made a passage in the streets out of the concealed ditches dug by the Jews trying to hide. My mother fell into one of these ditches. They dragged out 400 and took them from Oshman to Zhelanke, 6–7 km from Oshman, held them overnight in a barn. At dawn, they shot them all and threw their bodies into a common grave.

When we came to Zhelanke after the war, in the place where the mass execution had taken place, we found clothing fragments. The mass grave was overgrown with grass. The grave was instantly noted, because the grass on top had a brighter color. The peasants of the area told us that the Latvians, under command of the Germans had stripped the victims before shooting them.

The living survivors installed a memorial stone, but we don't know if it's still there, none of us stayed there. When I visited Zhezhmir, I learned of my mother's death. My little 11 year old sister remained in Oshman where she was found by some friends who took care of her. After the liquidation of the Oshman ghetto, my sister joined me in Zhezhmir. We both wandered through the various murder camps, where the grisly daily scenes of murder and destruction were played out.

Like some nightmare of the Hitler murders, we had survived to see the stigmata of our murderers. Today my sister is a doctor, working in Israel in Bar Shive.

[Page 194]

Under the German Regime
by Pesakh Gershenovitz

June 24, 1941, in Olshan, there were Jews from Vilna and Oshman, fleeing the Germans. Panicked, near the Polish–Russian border, they stopped to take a few breaths then ran on, hoping to get to Russia sooner. Panic ruled in Olshan, nobody knew what to do, whether to abandon one's own little corner to become homeless, or to stay and see their grim destiny. Panic increased still more when the Soviet soldiers and civic officials, who had been in Olshan for two years, fled back to Russia with their families.

Terrified I decided to go with my nephew Zelig Weiner to Russia. I followed quickly with my mother, sister and children. With us were Avrohom Koslovski, his family, Beryl–Leib Plotkin, Israel Berkman, Velvel Tchernovski, Teibel Korbonovitz, Moshe Ragovin, Moshe Gurvitz, Isaac and Zelda Soleducha, Moshe and Ester Koslovski, Israel Miilner and Avrohom Peibushak. We were in a procession of people from Vishniev, Volozhin, and Rokov, a border town. The road was flooded with people on foot, in cars and trucks, wagons

The first day, one could still travel by day. Here and there, we had to stop because of discarded bombs. The train station was in flames, and Vishniev was like a cemetery. People were hiding in their houses. In Volozhin, the upper part of town had been bombed, dark clouds of smoke coming from the chimneys. Going on, we traveled at night and hid in the woods in the day. German planes flew low overhead sowing death and destruction. The road was filled with thousands of fugitives. On the way to Rakov we met some more Olshaners: Meyer Meltzer, Dora Soleducha, Reuben Liond, Nachum and Miriam Schneider, Elihu Koslovski, Aaron Voronovski. At the border, the Soviet guards wouldn't let us in, waiting for their orders. They told us to wait until morning, and ignored our pleas. We returned to Rakov, where the Jews were confused, terrified and helpless. In the morning we returned to the border; the guards were gone.

The road to Minsk and the adjacent fields were littered with soldiers and frightened confused civilians. Some turned back, hearing of German parachutists and motorcycles. We could see clearly the flames in Minsk. We assumed that the Germans were in Minsk already, so we decided to return to Olshan. In Haradak, we got the news that the Germans had driven all the Jews into the marketplace, and abused them all, young and old. Near Volozhin, we were halted by a German patrol, who searched us for weapons, then let us go. From Volozhin, we followed the trail to Zavrezia.

Near Olshan, we were attacked by a band of the town hooligans. who beat us mercilessly. At dawn we arrived in Olshan, beaten and weary. Someone informed the Polish–Nazi police that Rogovin was in Zabrezia, so three cops drove off to Zabrezia to bring him back in ropes to Olshan under arrest. It cost Reb Khodesh a lot of trouble and money to get this 17 year old boy released back to his home in Olshan.

In March 1942, the Rogovin family, including Mottel, Rachel, Moshe and Pesach, and others traveled from Olshan to Volozhin, to the killing fields of May 1942. Among the murdered Jews of Olshan and Volozhin were four men from their family. Their only daughter Chaya survived, and lives in Russia. Another report relates that Moshe Rogovin, in a fight with a Nazi murderer, tore his gun away and tried to escape, but was shot .

The Tragic Death of the Pharmacist Abramovitz, the First Victim in Olshan

In the first bloody months of Nazi rule in Olshan, the following Jews were arrested: Bruch Abramovitz, Jacob Soloducha, Velvel Liond, Joseph Koslovski, Chaim–Leib Chernovski, Avrohom Koslovski, and Zelig Weiner. They were all taken to Oshman and all freed except for Bruch Abramovitz, who was thrown into jail. Isaac**Error! Bookmark not defined.** and Shmuel Koslovski were charged with involvement in the killing of an official, Rotschke in the town of Trov, when the Soviets were in power. They were alleged to have been angry at him because he had disrupted the Koslovski house during his service in Olshan.

These arrests elicited much concern in the Olshan community and the Judenrat, who managed to ransom the prisoners with 6 ounces of gold. Only Bruch Abramovitz remained in prison, because he had been accused by the local Poles of being an active communist. Later, Shepsel Kaplan said that he had not been a communist, but had been active in Olshan institutions, especially in the Cooperative Bank. During the Polish period, Bruch had given a talk about cooperatives. His Jewish enemies, whom Bruch had opposed during the Polish period got revenge when the Germans took over, and accused Abramovitz of serving the Soviets. And that's why he was shot in the first month of German rule.

Trapped in a Gypsy Aktion

In July 1941, the boy Leib Koslovski, from Oshman Street, ventured out, to get some bread, and to collect a debt from a Christian. He encountered a German Aktion, aimed at murdering the gypsies, then in Olshan. The Germans rounded up all the gypsies, including the Jewish boy, and killed them all.

Nazis Force Jews to Drag Two Soviet Tanks

Among the German edicts, an order was given to line up the Jews like horses, to haul two shattered Soviet tanks, standing by Schloss Street. The order was carried out by our 'good' neighbors, the White Russians, who willingly served the Germans in managing Olshan. The tanks had to be dragged to Trov, 12 km distant. How were they going to do this? They had no option. All Olshaners were put to work, everyone who could move. Beryl Kanon had brought very heavy boards and the creaking tanks were dragged out of Castle Street, by extreme effort. Sweat poured down our exhausted bodies. Our 'good' neighbors, Christians, stood on the street with folded arms faintly smiling, watching the enslaved Jews.

In fear of death we slaved away, bearing heavy loads for five km. up and down hill. I still can't comprehend where we got the strength to trudge and trudge, driven by fear. Time stood still, what would happen to us? Petrushevich, the German task–master, shouted, "Faster! Faster!" With bowed head and aching legs we labored without relief. When we delivered the tanks to Trov, we hoped for some rest. We knew that the Germans usually repaid our labor by beating us, but this time it didn't happen and we were overjoyed. We embraced and were happy that we would get home without being beaten. Near Olshan, at the bridge from Aaron Schneider's water mill, we were met by our family and friends, who had been terrified by our ordeal.

[Page 199]

Olshan Jews in the Concentration Camps
Work Camps in the Area of Lithuania
[Zhezhmir]
by Shepsl Kaplan

In 1942, 600 Jews, mostly young healthy young men and women from Olshan, Kreve, Smorgen and other towns were brought to Zhezhmir, near Kovne, to build the highway from Kovne to Vilna. Another group, mostly from Oshman, worked on the same road from Vevye to Miligan near Vilna. In the synagogue and the nearby cinema, the Germans had formerly kept Soviet prisoners of war. Because of the filth and the minimal rotten food, mostly potato peels, a typhus epidemic broke out. Many died, including Peretz Tchepelinski, Reuben Sogalovitz, Leib Koslovski and others from Olshan. Against great odds, the Jewish doctor Gordonovitz, his medic Anolik and his wife, Matilda, isolated the ill and saved them from the SS camp director. Thus the camp was salvaged from the threat of total destruction..

In the spring of 1943, after the liquidation of the last ghettos around Vilna, 1000 more Jews, mostly from Oshman, were crammed into Zhezhmir. Many of these were children, and they were stuffed into the same two houses where the typhus epidemic was raging. The 'Death Squad' led by the camp director, Shtoltzman, was ruthless, but the senior Jews weren't treated so badly. Every week several of them were driven in a truck to bring back products from their homes. They also carried letters and greetings for all.

There was the case of a 14 year old girl, who developed appendicitis in 1942, and thanks to the intervention of Reuben Segalovitz and Yivdal Rudnik, she was sent back to Olshan. This news was unbelievable. It was so much likelier that she would have been deported like the 23 Jews sent off in a truck to a field 3 km distant, where they were massacred.

Forced by the 'Death Squad' to work faster to finish the highway, the situation was hellish. Among the merciless sadistic slave drivers, stood out Georgi, who had a criminal past that he bragged about. At the smallest mistake, he would exact ferocious punishment. Usually this would happen to Jews who had never held a shovel in their hands. Like an aroused wild beast, he'd beat the Jews with his stick and kick them. The more he beat them, the angrier he got. None of his victims escaped his beatings.

Summer 1943, the work on the road was finished, and the Death Squad moved 300 men to Pskov, in occupied Russia. The remaining Jews were destined for execution since they were now useless. The bewildered Jews had maintained contact with the Kovno Judenrat, to whom some letters had been sent beseeching help to escape the fate of the camps in Oshman, Kovno and Ponor. This time the Kovno Judenrat appealed to the regional commander to allow the able bodied to transfer to the Kovno ghetto.

One day the Jewish officials of the Kovno ghetto arrived together with the leader of the German work force. 800 men, women and children were transferred to the Kovno ghetto in June 1943. They were welcomed warmly by the Kovno ghetto administrator. A number of the new arrivals were quartered in the cinema 'Latinika'. But soon the administrators began to treat the Zhelzhiners as second–class and assign them to the worst places and hardest labor in the ghettos. Because of this, the Zhelzhiners volunteered to provide 300 men to work in the Kashidor camp.

The Leaders of the Kashidor Camp

The work in Kashidor was difficult and exhausting. It consisted of digging ditches, loading and unloading trucks, chopping down forests. In four months, there were five camp administrators, including Corporal Mutz and pay master Shtieglitz. Their relations with 350 Jews were not bad, they breathed more freely. Stieglitz and Mutz allowed the Jews to enter town to get supplies for the camp. They also allowed the train crew to deliver and unload potatoes and other products in the camp. The work was controlled and assigned by the military administration. For fear of being sent to the front, if the camp had been liquidated and the Jews deported, the camp's military officials consistently praised the Jews to their superiors in Kovno, asserting that they were diligent and performed useful work.

Each of the five camp directors in Kashidor had a different relationship with the Jews. The first, Sergeant Sharke, was a troubled man, who often flew into a demented rage. When he ordered an assembly, it was suspected that everyone was to be taken to be gassed, causing a general panic. When he heard about this rumor, he visited every barrack, he reassured everyone, swearing on his life that he had personally ordered that the Jews would not be harmed. Apprehensively, the Jews went into the baths, and in fact came out washed and clean. The German guards photographed Stieglitz with a Jewish girl on his lap, and a report of this was sent to the Jews of the camp. Stieglitz was transferred to the Front, and was succeeded by Sergeant Mutz.

Mutz used to go to the town to procure supplies. Wherever possible, he allowed the camp Judenrat to handle their affairs. Mutz was also sent to the Front. A day before he left, he was advised of the upcoming children's 'Aktion'. He selected the 12 year old Aaron Kaplan and saved him from death. Mutz's successor Sergeant Kashin, a professional soldier, was told of the impending children's Aktion. On the third day of the order, Kashin summoned the Judenrat and ordered them to send the Jews out to work.

He declared,"I have believed, then not believed in the gruesomeness of the Germans against adult Jews. Now I have seen the truth. Our German culture has been degraded by the war against these young children. We have already lost the war. I am ashamed to be a German."

[Page 204]

The Nazi Murder of Children

Extermination of Children by Germans in Kashidor Camp
by Shepsl Kaplan

In March 1944, the Germans killed all the children from 1–12, who had been living with their parents in Kashidor. Of the 24 children in the camp, 22 were murdered. Three children survived, including, by luck, my son. These 24 children had been the only consolation and hope for the Jews in the camp, and the German atrocity struck at the heart of the 350 Jewish prisoners. This happened despite the impending defeat of the Germans. On March 27, at 3 AM, an SS special commando group of 100 drunken Germans and Lithuanians, armed with machine guns, surrounded the camp. All the Jews were summoned out, and it was soon obvious from the demeanor and disorder of the gunmen, that something terrible was going to happen.

Soon the SS commander ordered the 24 children, whose names were on his list, to be brought out. When the stunned mothers did not comply immediately, he ordered his men to get the children out of the barracks, tearing them away from their mothers, who tried to run after their children. They were beaten back brutally, and any of the older children who tried to escape, hoping for protection from their parents, were threatened with bayonets. The murderous band tore infants out of their mothers' arms. The hellish scene of weeping and wailing by the mothers and children was accompanied by wild yells of the militia, sounds which I will always recall when I think of this terrible scene.

Under a hail of blows, the mothers struggled to approach the commander and kneeling begged to be taken with their children. They were ignored and he stood like a statue while his underlings beat the women savagely with their bayonets. The women lay there, bloodied, anguished, at the feet of the commander. He was intent on the rows of the 350 Jews and that two missing children had to be found among the ranks. The two children were: Alek Radonski, from Kovne, 11, whose height enabled him to be concealed by his father Dr. Radonski, and Yosef Lipkovitz, 8, cleverly wrapped and agile, had slipped away from the doomed group and hid between the feet of Chaim Svirski of Olshan, who died after liberation.

The third child was my son, who had not been counted in the original list because he was mistakenly identified as four years older and had stood with me, among the work crew. The commander pointed at him and told his underling, "He comes too", and he took off to search for the 24th victim. By chance, on that same day, the former camp commander of Kashidor, Sergeant Mutz came home on leave. My son had worked for him, saving donuts for him and polishing his boots. He had come to pick up his belongings, to leave for the front. His departure was delayed because the camp was blocked, so he had witnessed the whole affair about the children Aktion. When he saw my son being selected, he approached the officer and asked him to spare this boy, who had been one of his best workers.

Confused by all the clamor of the suffering women, and by the improper surprising request from Sergeant Mutz, the officer gave the order to load up the 22 children on two hay wagons, to the nearest train station in Kashidor. There they were jammed into an underground bunker. After a whole day they were loaded into a special train, together with children from other camps, and carried off to their deaths. No one of these children returned. Later it was learned that this Aktion included all the camps and ghettos in Lithuania and had lasted two days. Among the rumors about this event, it was said that the Germans had utilized the children's blood for transfusions for their wounded soldiers on the Soviet front.

[Page 207]

Childhood in the Shadows of the Gallows
by Haya Altman Abramovitz

My childhood ended at age 9, when the Germans drove us into the ghetto. I had suddenly grown up. I understood that that my dear mother must not leave the boundary of the ghetto, and I used to weep and implore her not to seek food from the Christians. I had heard that whenever Jews were caught outside the ghetto, they were severely beaten, even shot. So i didn't let my mother go to the peasants. I decided that I wouldn't be in such danger as an adult, so I took along some items to trade with the goyim for food. so I used to go to the Christians and bring back some potatoes and other food items on my back.

The crowding in the ghetto was terrible. We lived at Shepsl's house. In one room we slept in a double bed, my Bubbe Elke, together with Mama and my little brother, and I on the floor. Later my sister was taken to the Zhezhmir camp, along with all the other youngsters from Olshan. Our room was pervaded by longing and weeping– why were we Jews suffering so much?

A year passed and in 1942 the Olshan ghetto was liquidated and we were moved to Oshman. We moved into a shul. Nearby we had some friends who took us in. The Olshan Judenrat sought lodging for us. When a little room was found with another family, there weren't enough beds, so Bubbe Elke and her mother Milkhe stayed in the shul.

One morning when we were all asleep, my Mama woke me, "Khayele! Khayele! Get up!" I felt my mother's distress and fright. She had dressed Mairkhen, my little brother, and told me that I should stay here with him in the room. "And where are you going, Mama?" She told me that all adults had been summoned. I started to weep– I wanted to go with her.

The Germans Take Away My Mother

We were among the last to arrive at the place, where groups were already standing. Mama held our hands and led us to the shul, where Bobbe had stayed. I saw police with cudgels in hand and I suddenly felt that my brother and I were being torn from Mama's hands, which I could no longer feel. We had been thrown into the shul basement, along with many people, weeping and sobbing. I tried to rejoin my mother, but the police didn't let anyone out. The lamentations intensified inside the shul. We thought we were going to be incinerated because we already knew that had happened in the Volozhin and

Vishniev ghettos. We were kept until evening, when the last of the chosen adults were sent off and then we were released. And that's when my troubles really began.

Where should I go with my little brother? Who could give me advice? I didn't go back to our little room. I wandered on the street with my brother. Then I heard that all the mothers, fathers and grandmothers had been sent to Zelianke. I ran to the Judenrat and begged them to get the release of the mothers whose children are suffering. I hoped that perhaps she could buy her way out since she had a permit from the Oshman Judenrat. That night I returned to the little room, now without a Mama. Only God could hear our weeping. Unfortunately, our own Vilna police had no pity. they were indifferent to our innocent parents. We passed the night, and next day seemed dark and hopeless.

In the Truck Leading the Children to Death, the Radio Was Playing

There were a few children in the truck. The radio was on, and the cries of the mothers were awful. My brother and I were weeping and he said, "Save yourself– Nechama is all alone." The truck stopped at the school and when the door opened, I begged the Germans to let me go–"I am able to work–I have my card." The German yelled at me. "Get out!" I ran out of the truck and didn't realize I had left behind my dear little brother. I could only think that I wanted to live.

As soon as I got out, I went to a room where I met a very pale terrified woman. I told her that the Germans had released me; I wanted to hide under the bed. She told me in a tremulous voice that her child was hidden in the bed. I hid behind some wall hangings, but then some Ukrainians broke in, saw my feet sticking out, and dragged me back to the same truck with the same driver and radio. Again I begged him, reminding him that he had released me before, so he let me go again.

I returned to the room, confused and helpless. Then I heard dogs barking to hunt down the children. In the evening in the nearby shul, some Jews had met for prayers. I didn't dare show myself on the street, but I asked one of the praying men to let my sister know that I had been saved and she should come to me.

Our re–union was very moving. We embraced, wept and rejoiced. She didn't ask about my brother, she was so happy that I had survived. Our own survival was paramount under such circumstances. At night when the Germans had left, we went back to the same room as before. Our bed was now free, but our brother was gone. Then we realized that the *Aktion* wasn't ended, the trucks were still there, ready to load more innocent victims.

Often during the night we heard a child cry, and we knew that it was being hidden in a bunker. But it was useless, the Germans knew where to find them. There were instances where a Jewish policeman was helping the

Germans to uncover the bunkers, and even a case where the policeman had helped to disclose his own family.

My Sister Hides Me in a Laundry Tub and I Am Saved

The *Aktion* lasted all day and night. On the second day, my sister and I went to the laundry workshop. She had hidden me with the laundry in a tub, under a long table. We hoped that the Germans wouldn't search in the workshops where able–bodied workers were, but they realized that children were hiding there, so they searched all the rooms, even came to our room. But they didn't find me, though one kicked my hiding place. I heard everything and almost suffocated with fear. It seemed a long time before I could get out of the tub after the Germans had left. My sister calmed me and told me that the Germans had gone but we had to wait a little longer. Slowly I climbed out and took some deep breaths. The people in the shop were overjoyed to see me, but I was unable to calm down, imagining that that I was still being hunted.

The *Kinder–Aktion* and our ghetto–these were the two most awful days of my life. It was difficult later to describe life in the ghetto. Only after things calmed down did we understand what had happened. Brothers and sisters lost each other. How could you save yourself and let your little brother go to his death? Deeply inscribed in our memory is the story of Chana Bruch**Error! Bookmark not defined.** Hirsh, who came home from work to find that her children had been taken away. I stifled my tears as I looked upon this beautiful woman. The murderers broke us down and left open wounds which will never heal.

[Page 216]

The Killing of the Children
in Zhezhmir Camp
by Haya Kzurer–Katz

On March 27, 1943, the Germans carried out their plan to exterminate the children in all the camps in the Lithuanian region. With German efficiency, the action occurred in all these places so that no child could be hidden.

The camp was surrounded, and all the children were assembled. The mothers came with the children and everyone was packed into the trucks. We later learned that in the other camps, only the children were taken, only in ours were the mothers also taken. My sister was 12 years old, but small for her age. She was taken immediately and I went after her. She was already sitting in the truck and I was climbing up the step to enter, the officer in charge yelled at me. I explained that I was getting my younger sister. The SS man shouted at me. "Take your sister! And get out of here!" Thus we were saved from death.

When we entered the camp, I dressed my sister in a long dress, an elaborate hair–do, and high heels, and she was able to pass among the adults. A German passed through to make sure that no children had been hidden, he stared at my sister and laughed because she looked so strange. He waved at her as if to say–she should stay.

The same day, a boy named Lazar Gobi was shot. There had been some contact with the partisans, but very few knew about it. Money was collected to buy guns, and Lazar was involved. He already had a little gun, and when the Kinder Aktion was being carried out, the Germans found his gun. They discovered his hiding place and shot him on the spot.

Actually six children under five remained hidden on their own when they heard about the Aktion. Their mothers didn't know where they were. A little girl, four or five, Goldele Abramovitz, stood behind a hanger and didn't utter a word all day. When this was reported to the camp director, he said, "Since there are no children left in the camp, I must report this." But he added, "If anyone is able, he must take the children out at night." The neighborhood was unfamiliar, so the children were not taken out. In the morning the weeping children were loaded by the SS man Keitel into a taxi. The mothers had been told to dress them warmly to protect against the cold. After driving a few km., he took them out and shot them, as related by some peasants. The Germans also took mothers, and young people who appeared sickly like Sara–Malke Soladucha and her daughter Mirke.

[Page 217]

The Tortured Jews Flee
to the Partisans
by Shepsel Kaplan

After the Kinder–Aktion in Kashidor camp, many Jews fled to the forest and joined the partisan brigade, *Svobodnia Litva*. The escape happened in mid–day in sight of the German guards, who were supervising the prisoners at their work. The workers were divided into ditch–diggers, road work, and foresters, assigned to fell trees. The forest workers established contact with the partisans, and in March 1944 received a message from the partisan leader, that a number of them should join the brigade. The message spread with lightning speed, that all the working camp residents should meet at a specified place in the forest. In a chaotic disorganized manner, the inmates suddenly left their work sites and ran off into the woods and to their families in camp. The Germans were initially confounded by this unusual event, but quickly rounded up the rest of the workers, to herd them back to camp. The forest brigade disarmed the Germans and took them prisoner. Next day they released them back to camp, but kept their weapons.

The remaining 300 Jews were locked in a barrack under heavy guard, and for three days were given no food or water. On the fourth day, a special commando unit from Kovne came to liquidate the 300 Jews. The commandos began their retaliation on the Jewish patriarch Roth, a Czech Jew, recommended by the Kovne Judenrat. Roth had dutifully carried out all the orders from the Judenrat, and hadn't flinched from his assignment to choose ten Jews to send to a certain death.

The Germans accused Roth of having concealed the flight of the 50 Jews. The commando leader tortured Roth, tore out all his hair and beat him savagely. Roth barely survived because of his athletic strength. Together with the camp doctor, Rodanski, they were sent off. Rodanski was shot and Roth was freed, to go to Aleksat. Together with the commando leader, Roth visited all the barracks to translate into Yiddish the command. "You have ten minutes to surrender all concealed weapons, or else be shot. You have a few minutes to live. Give up your guns, it's not worth dying on the spot."

After ten minutes, the inmates were expelled from the barracks and it was ransacked but only a bottle of juice was found. With this, the guard split the head of a Kovno Jew, to whom the drink belonged. They then savagely beat the Jews with clubs and rifle butts. The scenes were so gruesome and indescribable. After two hours of torture, they herded the Jews 3 km away from the camp, into a field next to a rail line. There was no let–up in the beating, and shooting over their heads. We were crowded into cattle cars and taken towards the death camp Shontz.

Nobody could survive this camp. The strongest man could only survive a month. But then a strange thing happened that no one expected. The train stopped along the way and we were unloaded into the prison camp Aleksat, 7 km. from Kovne. It was a mystery as to why we were sent to Aleksat. The Kovne Jews said that the unexpected change was the result of the influence of the Kovne Judenrat on the man in charge, Gecke (though he wasn't there that day). The 300 Jews were sent to Aleksat temporarily until further orders. It was probably just luck, since camp Aleksat needed the slave labor of the Jews from Kashidor, whose fate had seemed so certain.

Pain and Destruction in the Aleksat Camp

When the Olshaners arrived in Aleksat, they joined about 1000 Kashidor Jews, men and women from the Kovne ghetto. They were quartered in the Lithuanian army base together with thousands of Russian prisoners of war, who would all succumb to hunger, slave labor, shootings and various other privations. In the *kaserne* was an execution wall. All the walls in the rooms of the three story wooden building were covered in Russian, telling of the terrible hunger, gruesome beatings, executions by shooting. The longing for home and family evoked compassion from our souls for the innocents who perished here.

Aleksat was considered one of the worst camps in Lithuania because of the heavy labor in the fields and the two camp directors, who were murderers and sadists. There were two separate detachments for men and women. Twelve hours a day we labored loading and unloading heavy stones and other materials. German soldiers stood and ensured that no one raised his head or straightened his back, punished by severe beatings.

The camp leader for men was an SS man, Mia; the Kovne Jews dubbed him 'Leibele Fliess'. He was a cold–blooded animal. Four times a day, at every opportunity he would savagely beat dozens of Jews to the point of exhaustion and unconsciousness. His helper, in charge of the women, did the same. She was dubbed 'shorn head'. At every assembly, like a crazed animal, she'd use her whip, which she always carried with her, on the heads and faces of the women, who were driven to their labor bloody and beaten. Some collapsed when they came back.

The children in the camp were separated, boys with their fathers, girls with their mothers. In the month that I was in Aleksat, I didn't see my wife or daughter. Contact between men and women was disastrous. One could not even stop to have a few words at a chance meeting. If it weren't for the mealtimes, which supported relationships, the children could not have survived a month of hard labor.

For the month I was there, the food was tasty and adequate. But the camp chief used all legal and illegal means to restrict the food, to ensure that all food must go into the pot and not be stolen. There must always be some dry wood so that meals would be at the right time. He sought out places to gather dry wood, and at night he'd take a group of inmates on a truck to gather wood for cooking. When this went well, he'd slap the shoulders of his workers fraternally. It was quite different if the group was not so successful.

The Death March and the Escape From The Forest

In May 1944, the Germans shifted 250 of the 300 Aleksat prisoners, to the Roudamflime camp, near Koslov. This camp, our last before liberation, was deep in a forest of giant ancient pines, far from any settlement. After three months, we fled into the forest and joined up with the Red Army, leaving behind dozens of victims–such as my wife, Bunye Kaplan, Zelda Soleducha from Olshan, Chana and Leah Brudne, and two sisters from Smorgen. They were killed as they were fleeing into the forest. Dozens were captured and executed on the brink of liberation.

The Kovne Judenrat made the decision to shift the Koshidor inmates to Roudamflime, because it had to fill the gap left by the murder of the Soviet prisoners who had been working there. At that point we were thankful to the Kovne Judenrat, although we knew they weren't doing it for our benefit to release us from hell, but to avoid sending those Jews who wanted to stay in the ghetto. The Judenrat had preferred not to mix the Jewish groups, so the Kashidor Jews were used to fill the now–empty Roudenflime camp. But we were glad to get rid of 'Leibele Fliess' and 'Shaved Head' and their bloody massacres which were inflicted daily on the Kashidor Jews.

In this new camp, we were driven into wooden barracks surrounded by barbed wire. The walls were infested with cockroaches. Russian prisoners had lived there before and had inscribed on all the walls descriptions of the horrible treatment inflicted on them–hunger, sickness, execution. We knew that we could expect no better fate.

The regimen here was easier than in Aleksat, but the food was much worse. In May 1944, 50 more Jews were brought from Vilna. The labor was done in deep sandy pits. On three giant mounds stood three machines which ground up the turf which was then taken away to be dried. In this remote corner, we often thought that we'd be forgotten and be left over until liberation, but it turned out quite differently.

At mid–day in July 1944, we were suddenly assembled and informed that we had to march off to Kovne. We were allowed to take a small pack, but leave everything else behind. And in a few minutes all of us, including the sick, had to be ready to march. We were surrounded by 70 armed Germans, Letts and Ukrainians. We were told by the commander that if any bandits (i.e. partisans) came our way in the wilds, at any suspicious sound or a gunshot, we must fall prone with our faces down, or else we'd be shot.

Divided in four columns, the women in front, we started our last march. We were driven through a forest on a winding path, about 20 km. from a train station. The day was hot, the sweat mixed with dust covered our bodies and faces, ran over our eyes and we couldn't see more than 3 meters ahead. The suspicious behavior of the senior Jew, Dr. Bloisberg, who had just returned that dawn from Kovne with the troop of Germans, Letts and Ukrainians, raised the anxiety level . He had kept to himself, hadn't uttered a word, like the deceptive men of the Kovne Judenrat. He knew well about the horrors of that ghetto, how the Jews were driven into one area and the ghetto was liquidated. The houses were destroyed along with the people. On all sides the Jews fled and were shot down by the thousands.

In the course of the march, Dr. Bloiberg had kept his distance, and we suspected that he planned to escape with a few of his companions, and he disappeared unnoticed. [After liberation he returned to Kovne]. It was obvious that Dr. Bloiberg had sold us out. We were on our last march, and we had to flee into the forest to survive.

In the course of the more than three hour march with 10 minute rest, a large number of us had conferred and decided on a favorable moment to start running into the woods. Despite the inevitable costs a few would survive. During the rest period, families got together. The Germans didn't notice. The Jews agreed on a meeting point in case they got lost. Isaac Soladura lagged behind to confer with two Ukrainian guards serving the Germans, who foresaw their fate and they planned to escape with the Jews to join the partisans.

In close array, about 10 km from camp, in a spot where the forest was dense and the sun was setting, the two Ukrainians fired their guns, a signal for the Jews to start running on all sides. Fearful of an attack by the partisans, the Germans fell to earth and started firing. A number of Jews also lay down, who were too scared to run, or hadn't been informed about the escape plan. The shooting lasted about ten minutes. It seemed that the Germans were convinced that the shooting was one–sided, so they got up, ordered the others to stand and resume the march.

One week later, the fugitives re–assembled at the appointed spot and organized a group. The responsibility for maintaining the group of 150 men was assumed by Yerachmel Gershovitz, Mavshovitz and 'Binele', all from Kovne. They knew the Lithuanian language , were armed with a gun given them by one of the Ukrainians, and they entered the towns, got bread for or without money, brought it back and each person got an equal share.

Contacts with Soviet Units and German Troops

Yerachmial Gershovitz, now in Israel, told me about an episode while seeking food. Once as several of us were leaving town with a load of food and in a good mood, we encountered a group of armed German soldiers, in brand-new uniforms. Automatically we hid in the forest, but couldn't escape. They held us and asked in Russian and German, "Who are you, where are you coming from, what do we have in our bags, what were we doing in the forest, and where did we get a gun?"

It became evident from their calm 'German' attitude, their Russian speech and their radio receiver, that they were not German enemies, but a Soviet detachment. We told them we were a group of 150 Jews, escaped from a camp, hoping to join the partisans. They listened to us amicably, identified themselves; there was no reason to fear them. They promised to visit our group and to help as much as possible. In the morning eight men arrived, a lieutenant, two sergeants in brand-new German uniforms and five Soviet soldiers. We asked them either to take us with them or to help us unite with the partisans. The officer answered that it was impossible to take an unarmed group with them, and that the partisans would probably feel the same way. The only solution was to head in a different direction, and he suggested that he would lead us to a safer place, undisturbed by shepherds, hunters or gatherers.

In town, when we asked the Lett how he knew about us, he answered that everybody in town knew about the 20 men in the woods. We were dubious about him. He finally showed up two days later, with some bread, and next day led us into a thick forest with dense shrubbery. Every time we came to his place some suspicious activity was happening around his house. Only later did we realize that he was an agent for the partisans.

A majority of our group decided to trust the Lett, because we didn't have any other choice, and of course he could have betrayed us early on. That night we spoke to the Lett, promised to pay him for his help and asked him to lead us to that safer place. He didn't show up for two days, and we stayed put. Josef Potashnik and I went to him again and he explained that some important things had delayed him, and asked our pardon. He gave us a loaf of bread and said he would come at dawn. On July 20, he came and led us for two hours on a trail to a thick forest, where the weeds were six feet high. He told us to enter the woods carefully one by one, and the last one should restore the trampled trail. The forest was one km. from the town of Agurkishki.

The Punitive Squad Fires on Our Group

Two hours after we entered the forest, we heard heavy firing from all sides. That evening two girls from our group headed for the Lett to find out what was going on. They were met by his wife on the trail, who told them to run back into the woods. A company of Germans had arrived at their house with the goal of wiping out the partisans and the Jewish fugitives. We learned later that one of the shepherds had observed us and had brought on the punitive expedition.

From dawn to dusk, the shooting lasted without a halt, and could be heard from 10 km away and lasted for nine days. From a nearby trail, our enemies found a way to keep firing at us in the forest from all directions. We could hear them clearly, in German, Russian and Lithuanian. Fortunately they didn't venture into the forest depths, only as far as the thistles.

About 40 Jews were killed from the gunfire. A few from the group were captured in the town where they were seeking food. They were severely beaten and some were forced to lead our enemies to the location of the main group; they were all shot immediately.

Elia Kozlovski from Olshan, was caught and tortured, but did not reveal the location of his parents, brother, sister and others. Several days later his parents found his body and buried him.

The Consequences of Liberation

The Latvian came to us on the 10th day. He brought a pack of food supplies, and also the happy news that we were free. His area was now occupied by Soviet tanks, soldiers and officers. We shared a drink of congratulation and he invited us to come visit his home.

We didn't walk, we ran to his home to see the people who had liberated us. There we met the Soviet soldiers and officers. They were friendly and cheered and consoled us and urged us to help defeat the Nazis so that no trace would remain of them.

Their friendly words moved us to tears. The feelings of unavoidable doom had suddenly lifted, and we felt so thankful to our liberators. We stayed at the Latvian's house for two days. His wife cooked the best for us. And they had quite a lot, enough for everybody including the hundreds of Soviets who passed through their home. We slept on fresh hay in the barn and in the morning we went into the field to help gather and prepare the freshly cut corn.

On the third day we took leave of this wonderful Latvian family, whose name, unfortunately I don't remember. In gratitude, David Lifkovitz presented the wife with his last possession–a gold watch and chain. We left behind a letter in Russian, warmly thanking this remarkable family from Agurkishki, who had saved these twenty Jews from certain death.

The Death of Bunye Kaplan on the Eve of Liberation

Four years of bloody terror had ended for me, my two children, Rivke and Aaron, and 150 Jews of Olshan. Kreve, Smorgen,, Oshman, Vilna and Kovne, liberated by the Soviet army. For me, liberation brought a deeply tragic component to my soul. On the brink of liberation, I lost the dearest part of my life–my wife Bunye, the mother of our children. During the course of that bloody trail for four years, fate had held us together, only to lose her, leaving me with the tragic memory.

She has been gone for 15 years. Night after night I lay sleepless and agonize. During the day, my heart is weighed down, and to my last breath, I re–live our sad experience. Broken physically and spiritually, my two children and I returned to Olshan, but we found no home there. Out of 1000 Jews, there remained 100 wandering shadows. All the others had been tortured like my Bunye.

How Bunye Was Lost

It happened as we were being hunted down in the forest by the enemy forces. During the 10 minute rest period, I had re–joined my wife and children. When a group of us decided to flee further into the forest, I asked them to flee with me. We planned to meet at plow number 3.

We were about 8 km. from camp, when, at an agreed signal, one of the Ukrainians fired his gun, and we all ran off in different directions. Concerned with a possible attack by the partisans, the Germans lay down and started shooting at the escapees. I held Bunye's hand and with our children, we plunged deeper into the woods. We jumped over logs, through thickets, fell and got up, and then I was hit by a tree branch which knocked me unconscious. When I recovered, it was night time, and i couldn't see anybody, my wife or children. I tore off my rucksack and with my last strength ran into the woods. I didn't know where I was. Exhausted, I sat down under a tree, thinking only about my wife and children.

At dawn, I thought I heard some steps and then I met a group of our refugees, among them my daughter Rivke. She didn't know what happened to her mother and brother. Then we all met at the meeting point. On the third day, another group of refugees arrived, including my 12 year old son Aaron. He was also unable to tell about how he came to be separated. By the end of the week, about 150 had assembled. The only missing ones were my wife Bunye and three other women, who had been seen running through the forest. This terrible event has remained as the saddest day of my life.

Back to the Old Home after Liberation

After we were free, the Soviets helped us get loaded into a truck which took us as far as Zhezhmir. There we visited our first camp, where dozens of children had died from hunger and typhus. then we went on a truck to Vilna, where we were stopped at a military post and identified ourselves. We were sent to a Jewish committee where we met some familiar faces, and stayed overnight. In the morning, August 2, 1944, we arrived in Olshan. Not much had changed, houses, streets, alleys, lake, pools, fields, woods were all there, but Jewish mothers, fathers, children were missing. The goyim, enemies of Israel, now occupied all the Jewish houses, and that was extremely painful for the returnees. Of the 225 families living there in 1939, only 70 souls returned.

For some time there had formed a collective in the big home of Velvel Tchepelinski after we had relinquished our individual homes. There were cases where the goyim had resisted returning the houses to the Jews. The Soviets had to exert their power.

We didn't stay for long in the shtetl. It was too horrible for the few Jews to get rooted again in their former lives. The hope to rebuild a family soon disappeared. A few who had returned from Germany, were initially content but then realized the bitter truth, that return was not possible. One by one, the 70 Jews began to leave their old homes, to wander into the greater world, to seek some consolation for their misery. I have established a home now in Israel.

The Trail of Pain– My Father's Death

When the Germans took our town on June 24, 1941, my mother was left with me, a 10 year old sister, but no father. We learned later that he had been in the Minsk ghetto, in the Judenrat. He spoke German well. Through the Judenrat he was connected with an underground organization.

One day the Germans issued a demand for a large amount of food provisions. all of our shelves were stripped. My father got the word from the underground that he should divert some of it. The Germans were tipped off about this, and he was taken by the Gestapo and tortured, to disclose his contacts. He did not tell despite the terrible ordeals.

At first we lived in our own home, in a state of terror. But then we were all crowded into the ghetto. We all had to work, clean the streets, cut the grass, chop trees. We were very crowded, 3–4 families in a room. Often the Germans would enter the ghetto and demand gold, soap and other valuables. The Judenrat was always busy going from house to house to collect for the Germans. Soon the Germans sent many to the Zhezhmir camp and I was included. Daily we were driven out to work. I was helped immensely by a girl from Kreve, Chana Kapelovitz. She really took care of me and my sister who came later.

We tried to conceal a typhus epidemic lest the Germans immediately kill everybody. The camp commander, Stoltzman, whom we called "Hoarse" because of his voice, knew about the epidemic but kept it quiet. After the healthiest and strongest of the youths had died, the survivors were extremely weak, our hair had fallen out, and we looked like ghosts. It was very difficult to recover from the typhus, but we managed to return to work. A few of us would sneak into town to try to barter some of our things for a little bread or potatoes.

Once, when I finished eating, I went into town also, but at the same time a guard came into the camp, and counted the roll. When I returned, the guard was waiting for me (he was called 'Reds' because of his face) he said he would handle it at the evening meal. I was terrified, and when I stood in line for the cup of watery soup, he called me out and in public, slapped my face, saying,"This girl has committed a serious crime. Without permission she has split off from the group to go into town." I was locked in, and after the intercession of the Judenrat, was told to ask for pardon, and to promise that it wouldn't happen again.

After the liquidation of the Oshman ghetto, the Jews were sent to various camps, depending on where they had relatives. Those without relatives were taken to Kovne and to Vilna. Thousands of Jews who had registered for Kovne, were taken to Vilna, and then all were shot in Panor. Later when the Oshman Jews arrived in Vilna ghetto, they found the remaining items and old photos of friends, and it was evident that they had all been killed in Panor.

My little sister had registered to come to Zhezhmir, and so we were re-united. When the adults went out to labor, the children remained in camp. They became very resourceful, wise beyond their years, and fully understood our dire situation.

New Camp, New Suffering

When the Zhezhmir camp was liquidated, we were taken to Ponyevyetz, where we worked building an airport. We lived in huts and living conditions were extremely severe. We were awakened at 4 AM for coffee, then on to hard work. When the front became closer, we were stuffed into cattle cars and taken further west. We suffered hunger and thirst and thought that we were on the final road. There was no hope of escape. Even if you could crawl out of a tiny window, where could you go? The area was totally strange, everyone was your enemy who would betray you to the Germans or kill you.

After a week we arrived in a forest. It was night time, we were treading on refuse and trash, as well as rucksacks. and we were terrified. The group before us started to shriek. I went further, our ranks swelled, and the terror spread so that we also started wailing. That was our first night in Shtuthof. We were driven into a large hall, where the SS men announced,"Here below you, are buried the Jews who refused to give up their gold. So give up your gold voluntarily, and you won't be harmed." We thought this would be our last night.

At dawn, we were led into a barrack, surrounded by electrified barbed wire. Contact with the wire caused several to lose their lives. The SS had separated families on either side of the fence. If anyone neared the fence to converse, our enemies at the guard posts above turned on the electric current. We were tormented by the assembly calls at any time of day or night, when the sudden sound blast blared–Assembly! Line up! They called the roll often, and shifted the inmates to other barracks, so that one could never know where you were going to sleep next night, or what might happen that day.

The first few days when we still had a few items, we tried to hide them between the floorboards on which we slept, but when we were shifted to another barrack suddenly, we were left with nothing. Every dawn, the SS men came in, some women among them, and selected out those who appeared ill or exhausted. Later we were told by some Polish political prisoners that the camp had a crematorium.

The frequent assembly calls served to confuse the people, to hide their fate and to eliminate any resistance. The food was awful. Soup was brought in a large wooden vat. There were cases where the bestial fiends amused themselves by throwing a woman into the pot, then telling the prisoners to eat. Several days after our arrival we were told to bring all of our belongings, to be disinfected in a bath.

Near the 'bath' we saw long lines of people waiting. We had broken up and tried to destroy anything of value, lest the Germans take it . When it was my turn to go in, a man in a white coat asked me my age in Polish. When I told him 16, he let me go. We were all naked, but we didn't go in the bath. Women and girls, older than me, were set on an examining table to see if they had anything hidden inside. After this painful inspection, we were taken out of the camp in prison clothes.

Later we were taken to a children's home, where we were fed well. We were taught a trade so that we might get a workers card. It was also important to show that we were able to work, in case there was another Aktion. It was a good connection for the orphans, since we were given part of the food brought in by Jews newly arrived in the ghetto. Some Jews worked outside the ghetto, and often, though terrified, would bring in food obtained by barter with the peasants. As there were strict controls, these Jews were often caught and severely beaten. Their products were given then to the Jewish police, who then donated some food to the children's home.

We were taught Hebrew and sewing, and then given a little work. So, gradually we adjusted to our condition. When the Germans sent off some Jews to another camp, our ghetto became smaller. From the children's home we were sent to eat at a strange family's home, and sometimes we sat hungry, unwilling to go to these strangers' home. But we got used to that too. Our bed was very crowded. We were three in a bed, with four families in the room. I was sent to a class in housekeeping, while my brother learned metal work. Until suddenly everything changed, the terrible children's extermination, called by the Germans, 'Kinder Aktion'.

We were terrified at seeing the faces of the Germans. There was chaos in the ghetto as people ran to hide in their 'melinas'. We also ran to the workshops, where Nkhoma worked, but they were already guarded and the streets were blocked. A loudspeaker from a car announced that no one was allowed on the street. Then we all ran into a two-story house, and with Nkhoma waited. We entered an empty room with a window facing the street where we could see all the action. But Nkhoma didn't want me to look out the window, lest we be seen by the Germans. We heard children weeping, and saw a mother trying to join her child in the car, being beaten back into her home. My heart was pounding, and I was overcome by dread. We looked for a place to hide. My sister had put me in the bed and covered me with pillows, but it was obviously inadequate. We were so confused, that finally we decided to await our fate. So we stayed in the room, hoping they would not come. Suddenly we heard the familiar steps of the murderous Germans. I wanted to show that I wasn't scared, though I was trembling inside. They directed my brother to come, but he started to cry and to beg that he wanted to stay with his sister. They didn't take Nakhman who lay in his bed kicking his feet. But they grabbed us and forced us into the waiting wagon.

German Peasants Bought Us For Labor

My 12 year–old sister and I were sent out as slave labor. When the Polish doctor who checked us didn't want to release my sister because of her age, he was directed by a SS woman to let her go. "They want to work–let them." So four of us girls were sent to do farm work. After three months when we were sent back, the Shtuthof camp was unrecognizable. Typhus and other major diseases had decimated the camp. Hundreds died every day, survivors looked like ghosts. Between the barracks lay piles of shoes, thousands of pairs of shoes of all sizes, adult and tiny children's shoes. The atmosphere was suffused with death.

The Germans tortured us in many ways. We were starved, made to sit all day on our legs and were beaten if we made a move. The Polish kapo Max was remarkable. He had suffered so much from the Germans and he took it out on the Jews. He beat us brutally over the head with a stick. In the next block where there were 500 women, he forced them to exit within one minute. In fear of another beating, they all rushed frantically to get through the door and even jumped out of the window. There was much bloodshed and weeping. In addition to the brutal Pole, there was daily physical violence. Gypsy women were used as observers, and they also beat their victims at random.

Suddenly an edict was announced: "Whoever wears trousers is to stand on one side; those in dresses on the other." My sister was wearing trousers, and I wore a dress. We would be separated, so I stuffed my skirt into my underwear and remained with the women wearing trousers, so I was able to stay with my sister. Then the healthier ones were taken out to dig ditches in Shtabov.

Amid all this misery, sometimes we tried to sing a little song:

"Oy, Shtabov, you are so close to me

Oy, Shtabov, how can I get rid of you

Oy, Shtabov, when will the time come

Oy, Shtabov, when we'll be liberated"

I was young then and wanted to survive, and we believed we'd be free someday, but it seemed hopeless. We couldn't consider running away because it was a German neighborhood, which could offer only death.

The Orphans in the Camp on the Eve of Liberation

When the Russian forces moved westward, we were moved back to Shtuthof, and the Germans planned to liquidate the camp. German punctuality had vanished and the camp fell into disorder. It seemed like the Germans were about to evacuate, and intended to take us along. They divided us in sections, accompanied by armed guards and SS men and we were herded westward, parallel to the Baltic Sea, deeper into Germany. Snow fell during the day, and at night it covered everything, accompanied by icy winds. We were half–naked and barefoot. We used wooden shoes covered with scraps from above, which became wet from the snow and soaked into the wooden shoes. Dozens fell along the road and were shot by the guards. And so we staggered along starving and exhausted, passing many bodies of our predecessors.

We stopped every night if possible, in a shelter like a cloister, or a barn. The nights were worse than the days. The wet rags adhered to our feet and we had to tear them off. Many women had frostbite. Death seemed preferable to life, but no one committed suicide. After a long march we reached a huge merchants barn where we were allowed to 'rest'. We had started with 1200 women, and in six weeks, only 190 were still alive. Many of them died after liberation, and succumbed among the masses of the dead.

Those of us still breathing lay starving in the cold, under unimaginable conditions, infested with lice. We were resigned, this must be the last stage. The German merchant, owner of the barn, would order some potato soup for us, that had been prepared for the pigs.

So, sick and broken, dispirited, with frozen feet, the few survivors were finally liberated by the Soviet army on March 10, 1945. We were housed in a German town. The houses of the Germans were empty and open, their owners had fled into the forest. I was taken to a Soviet army hospital, where it was recommended that my feet be amputated. I refused and eventually they got better and healed. When I had regained my health, my sister and I, after an interval in Russia, made our very difficult way back to our destroyed homes in Olshan. There was no one left in our family. We encountered Shepsel Kaplan, who took great interest in us, and he housed us for a while. Later when I sought work in Oshman and Vilna, my sister stayed with him. He was like a father to us–we'll never forget him.

[Page 241]

In the Extermination Camp Klage (Estonia)
by Aharon Shuster

My Survival in Olshan and in the German Extermination Camps

When the Germans took Olshan, they immediately loaded 200 Jews into a truck for a labor detail. We assumed that the captives would never return. But in fact, when they all returned in the evening, we rejoiced as if they had been gone for years. Then in 1942, the Germans ordered 150 Jews to work in Zhezhmir. Having heard of the mass killings, the Jews didn't want to go, but they had no choice for they and their families were threatened with death. On a beautiful sunny spring day, guarded by police like criminals, we went on foot to Kreve, joined by the Jews from that ghetto, and we were marched to the Smorgen ghetto for a few days. Then we were taken to the border, where we were taken over by the White Russian police and the German 'Death' squad. Some of us imagined that we were going to do some labor. We were taken to the Lithuanian train station in Kashindor, then driven to Zhezhmir.

There the Christian inhabitants were amazed to see us, for they assumed that there were no more Jews in the area since the Germans came; all the Jews had been murdered in the first weeks of the German attack. The trucks stopped in front of the shul, surrounded by a high barbed wire fence. Inside, we were lined up and counted, then directed to go to sleep. We were awakened early by the bell, assembled outside and put to work, guarded by armed Germans and Latvians. We worked on building a highway and a rail bed, to transport various construction materials, and to facilitate troop movements back and forth. After 3–4 months, the camp director sent a truck to Olshan to find some additional food to feed the slave workers. The truck returned with the heart–breaking news that the Olshan ghetto had been liquidated, that the last Jews had been taken to the Oshman ghetto, along with other ghettos, and had all been killed, including my mother Rachel. The terrible news horrified everyone.

The construction work ended by winter and we then labored in the forest. At dawn we washed our hands and face with snow. At night half–naked, we sat on stools near burning stoves and washed the lice out of our clothes. Typhus broke out, the camp was totally sanitized, but many died including Olshaners Segalovitz, Koslovski, Gurevitz and others. In the summer came new groups of deportees from the shtetls. Jews who had family in the camps were able to visit there. Thus the remnants of the Olshan ghetto, who had been saved in Ashman, came to Zhezhmir. And so I was re-united with my father.

The Kovne Judenrat Ghetto Receives the Camp Survivors who are Later Murdered by the Germans

The Kovne Judenrat did all it could to take in the remaining Jews, though many of them were killed after their slave labor was done. One Sunday in Fall 1943 trucks arrived in the camp and took almost everyone away to Kovne, leaving behind a pile of all their belongings. That Sunday, I had not been in the camp. With my brother Elia we had sneaked into the town to barter for some food. When we returned at night we were dismayed to learn of what had happened. We had been separated from our father, and decided to seek some way to get to the Kovne ghetto. The camp director announced that the 140 remaining Jews were absolutely forbidden to leave the camp.

In the morning trucks arrived to pick up the left–over belongings. I managed to tag along so was taken to Kovne. However the camp director noted my absence and demanded that I be sent back, which meant certain death. Thanks to the work leader of the Kovne Judenrat, Rabinovitz, I was sentenced instead to 15 days confinement.

So I was separated from my brother, who later died in Panor. While I was under arrest, most of the Zhezhmir group moved to Kashindor, and I was left in Kovne with my father until October 1943. Then the ghetto was surrounded; we were all packed into heavy trucks guarded by SS men and militia. As soon as the trucks halted, our enemies attacked us like wild animals, throwing everybody out on the ground. Mothers and children were separated, as were men from women and older people.

After the segregations we were packed back into the trains, the windows closed with barbed wire. That evening the train started to move, with armed guards on top. At every station they broke into the cars to beat the victims and confiscate their valuables.

Enslaved Jews Build a Secret Military Rail Line

On the sixth day at dawn we arrived in a desolate location. We were ordered to get out, and we thought this would be our last stop. Several youngsters started to run away, but were shot down. Looking at the bodies, the SS commander shouted, "Whoever tries to help these will suffer the same fate".

In groups of four, each holding the other's hands, under heavy guard, we marched past a swampy area with no signs of life. After several hours we came to a flat field where several small barracks stood, surrounded by high barbed wire. This was our new 'home', the first concentration camp, "Ivore", in Estonia. We were assigned 40 men to a barrack. Later we learned that this area was called the Estonian Siberia by the oppressed and miserable populace.

We were brought here to build a secret military railroad to connect this area with imports from Finland. Next day we worked in the swamp knee–deep, to smooth the surface with sand and rocks, brought in from the adjacent train station. After a 12 hour day we returned to camp, and had to respond to repeated roll–calls. After all this labor, we collapsed in the barracks exhausted, lying on the ground crushed together. After several months, many starving prisoners had died of the common diseases, typhus and dysentery, There was no medical treatment. If an inmate became ill for a few days, an SS man would come and give him an injection, putting him to death immediately.

Suffering and Death in the Slave Camps of Estonia

In January 1944, when the Russians started their Leningrad offensive, the camp was evacuated to the Estonian town of Kivaili, which had two camps, 1 and 2. In Estonia there were 23 concentration camps with Jews from various European locations. In Kivaili the inmates worked in the forest or in factories producing fuel.

I will always remember the road from Ivore to Kivaili, which straggled along the Finnish inlet. It was winter in deep snow, and we could barely move our feet. Some fell and remained in the snow. The guards collected the living bodies and threw them into the sea.

In spring 1944, the Germans liquidated all the Estonian camps by murdering the incapacitated prisoners, and evacuating the able–bodied ones elsewhere. My father and I were sent to the remaining concentration camp, Klage, about 50 km. from the Estonian capital of Talinn. Klage was located at a major junction and train line, surrounded by a forest and a huge thicket, where the previous Russian inhabitants had erected several 4–5 story buildings. 1500 Jews were kept in one of these structures, surrounded by a double fence of barbed wire. Klage had been established several years before by the Germans, and practically all of the original inhabitants had died of starvation and hard labor.

The majority of the prisoners were from Vilna and Kovne. From Olshan were Rebetzin Daicha, her daughter Milye, my sister Bes–Shiva, her daughter Lahla, our father Mordechai, Shlomo Koslovski, his wife Hanye, Ester Ziskind, Nachmia Meltzer, and Chaim Yosef Leibman and his wife.

The main project, on which we worked from 6 AM to 6 PM, involved making cement, then pouring it into various forms. A group also worked in the forest. The labor was constant, any pause was punished by beating on bare backs. Executions were carried out at a special hillock, where the victim was laid down. On both sides the SS men held whips with multiple lead points. Laughing wildly, they indulged their animal instincts by drawing blood. The victim had to count the blows, and if he missed one, they started all over again. After 15–25 strokes, very rarely did anyone survive. Afterwards, a doctor checked to see if anyone was still alive. The dead corpses were cremated in a nearby oven.

Once a group of returning workers picked up a few potatoes from a field. They were observed by the guards, who opened fire, killing a third of them. The rest of the group had to carry their bodies back to the camp for cremation.

Shooting the Young and Capable Jews, who had to prepare the Firewood for their Cremation

On September 19, 1944, the labor force was assembled ready to go to work, but then everyone was called out, and we were surrounded by a heavy SS detachment. It was announced that because the war front is changing, the camp must be evacuated for security reasons, and we were going to Germany. A transport would fill the empty wagons with wood and then a selection of men would be taken to the port of Kunda, on the gulf of Finland.

The director chose 300 of the strong younger men, who were then driven out of the camp under a heavy guard. Each one carried a load of wood on his back. Our mood was improved, as we believed the director's words. But that didn't last long when we heard a volley of machine–gun fire. The wailing among those still in the camp was mingled with the screams of the victims. It became clear that we were destined to be massacred.

We later learned that the wood carried by the 300 victims was used to create a fire which consumed the 300 bodies, leaving no evidence behind. When the SS detachment returned, they grouped the remaining Jews in groups of 50, and executed them.

So that's what these bestial barbarians did all day, accompanied by continuous screaming of the victims, from afternoon to night on the main plaza. In one corner remained a group of 200 beaten and hopeless men including me and my father. One evening, the guards were distracted for the moment, and had gathered at the camp gate. One of our group, waiting to be killed, suddenly shouted, "A little life is still good" and he started running for the exit, and then the others also started running. There was great tumult and milling around near the gate. The Germans opened fire, and in the confusion, I was separated from my father, and was swept away in the crowd.

How I Was Saved

I had only been in the camp for a few months, and didn't know that the older inmates had constructed some bunkers on the roof. I ran up the steps with them, but saw that my father wasn't there. I stopped, wondered what to do, then went back to the doorway, which was almost totally blocked by the dead and wounded bodies. I searched for my father but could not find him.

In this moment of mass murder, I felt a sudden revival of urge to live. I went back up the stairs to the room on the second floor. It was empty, holding only two story high storerooms. I heard footsteps in the corridor getting closer, so I grabbed a wooden shoe and smashed the only illumination, a single electric bulb. From a nearby room, I heard some wild screams, coming from the camp hospital. Most of the patients there couldn't move from their beds, and were shot.

In the room where I was, there was an alcove covered with a white sheet, for the belongings of the prisoners and I hid there. A German opened the door and commanded anybody there to come out. Then he searched all the corners, found nothing, then went to the corridor and spied the white sheet. He came back and poked into the alcove, and miraculously didn't find me. He was convinced no one was there and he left.

I stayed hidden there as long as I could, while the vermin from the alcove almost ate me alive. Little by little I emerged trembling and held still next to a wall near the window. It was late at night, a deathly stillness reigned, only a few moans from the dying. I ventured out into the corridor, and saw the flames spreading in all directions, cremating the victims, doused with gasoline by the murderers. Bewildered I returned to the room. A light rain intruded on the stillness of the night. Then I heard a loud sound of an engine, which suddenly halted. I heard the order in German, "Everybody out, get in now!"

From all directions the SS men ran and in a few minutes the loaded truck moved out. At daybreak, I saw the litter in the street, of discarded army rucksacks and other equipment and I realized that the Germans had fled. Weary and drained by all these events, I fell asleep. After I awoke, through the window I watched masses of military units filling the whole scene, soldiers, local residents fleeing the front, making a rest stop at the camp. They eagerly snatched up all the left over supplies and equipment strewn all over. I returned to my hiding place behind the drape. A few soldiers inspected my room. Only one stuck his hand behind the drape and touched my face. I came out, stood there, wordless, and he was taken aback.

An unusually tall soldier stood before me with his machine gun ready. He was a youthful Estonian with fine features, perhaps a student, who had been drafted into the German army. He was startled, pale as the plastered wall and speechless. Then he put his gun on his hip and in broken German said, " If you have survived, I won't hurt you", and he left. I remained hidden, petrified, and couldn't imagine what would happen next.

I didn't have long to wait. Incredibly, he had told a friend that there was still a person alive in there. And soon I heard more steps in the corridor. I hid again, but in vain. Someone opened the door, pulled aside the drape, and started to speak to me in good Russian. He assured me that I shouldn't be frightened, he would not hurt me. He was a corporal of Russian extraction, who had settled in Estonia with his family when he was a child, after the Russian revolution. He questioned me about everything intently. After a period of chatting, he looked at his watch and said he had to go. He advised me to leave the area because everything was going to be demolished; I should hide in the woods for a few days for the imminent liberation. He gave me his address and asked that I send a greeting to his family because he must go and didn't know if he'd ever come home again.

He left, and I sneaked down the stairs to the doorway. I saw that the entire area was flooded with departing soldiers. I hid again in my shelter, because there was nobody else visible but soldiers, and it would obviously be very dangerous to go outside. I thought I would look for other survivors who may have been hiding in the attic.. I ventured out into the dark corridor, and it was evident that the Nazis had dragged many Russian prisoners there to shoot them, after they had killed off the Jews. It took me several hours to get up to the top floor. I stumbled and fell over the corpses and was too terrified to get up.

It was night before I was able to crawl up to the attic. There was no sound and I didn't call out. I thought that they had all been discovered and killed. I didn't know what to do, and remained paralyzed until dawn. With my last energy, I tore up a board from the floor of the attic, lost my footing, fell into a pile of rubble, and just lay there.

As if in a dream, I heard a voice. I got to my feet, and there I saw two Jews. They said they were too frightened to speak up lest they be captured. In the attic there were 80 men. We stayed there for 6 days, not knowing what to do. At night, using piles of straw, we descended to collect water and food from the provisions left behind by the Germans. On the afternoon of September 25 1944, we heard an airplane flying low and could see Soviet markings. The next day we came down from the attic, to view the scene of indescribable destruction.

Germans Burn The Barrack With Wounded And Dead

About 0.5 km from camp, a special crematorium was created, with a chimney in the middle. Here were stretched out layers of wood alternating with bodies, about 3 meters high. Partially burned bodies were on the periphery, totally consumed bodies in the middle, because during the night some rain had fallen, extinguishing the fire. The whole area was covered with the corpses of those gunned down by the Germans. Among them was the body of Shlomo Kozlovski from Olshan.

The Germans had also killed an additional several hundred in a barrack, leaving no trace. We were told about this by the only survivor, a 21 year old from Oshman, Isaac Oshervitz, now in Israel. He had escaped by crawling over the bodies of the victims, many still alive, to get to the roof. He was seen and was fired on. He fell but was not wounded, and remained fully conscious, observing the Germans pouring gasoline through all the windows. As the fire was ignited he managed to jump out of a window to a nearby tree, where he stayed for a whole day. Then he wandered around for several days until he met us after the liberation by the Red Army. After the liberation, everyone tried to get back to his home town as soon as possible.

Rivke Davidson-Segalovitz

Women In The Ghettos And Camps, Oshman, Vilna, Kovne

At dawn on the second day after the Germans occupied Olshan, my brother-in-law David Segalovitz, wearing his tallis and tefillin, ran to my house. He had been driven out of his home by a mob of Germans, who then stripped his house bare, leaving everything on the street to be divided among the goyim who had been waiting nearby. David and his children, Reuben and Samuel, stayed with us for a while, until we were all driven out into the ghetto. Conditions became very difficult. We were forbidden to leave the ghetto. Often the Germans would come in the middle of the night, assemble the Jews, and confiscate their belongings while beating them.

The younger Jews were taken to Zhezhmir camp. Included were my husband Bruch-Shmuel and Reuben. After that, life became even more difficult for the older folks. Until the liquidation, we were driven daily to various hard labors, especially to fell trees in the forest.

After the liquidation, we were transferred to the Oshman ghetto, which was severely overcrowded. On the second day, at dawn, we were all driven out into the plaza, where the Vilna ghetto police separated us into two groups. One group, destined to be killed, was herded into empty houses. On the same day they transported the victims to Zhelanke, where they had prepared huge ditches. After severe beatings, they were all shot down, forming a mass-grave of 400 Jews. Those allowed to live, including me, remained in the Oshman ghetto for the next six months, in pain and misery. After the Oshman camp was liquidated, we were given a choice between Vilna or Kovne. I chose Vilna because my husband was already there.

From Forced Labor To Death

In the Vilna ghetto, everyone was forced to work. I worked in a garden near a hospital, along with about 30 men and women. Shabotai Abramovitz and his wife Gitl were among them. Later we were sent to Farubanek, where there were many women. We were kept busy digging and filling ditches, as if there was no other work for us. One morning we were sent out on a different road. We reached an open space surrounded by a high fence of barbed wire. A few tried to climb over the fence because they felt they had nothing to lose, there was no chance of getting out alive. The SS men immediately tracked them down with dogs and shot them. This bloody scene in early 1943 will be inscribed in my memory forever.

I can't remember how I got out of that alive. My only memory is that while fleeing I met a girl named Livke. We ran until we came to a village several km. from Vilna. We entered a house, but ran away again when we heard shooting. We saw some woods in the distance and thought we might hide there until night. Then we saw that the trees were standing in a deep gully full of water. We decided we had to lay down there, because standing up would have made us visible. We stayed there until evening, when the shooting seemed to abate.

Before we could think of our next move, we heard the blood hounds howling and we were dragged out by the SS men, who forced us to run after them on their motorbikes. It was night when we got to the station. All the Jewish captives were stuffed into sealed freight cars, in groups of 100-120. It was so packed we couldn't move. For three days and nights we had no water or food, and many died of hunger and thirst.

After these three horrendous days the door was finally opened and a little dirty water was given, which was accessible only to those near the door because of the crowded mass and the dead bodies. The door was quickly closed and sealed, and the train finally reached Riga.

Meeting My Husband in a Camp in Estonia

The train was in Riga for the day, but all the camps were too full, so it was sent on to Estonia. We were herded on foot from the train to Eivora, where I found my husband Bruch–Shmuel, and other Olshaners, Leibe Gilyes, Hinde Korbanovitz, Bas–Sheva (Benjamin's wife), Mordechai Natas and Shmuel Trobski. My husband approached me, and was beaten as punishment. We were together for several months, along with my nephew Leibe. We even worked in the same forest, but then my husband and nephew were sent to Echeda camp, also in Estonia. Leibe was killed there when he developed a foot ailment. A little later, my husband became ill and was murdered.

The Germans brought the Jews to Aveda from all the nearby camps, in order to murder thousands of them. Then one morning 100 women were assembled, including me. We were kept outside all day in the bitter frost. then we were taken to another camp, Kiveili #1, and things were a little better there. We were given food and cots to sleep on. Shortly after, 400 men were brought in from the liquidated Vilna ghetto. Among them: my nephew Hershel**Error! Bookmark not defined.** Golias. His four children were sent to the left, i.e. to death.

I was in Kaveili camp for several months, where things were a little better. But then, with several hundred other women we were sent to Stuthof, which was really hellish. We were crowded into barracks where the doors and windows were kept open despite the freezing cold and our half–naked state. It all seemed quite hopeless. We weren't allowed to speak one word. If the guard heard anyone speak, he would immediately pour cold water on her head. As we were packed together the water would immediately freeze our skins together and it was almost impossible to tear the skins apart. People died like flies. I was in this bitterly inhumane place for three weeks. In another selection of 300 healthy young women I was sent to Camp Rusalek, to experience new misery and pain.

[Page 254]

Tortured Women in the Estonian Camp
by Rivka Davidson–Segalovitz

Every day at 3 AM we were forced to walk 3 km. to a trolley line, which carried us to Danzig. There we labored to build a train track, rails and cross-ties. We unloaded stones and did other heavy labor. And that's how these exhausted women built a railway. It was a bitterly cold winter. The trail to the labor site was slippery and we wore heavy wooden shoes. Here too we were tormented by the deliberate poor fitting of the shoes. Small feet got large shoes, and large feet got the smaller ones. And above all we were hungry and almost naked. To survive such a day, meant to return with bloody feet. We didn't even have a piece of rag to bind our wounds. Every month , the weaker ones were sent off to Stuthof for execution, and replaced by younger healthier women.

Only a few of the original 300 survived these terrible conditions. The tiniest infractions were punished by death. Even a piece of string could be a fatal problem. Near our work place there a few towns. When we had a half–hour rest period, we'd sneak into a home to seek a little bread a potato, or a noodle. Anyone caught going into town paid with her life. First she would be obliged to kneel all night in the frost outside, and then be sent to Stuthof for execution.

Once I was on the verge of such an outcome. We were working close to a house owned by one of the rail officials, and some of the girls would sneak in to get some food, when they found that the lady of the house was generous. So I decided to test my luck to try to get some yarn to repair my cloak, which wouldn't stay on me at work because it had only one button. Instead of yarn, one of the children brought me a torn old jacket. My joy was short–lived. When I returned to the barrack, the supervisor ordered everyone to exit, one by one, for inspection. I was taken aside and interrogated as if I had committed a major crime, punishable by being shot. A transport was scheduled for morning to Shtuthof, and I was to be sent. But I was saved by a Kovne lady, Sarah.

Sarah had a special assignment; she brewed coffee for the supervisor. She had three daughters, pretty girls, who worked as 'blitz–girls', i.e. prostitutes for the SS men in their quarters. Thanks to Sarah that I am alive today. The supervisor decided not to report me to the camp director. All the others caught that day were sent off to Shtuthof. For my crime I was to be punished by a public lashing. Again Sarah had my sentence reduced to five lashes.

Bestial Assassinations of Jewish Inmates Just Before the German Collapse

When we finished our work on the train track, we had no more assigned work. The Germans were preoccupied and realized that their end was near. They gathered all the young healthy women, including me, and crowded us into a large beautiful house, abandoned by the German officers. We stayed there a few weeks and then were moved to an open field for a few days without food or water. For the next week we were driven on foot through fields and forests. It was mid–winter and freezing cold as we trudged through deep snow in our wooden shoes, which clung to the snow. If anyone stopped to get the snow off the shoes, she was shot on the spot. Likewise, if one tried to take a bit of snow for drinking water. The road was strewn with dead bodies of those perishing from hunger or being shot.

The last night before liberation, we were driven into a large dark barn, where we stumbled around over irregular piles. Only at dawn could we see the horrible sight of the corpses piled up behind the locked gate. Six weeks before, 1200 women had been brought here, stricken with dysentery, typhus and starvation, and only 50 had survived.

We wanted to get out of this barn, and saw that there were no guards. They had all fled, leaving the barn locked. We pried up a few boards, and a few of us were able to get out. We saw some houses in a little town. A few of us checked them, and soon came running back, joyously carrying bread for all given them by the Russian soldiers. The barn was unlocked. We all celebrated our recovery from death into a future life. The Russians carried out any remaining women, then, after burying the corpses, burned down the barn.

After four years of inhuman awful slave labor, suffering in the ghettos and concentration camps, we had seen the end of the Hitler era, and we were free.

[Page 262]

From Camp to Camp
by Henye Tchepelinski

The Tchepelinski family [listed] was separated at first, then re–united in the Zhezhmir ghetto. My father died before the war. Prior to the liquidation of the Oshman ghetto, my brother Velvel ran off and hid among the peasants. The rest of us, including my husband Pesakh, my mother, me and my child, were sent to the Kovne ghetto. We were assembled, beaten, and my husband and I were herded into a sealed truck, while my mother and child were sent off, never to be seen again. Along with the corpses of those who died on the way we arrived in the port of Kunda, Estonia. Men and women were sent to separate camps, to start our wretched paths.

The victims from various ghettos were set to work in a factory with a special project. The camp supervisor, Adolph Klee, tormented us, especially the men, by waking us in the middle of the night, to assemble in the yard stark naked, to sing until roll–call at dawn.

One day, the SS came, divided the group, right to left, determining who would die. The camp had to be liquidated and we all tried frantically to be allowed to live. The camp was chained shut, and no one was allowed to go to work. However, my partner Lipke and I, as washerwomen, were let out by the guards, and we fled. We didn't know where to go, the woods and the surrounding area were foreign to us. It was harvest time and we hid in a corn field.

At night the guards were looking for us, we could hear them shooting. We arose at dawn, took off our tags and sought some food. We knew a little Estonian, and I was acquainted with a peasant who had agreed to hide us. When we arrived at his house, we were met by the SS camp commander and the guards, who had been alerted and our lives were in their hands. They did not shoot us. In fact, as we learned later, we were actually caught by chance. The camp was to be liquidated, but the young SS man had a fiancée and had gone with her to be married, and had encountered us unexpectedly. Our hands were bound and we were led through the streets of the capital, Talinn, back to the camp. The camp director just wanted to know where his laundresses had gone, and we told him we were seeking food. That night, at roll–call, he had to decide on our punishment. He decided that our heads would be shaved, like the men.

So we were transported along with thousands of women in a ship to Stuthof. Among the men on the ship, my husband Pesach Rabinovitz died en route. In Shtuthof were many Olshaners. We were herded into a house and stripped of all our belongings, left naked as newborns and given prison uniforms. My number was 69858.

Our brigade consisted of 11 women ; we stole beets and potatoes from the field to survive. Our straw was infested with lice. I became friends with a woman from Olshan, Rivel Segalovitz. A few nights before liberation she supported me when I thought I would die of starvation, and in fact we were soon freed in Danzig in 1945.

[Page 265]

The Vilna Camp in the Cheap Houses
by R. Abramovitz–Shkop

The last step in the fate of several hundred Vilna Jews was the HKF camp [Heeres Energy Co], which employed the ghetto Jews in refurbishing used cars and other transport vehicles. Just before liquidating the Vilna ghetto, in September 1943, the HKF negotiated with the Gestapo, to move the Jews and their families into a separate camp, designated as the "Cheap Houses", on Suvotch Street. Mayer Flage, the supervisor of HKF told us that we would work only for the HKF, which belonged to the Gestapo. Our boss would be Ernest Weis–Alen, a cold–blooded murderer.

Internally, the camp was directed by a Jew, Kolish and his brother–in–law Lalke Gurevitz, as well as Jewish police. We were not under guard, but there was a high fence reinforced by several rows of barbed wire. But this was inadequate for the SS, who utilized several Jewish spies. One of these traitors, Niki Drazin, transmitted to the Gestapo daily reports of all the activities in the camp. I can still see before me his ugly figure in a long brown leather coat. However his fate was the same as all the others who were betrayed by him.

About half the men, including my husband Lave Shkop, were taken to another camp, Pantzerke. The rest of us worked at various tasks–upholstery, locks, electrical devices, cabinetry, etc. The women worked in the 'tailor room', repairing uniforms, direct from the front. Three or four families lived in a small room. While I worked at the uniform repair, my friend Esther Woloch took care of my two year old son.

To inform us about the consequences of disobedience, we were called out the first week after arrival and assembled, to witness in public the hanging of a man and woman, who had been hiding outside the camp. Their 10 year old daughter was made to witness this horrid spectacle.

Ernest Weis the murderer used to visit often. After every visit he selected 20–30 persons to send to Panor to satisfy his thirst for Jewish blood. We knew that our days would last only as long as we were useful. In early 1944, Pantzerke was liquidated and the men were brought back to camp. The end was approaching faster than we expected. At dawn March 27, 1944, the Gestapo surrounded the camp, and tore away from us our dear innocent children, including my 2 1/2 year old son Baruchl, who was named after my dearly loved uncle Baruch Abramovitz, the first victim of the Germans in Olshan.

While we awaited further events, we started to build hide–outs. We discussed weapons, tunnels under the camp, but the possibilities were slim and the time was short. In June 1944, when the Russians re–took Minsk, we were surrounded one morning by the SS, armed with machine guns, and it seemed that this would be the end. Everyone panicked, and people ran everywhere like frightened mice, trying to find a rumored secret exit, to no avail. My husband's friend, a policeman from Oshman, had promised to help save us but he backed out at the last moment at midnight. But Lova didn't give up. I still don't know how we did it, but by 1:30 AM we sneaked through the SS guards and got into the workshop. And there we found the secret exit, a small window with sagging bent bars, four meters high leading outside the camp into a potato field. There were only a few escapees, but others followed at dawn. The Gestapo discovered the window and chased the fugitives, firing their machine guns.

We ran and managed to hide in the cellar of a burnt house. Those who were caught were shot immediately, others were sent to Panor, and many are buried in the 'Cheap Houses'. The few who had enough patience and some food for a few days remained free. And that was the fate of the Vilna Jews in the HKF camp, including Malke, his son and wife and several Ashman families.

Lova, his friend and I left Vilna and wandered in the woods and trails in constant fear of the Germans, or the 'White' or 'Black' partisans, with no food, swollen and lacerated feet. In 12 days we finally reached Olshan, No one had recognized us; we feared our own shadows. For a week we hid among the peasants in Slobodi, as Poles. The peasants had known me since childhood, but didn't recognize me now. When the Russians re–captured the area, we stayed in Olshan. The first Jew we met was Velvel Tchepelinski.

Now we live in America and have two children. In our hearts remain sadness and open wounds. Lova's parents and brothers–killed with the men of Oshman; my father–murdered in Estonia; my mother in Panor, others in Volozhin and Shemberg. My Baruch would have been 19.

[Page 268]

My Survival in the Years
of the German Final Solution
by Abrohom Potashnik

After the Germans had secured Olshan, the war spread to Russia. The Jews gave up hope for any assistance. The Poles of Olshan were jubilant. The Germans directed all Jews must wear a yellow star on their sleeves. The Polish and White Russian police were given a free hand to do whatever they wanted to do with the Jews. Every night they would ransack the Jewish homes, beating the Jews and forcing them to do hard labor in the fields, forests and streets. In December 1941, things got even worse. The police and Gestapo had seized all the furs from the Jews, and then in March 1942, they confiscated all the cows from the ghetto. Even the poorest of Jews had some tiny fur to shelter against the cold, and the loss of the cows meant no milk for the babies.

In preparation for the liquidation of the Olshan ghetto, the Germans directed the Judenrat to select 200 work–capable men and women, to be stationed at the gate; they could bring their food. They were lined up in rows and taken by train to Zhezhmir. The ghetto was gradually emptied, the Olshan Jews were driven to Oshman, as were those from Kreve, Smorgen and other *shtetlach.* Most of these were shot, including my mother Chane Sarah**Error! Bookmark not defined.** Potashnik.

Germans Allow Family Re–Unions, Masking their Extermination Plans

In order to minimize contacts with the partisans, who were increasing in number near Vilna and White Russia, the Germans authorized family camps, to unify families, and allowed them to bring their 'soft' goods and food. So the Jews of Sol, Smorgen, Oshman, Michaleshak Svir and Olshan– the last remaining old Jewish communities–were packed up into freight cars in April 1943 and brought to Zhezhmir and Vevye.

Some of the Jews from the smaller communities had volunteered to join the Kovne ghetto to unite with their families. In 1943, a train from Vilna with 4000 Jews was halted in a forest near Panor Camp. There a band of Latvian police units opened fire with machine guns, and only a few Jews escaped alive. Several women made it to Kovne, and related the details of this massacre.

Another transport of Jews, assembled from various camps directed by the Kovne Judenrat, eventually was taken to Kashindor Camp. Some of these, assigned to work in the forest, joined up with the partisans and didn't return to camp. To prevent further escapes, the Gestapo doubled the guard, and threatened execution. The prisoners were assembled, beaten and taken on the train to Aleksat, which was the designated camp for Soviet prisoners. They were assigned to work at the airport, digging ditches, hauling earth, and carrying loads of cement. This camp was 30 km. from Kovne. Then in May 1943 we were taken to Koslov, where there were about 400 Jews from Vilna, Smorgen, Oshman.

When the Red Army neared Vilna in June 1944, we were directed towards Kovne and told that we must drop to the ground prone if any partisans appeared, or else we'd be shot. We lined up in groups of five, holding small packs. Guarded by soldiers armed with machine guns and hand guns we were marched toward Kovne. After about 10 km, at the approach of dusk, 140 men and women ran off into the woods. The rest of us were brought to the Kovne ghetto, to join the ranks of Jews already there.

From the ghetto we could hear the bomb explosions, used by the Gestapo to destroy the bunkers used by fugitive Jews. Wednesday, July 12, 1944, at dawn more than 2000 of us were ordered to line up in groups of 100, guarded closely by Gestapo armed with automatic rifles, and marched through side streets of the town to the train station at Aleksat.

Accompanied by dark clouds, thunder and heavy rain, many Jews tried to escape, but the Gestapo men opened fire and many Jews were shot. Only a few got away. By the heavily guarded ramps stood 40 freight cars with barred windows. The Jews from the work camps around Kovne were also brought in, so over 3000 Jews were jammed into the cars like herring in a barrel. The train didn't stop at any station on the way to Germany. At Tugenhof, near Danzig, the train finally stopped and unloaded the women and the children.

Suffering in the Kaufering Camps

The men were sent to camps near Landsberg am Lech. In the summer of 1944, the 11 camps there were named Kaufering, because that was the closest train station. These camps lasted barely 9 months. Here the Jews built underground factories, while additional transports brought in thousands of additional hungry thirsty Jews, including me and my brother Yeshua. He died in early January 1945.

The camps were surrounded by barbed wire and guard posts stood at all 4 corners, with heavily armed SS men, ready with machine guns and grenades. The barracks were flimsy, painted green, and housed Jews from Vilna, Oshman, Smorgen, and Krever. Olshaners included Sholom Kaplan, Ephrim Afrimovitz, Bruch-Hirsch Gurvich, Asher Gurvich, Yikosel Koslovski, Yeshihu

Leibman and his nephew Israel, Shmuen Gurvich from Kreve. In camp 5 were Boris Potashnik, Mordechai Segalovich.

The SS guards were experienced in tormenting us. They were all murderers and sadists, who patrolled the camp with heavy clubs, beating and slaughtering without pity. All of our belongings had been taken away, and we were clothed in the usual striped concentration camp garb, with a pair of wooden shoes. There were 20 men in each barrack, and we slept on the hard ground. In September, with onset of heavy rains, the barracks were flooded, then in December winter brought high winds, snow and frost. We were allowed to install shacks from plain boards, which sheltered 40 men at a time.

Shivering from the cold and our skimpy clothing, we fashioned undershirts from the cement bags. Once the Germans caught five boys who had wrapped these bags under their clothes. For this crime, the Germans made a public spectacle and the boys were hung. In January, we were issued torn and dirty jackets, specially labeled to identify us as imprisoned slaves.

We were awakened at dawn by a shrill whistle, and had a half hour to get dressed, wash up in cold water without soap. At 5:30 a second whistle summoned us for roll–call. Anyone who was late was severely beaten. The path to our work site took another half hour. The snow clung to our wooden shoes. We were exhausted by the time we got to the site, while being beaten by the German supervisors, who had been selected for their brutality. Many Jews were injured at work and many perished there.

After work, we returned 'home' to the camp, drained, with swollen injured feet. Especially in the last few months we were starved on a diet of 120 grams of bread daily, a pat of margarine, and potato or cabbage soup. The tortured slaves often died suddenly, either at work or at night, unable to arise, from freezing or from beatings, which seemed to get worse as liberation approached. The inmates died like flies from starvation and weakness. It should be noted that the Germans intensified their brutality in the camps and in flight even as the end of the war was near.

On April 23, 1945, the order was given to move the Jews on to Tirol, the start of the infamous Death March. Many hundreds fell on the way and on April 30, the SS guards fled. On that day we were in Alloch, near Munich, liberated by the American army.

[Page 273]

The Mass Burial Ground of Zhelianke
by Aaron Shuster

In Zhelianke, near Oshman, was the common mass burial site for Jews of Olshan, Oshman, Kreve, Smorgen and others, tortured to death by the Germans in 1943. The victims were assembled in Oshman. After a precise tabulation, the Germans selected those to be killed, and they were brought to Zhelianke and then to the execution site. Guarded by Vilna ghetto police, they were locked up for the night, then shot down in the morning at the edge of the woods.

After the war, Jewish survivors returned to this place where their nearest and dearest had been murdered. The horror of this site was indescribable, a huge ditch between the woods and the adjacent field, on which peasants' cows now grazed. The grave site was distinguished by the dark–green grass, beneath which now rested the bleached bones and shoes of the victims.

As far as possible, the remains were gathered together in one place. Local peasants showed us another solitary grave of a woman who had been shot there. She had escaped from the barn and had wandered around for a few days before being shot down by the Germans after the mass execution. We dug up this woman's grave and we recognized the garment wrapped around her. We identified her as Malche Katz from Olshan, Simon Katz's wife. Our group established a memorial site with grave stone inscribed "In Memory of the Murdered Jews". Every year we held a memorial service, and the relatives would say Kaddish. We left an annual payment for a local peasant to take care of this site.

To our great sorrow, in the year that we left, 1957, the memorial site was damaged by shepherds and their cows. I am sure that the remaining Jews of Ashman continue to hold an annual memorial service on this mass grave of Zhelianke.

Olshaners and Krevers mourning death of a brother at his grave in Zhelianka

Page 276]

The Shemberger Mass Grave
by Ziml Abramovitz

A Remembrance of My Two Brothers Isaac and Gershon Abramovitz

Isaac Abramovitz z"l

Gershon Abramovitz z"l

On the 19th memorial reunion in New York, the famous Holocaust researcher Mordechai Bernstein, gave a dramatic presentation about how he discovered a previously unknown cemetery containing 1755 unidentified bodies. This had been part of the Dachau camp complex, where so many lives were destroyed from October 1944 until April 1945, shortly before Hitler's downfall. Among them were 347 from Vilna, and 50 from the other *shetlech* in that region, Oshman, Olshan, Podbrodz, Smorgen, Svir, Sventzion, Trok, Voloshin, Kreve, Lide, Ivie, etc.

Every name was recorded with birthdate, nationality, and origin, and date of burial. As Mordechai Bernstein related: "I was there at the cemetery, a huge stone , and on the pedestal I read the inscription in French: "In Memory of the 1755 Victims of Nazi Barbarism, Who Lie Here" , signed by the French authority. Behind this stone stood a forest of stones, each with a number from 1 to 1755. There, theoretically, lie the bodies of these tortured victims, but in fact they cannot be individually identified."

In these slave camps, only men were brought, who could still be exploited for labor, but they died like flies from the unbearable punishment. Their bodies were carried out to a field behind the town and discarded, sometimes covered with a little sand, and so developed a huge pile of bones. When the French army took the town, they found these piles of bones and knew their origin. They ordered the local SS and other camp guards to bury the remains.

When the French found these remains, they issued an order that 1755 graves should be created, each one containing a symbol such as a bone or skeleton, and that a stone should be erected for each, numbered as noted.

Leafing through the records I was shattered to recognize a number of familiar names, of well–known Jewish families from Jerusalem–Dlita and their suburbs: Chvolles, Pupke, Kovarski, Klotchka, Kinkulkin, Stolper, Shulkins.

Standing there at the Shemberger "Bone Monument", in front of the stones atop the countless Jewish bones, an unheard voice rose from these thousands of mounds:

"Remember us! Know Who Lies in This Place. The Voices of Our Bones Must Be Heard!"

Among the records kept so punctiliously by the heartless German assassins I found my brothers Isaac and Gershon, and also Motel Koslovski from Olshan.

Memorial stone in the Shemberger cemetery for the 1755 victims

Isaac was killed on November 27, 1944, at age 21. Before the war, he had been a student at Epstein's Vilna gymnasium, excelling at mathematics. The Nazis sent him to various concentration camps and ghettos and finally to

Shemberg. Gershon, tall, handsome and athletic joined his father's flax business and managed the facility in Vilna. During the Soviet period, he was the chief flax broker, and expected a successful future. Along with Isaac, he suffered through various camps, ending in Shemberg on April 5, 1945, just three days before liberation by the French.

Shemberg is just part of the horrors inflicted by the German murderers and their accomplices. My mother Gutl rests in the giant mass graves at Vilna, and in 1943 my father Shepsel Abramovitz ended in the huge death camps of Estonia. In the mass graves of the Olshan Jews in 1942 in Zhelianke and Volozhin, were buried my aunts, uncles, cousins, the whole Voronovski family, Malke Katz, and others. In the Kinder–Aktion in the Vilna ghetto in 1944, my sister's 3 1/2 year old boy perished, named for my uncle Bruch Abramovitz, who had been the first victim in Olshan, deliberately killed in the first days of the fascist attack on the Soviet Union. No trace of his family remains.

In my heart, I feel open wounds, which will last until my last breath, the memory of the suffering of my nearest and dearest ones. I hope my words, inscribed with great pain, will reach all those remaining in my family. I'll never forget them and will always bear their memory in my heart.

All the fascist murderers and their allies should be cursed for all eternity.

[Page 283]

Confusion and Resistance

The Heroic Death of Shmuel Tchepelunski's Partisan Group
by Michal Koslovski-Gurevitz

Shmuel Tchepelunski

Shmuel Tchepelunski was born in Olshan in 1915. His parents, Rivka and Haichl prospered with their restaurant business, had a nice home, and imbued Shmuel with their national Jewish spirit. In the town they were well-known and respected. After finishing public school, the tall broad shouldered Shmuel joined the *Hashomer Hatzeir* and was active with the eventual goal of going to Israel. The Holocaust destroyed his hopes..

In 1942, Shmuel along with 200 Olshan youths was sent to Zhezhmir for slave labor, and then to Kashidor. These youths continually thought about escaping to join the partisan fighters in the woods. Despite severe restrictions and great dangers, escape was not too difficult, but connecting to the partisans was much harder. In 1941–42 such attempts failed due to starvation and freezing weather, and also because of attacks from White Russian and Polish gangs on the trails, the towns and the forests. Besides, no one wanted to endanger the lives of their families, who would be identified and then shot by the Germans.

After the German children murders in Kashidor, it became clear that the Germans intended to kill everyone. Shmuel and his friends planned to escape to the partisans. He was one of the forest workers who had made contact with a partisan unit, the *Svovodnaya Litva*, in the Rudnitzki forest. In early 1944, Shmuel and his group disarmed their German guards and fled into the forest. They knew what would happen to those left behind in the camp. They met the partisans and made a plan to save the 300 Jews left in Kashidor.

After a 50 km. flight through fields and woods five days later, Shmuel along with Sholem Milikovski from Kreve, Avrashke Landsman from Sumilishki and two Christians attracted by his leadership, met up with some partisan contacts who lived on the edge of the forest near Kashidor. The Latvian contact however turned out to be a German agent and a traitor. He didn't tell them that the camp had already been liquidated, and advised them to proceed to Kashidor to rescue the Jews. He informed the Germans, who arrived heavily armed and despite a heroic defense, the five were killed. In a few days, the partisans burned the farm of the Latvian traitor who had escaped earlier with his family.

[Page 285]

In Battle Against the Germans
by Ziml Abramovitz

In June 1941, when the Germans entered Olshan, I was in Kiev, Russia, where I was studying bookkeeping. My only thought was to go home, but when I got to Vitebsk, all the roads were closed. I encountered a stream of refugees from the Vilna region, who had decided to flee their homes. With them I was evacuated deep into Russia, to Bashkirye, in a Kolchoz.

After a few months, men were being called to mobilization points. Despite the huge losses of the Russian army at that time, the remnants of the Polish army were not taken, but were sent to work battalions. I was 17 and I wanted to fight against the Germans. I thought that when I had trained to be a soldier on the battlefront, I would ask to be sent off to join the partisans in our area. In order to be accepted into the Red Army, I tore up my passport and at the mobilization point I said I was born in Olshan, in the Minsk area. So I was deemed 'kosher', and was accepted into the army. After three months of training I was qualified to be an instructor for sharp–shooting.

With the Soviet Liberation Army

In the summer of 1944, shortly after the liberation of the Olshan area, I got the first letter from my home, from my sister Rive, the only remaining survivor in my family. In her letter she described the horror and devastation which had occurred to us all. At that time I was just finishing officer school to which I had been sent because of my distinguished record in the war against the Germans. I took part in the battles in the Ukraine. I was in the first Ukrainian front, the 92nd infantry division. I helped to liberate Poland, and when our forward march had paused near the Veisel, I was sent by staff from the front on other important dangerous missions.

On Jan 18, 1945, our division participated in the liberation of Tshenstachov and a large labor camp, where most of the inmates were Polish Jews. They had been working in a munitions factory. On leave, I visited the Jewish camp survivors. I found them in the houses which had previously been occupied by SS officers. The houses had not been touched; the SS were concerned only with saving their skin. I saw young and middle–aged women, skinny, prematurely aged, who couldn't get accustomed to their freedom, their relief from the constant threat of destruction. They also couldn't believe that a Jew, an officer, a Pole could be their liberator. For one whole night they told me about their terrible experiences and suffering.

In a few days, after taking Krakow, our division was distinguished as the 'Krakow Division'. The main highway to Breslav [today Vuratzlov], was strewn with dead Germans. I recall an episode: After an artillery assault, we took a town near Breslau, from which the Germans had fled. My unit was directed to search the houses. My group, with six soldiers, entered a beautiful undamaged house. When we entered a bedroom we found an elderly woman in bed wearing a wig on her head. After considering this 'invalid', we tore off her outer garments, revealing an SS officer, and then we found another one hiding.

They took off their disguises, and begged for mercy. They were innocent, just soldiers. But when I told them that I was a Jew, they quickly fell silent, expecting the worst. The two German murderers were degraded and frightened, their heads bowed, trembling in front of a Jewish boy from Olshan. My immediate impulse was to put an end to these criminals, but I had to obey my strict orders to bring them back to the base.

As we got further into Germany, the fighting became more difficult and bitter, and we suffered heavy losses. Bur our determination to destroy the fascist monsters persevered and we defeated them. On the Czech–German border town of Vakenov, I was severely wounded. That was the month of the German capitulation.

[copies of the Russian declaration and medal 'For the victory over Germany in the Great Fatherland War 1941–45'.]

I went through several army hospitals in Germany, Poland, and then back to Russia, where I was discharged as a war invalid. I was selected for the order of 'Fatherland War', with medal, and came home to Olshan at end of 1945. The only survivor from my large family was my sister Riva, who is now in America. The rest of my family was killed by the Germans.

[Page 289]

Kashidor Camp and the Escape Into The Forest
by Sima Soladucha–Rudnick

There were many Olshaners in the Kashidor camp, including my brother Yossl, now in Israel, and my sister Zelda, who later suffered a miserable death. In Kashidor, there were many youths as well as mothers with their children. Life there was a little easier, there was more food. There was still some hope for the future. There were quiet moments when young couples got together, unable to contain their youthful emotions. But this didn't last long. On a clear morning, we were assembled and the camp was surrounded. We were panic-stricken, we ran back and forth, confused. Later we found that the little children had been taken away.

The Germans grabbed these innocent souls away from their mothers' hands, crowded them into wagons and drove off. My mother climbed up to be with her children, and my father was sent to a slave labor camp where he perished. Then we had to go to our labor, loading and unloading wagons, felling trees. Even the women were used to cut the branches and do other tasks, which normally were done only by men.

We had heard a lot about the partisans, fighting in the woods. We all dreamed of joining these fighters, but this seemed impossible. Finally a few workers broke away to unite with them, assisted by a Latvian woodsman. We agreed on a place, day and time to meet. In April 1944, at the pre–arranged time at noon when the guards were having lunch, we silently stole away in the forest, hoping to meet up with the partisans.

Sadly, the agreement had been delayed except for those who had originally planned the meeting. We wandered around in the woods for a few hours, but the guards had been alerted. They forced their captives to return to the camp. But I had split off, following a Kovne woman, who was determined not to return. She also heard that her husband had a gun and was waiting for an opportunity. At that moment, I forgot about my brother and sister, who had been forced to return to the camp and would face certain death. Along with a few others like me, 20 of us got together at night. One of us, Isaac Ziskind, fortunately knew the forest warden, an agent of the partisans. Every day he brought us some food, and also some old coats for shelter, since we had dropped everything during our flight. I'll never forget how free I felt, getting up from our shelters on the ground. We'd wash our faces in the dew on the leaves, and even swallow some drops since we didn't have any water.

After two terrible weeks, we found our meeting place, then wandered two more days from town to town, in great danger of being reported by the peasants, and finally found the partisans. The partisans were divided into sections, each with a commander who made assignments. We were assigned to do domestic work, cooking and washing clothes for the men. Every day they went out on their missions, such as laying mines, destroying wagons, burning German–occupied towns, tearing down electric junctions, and other such important tasks, often very dangerous.

We were threatened by airplanes firing into the woods; at night we often had to retreat into the swamps. I was with the partisans for four months. On July 8, 1944, the First Latvian brigade, to which we belonged, was ordered by their top command in Moscow, to march on Vilna. On the way we met up with the Red Army, which had cut off Vilna, on the way to Kovne. All the partisan brigades took part in the Rudnitzker attack.

The partisans took over the administration in Vilna. Many of them had volunteered to join the Red Army, others served as the civilian police, to clean up any remnants of the Nazi presence. Along with two other girls from Olshan, we returned. No one was left of my family, but luckily a brother, Yosef Soladucha survived, now living in Israel.

„ЗА ПОБЕДУ НАД ГЕРМАНИЕЙ
В ВЕЛИКОЙ ОТЕЧЕСТВЕННОЙ ВОЙНЕ
1941—1945 гг.“

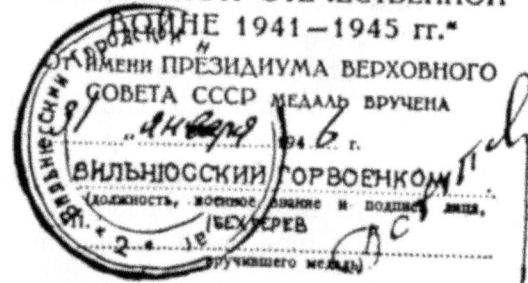

Footnote- also known as part of the 'Kroyova' Army, the Polish underground army after the German occupation of Poland

[Page 292]

Armed Partisan Battle
German Attack on Soviet Union and Escape from Olshan
by Reuben Liand [Roman Liandov]

On June 24, 1941 when the Germans were approaching Olshan, I was 19. I knew what to expect, and decided to flee. Along with three others, Sarin, Fodiev and Meltzer, we left at noon on bikes, on the way to Minsk. The road was clogged with Russian soldiers, who were fleeing in disorder. When we got to the train station in Bogdanov, 12 km. from Olshan, German airplanes bombed the station and we had to keep going. On the road to Volozhin, we passed the bodies of civilians and soldiers, wounded or dead from the airplane bombings. We were also forced to hide a few times to evade them. We were held up briefly at a Soviet control point, mistaken as spies.

We reached Volozhin by night and were told that the Soviet civilian authority had fled. We sought out a former Olshaner, Elia the Watchmaker, now living in Volozhin, and spent the night there. Before dawn, we left on the road to Rokov. There we met many Jewish families on wagons and on foot. In the woods near Rokov, German airplanes strafed the woods constantly and we had to remain hidden. After 3–4 hours we finally got to Rokov, where there were many Jewish fugitives. The sandy road to Minsk was also clogged with weeping refugees carrying packs and little children, and we could hear gunfire in the distance.

At the Former Polish–Russian Border

Thousands of people were crowded at the border. Posted on boards fastened to trees were warnings inscribed in large letters in Russian: "Unauthorized entry over the border is prohibited under penalty of death". We pressed forward to reach the Soviet guards, who told us that the border was closed to civilians, and that we should return; at night, anyone found near the border would be shot.

People hurried back towards Rokov, and we joined them, after we found that the decree would not be canceled. In the shtetl there was no light in the houses, but no one slept. We sought shelter, but were repeatedly turned away because every place was full. We spent the night in a wooden shed, which had a roof. At dawn we headed toward Radoshkevitzi, near the Polish border, but on the way learned that the border was closed there also. We were advised to try another route to the border and we hastily decided to steal across using byways and fields. As we approached our destination, there was no forest and we could be seen from afar. We were unconcerned and careless. We went through thorny thickets where we had to lift or push our bikes. We encountered no one.

From a distance we saw a road with many soldiers. It became evident that these were retreating Soviet soldiers. We followed them and arrived in Zoslov, the first Russian town with a train station. Above, an air battle was going on between the German and Soviet planes. We could see pilots jumping from their burning planes in parachutes. A train loaded with soldiers and civilians was slowly leaving the station. We entered Zoslov and our spirits were lifted— we were behind the Iron Curtain! At a restaurant, the waiter brought us some bread, but demanded to see some I.D. We snatched the bread from the table and ran out. On the street, people were excited and fearful about the news that the Russians were abandoning Zoslov, and German tanks were approaching.

On our bikes, we got on the trail to the capital of White Russia—Minsk. German planes were strafing the road and it seemed safer for us to lay in the ditches until they passed. Gunfire and missiles whizzed over our heads. We could see in the distance that Minsk was burning. The towns in the area were filled with refugees, fleeing the almost constant bombardment. We spent the night in a small clearing near the Soviet soldiers, so that we might flee with them. Exhausted, I slept til morning, and we were again on the way to Minsk, which was in flames from the bombing. The road was filled with bodies of dead and wounded. Parents were searching for children, who were terrified, weeping and lost. We passed abandoned military vehicles and tanks, which had run out of gas.

In the forest we were suddenly halted by four soldiers, guns drawn, who told us to raise our hands. They asked if we had any weapons; Sarin and Padaiev had to give up their revolvers and we were all searched. We were taken off the trail and ordered to sit, guarded by two armed soldiers. The other two led off our companions, Sarin and Podaiev. After two hours, which seemed like ten, they returned. We were set free and quickly resumed the road to New Borisov. But we never made it because soldiers and civilians were streaming toward us; German units had cut off the trails in the woods. Confused, we finally made our way back to our last stop, and decided to stay there.

Among the Peasants in a White Russian Town

Now we saw few refugees. We were in a remote hamlet, and we asked some peasants if we could buy some food. The answer was, *Nyet, golubchik* [No, little dove]. We sat down with a group of peasants who were chatting. They asked us where we came from, since our clothes indicated that we weren't local, and our bikes weren't a Russian brand. We told them that we came from Olshan. One of them went off and returned shortly to tell us that he had talked to his wife and she was willing to cook us some potatoes. And in a half–hour, he invited us to his home.

His wife was awaiting us there, and also his 17 year–old daughter. The table was set with a white tablecloth and three pieces of bread. We washed up and sat down, as our host set down a large bowl. Our hostess put on a white apron and brought in a pot of hot potatoes, which we quickly polished off. Sarin offered 50 rubles which our host declined. I stuffed them into our hostess' hand and she thanked us.

The host went into the kitchen, then returned and told us not to get up, because his wife was preparing some more food. The smell of pickled onions pervaded the house. He brought in a freshly baked loaf of bread and a knife, while his wife served a *skovorade*, scrambled eggs cooked in lard. We cut up the bread and ate all of the eggs. We thanked them and declined any more food. The peasant invited us to stay overnight; his wife had already prepared a room. On the wall was displayed a decorated icon of the Virgin Mary; a small candle was lit below it. The windows were covered by drapes so we could not see outside. After a few minutes we undressed and lay down, but didn't fall sleep because we could hear gunfire and airplanes. When we looked out, we could see shadows of the planes flying and shooting overhead. Suddenly some gunfire hit a window in our house. Before we could get fully dressed, the watchman ran in from the street and led us out from the house into a cellar which had been dug out under the house. There sat our hostess with her daughter. I was trembling from the cold and from fright. The hostess crossed herself and prayed. The earth shook from the bomb blasts. The daughter, Stasha, who was also trembling, fell into my arms and I also held her as if we had been old friends.

When the shooting stopped, we emerged from the cellar. The sky was red from the burning towns. We went back into the house and got some sleep. When we arose in the morning it was raining, and there was little movement outside. Our hostess served breakfast and we sat down with everyone. Since we had eaten so little for several days, we really appreciated the groats, hot milk, oat *latkes* with *skovorade* of pickled ham.

Afterwards I again offered them 50 rubles, and we intended to leave, but it was still raining, so we waited until noon. The hostess told us to wait until afternoon, but the rain continued. Sarin and the peasant went out in the rain to find out what was happening. On return, they had several impressions. They were told that Minsk and Barisov were already in German hands. Our group–Sarin, Fodiev, Meltzer and I– decided to leave. Our host showed us the way to avoid Barisov and get back on the road to Minsk.

Sarin and Fodiev tore up their documents. They hid their party registrations and revolvers in a crevice under the roof of a stable. We marked the place well in case it would be possible to retrieve them. We checked our bikes, pumped up the tires, but then decided to stay the night again because of the continuing rain.

The Germans Arrive and are Greeted Warmly by the White Russian Peasants

My companion, Meyer Meltzer, older than I, had formerly been in the Polish Army before the war. He had repeatedly urged me not to come with him. He had been captured by the Germans in 1939 and had been freed as a resident of Olshan, which had been annexed by the Soviets after the Polish collapse. They had not noticed that he was Jewish, and had let him go.

He tried to make me aware of how I would seem to the Russian soldiers when we were stopped at various points. He was Polish, a *zapodnik* [person from the east], he felt less concern for the Soviet citizens. But I could be killed either by the Germans or the Russians, so which town should we choose?

Sarin had wanted me to go with him back to Olshan, so before going to sleep, in Meltzer's presence, he asked me if I was staying or going with him. I said I would go. He said he would wake me at dawn–and those were the last words I heard from him. I fell asleep, and as if in a dream I heard him ask if I were going. But I fell back to sleep and I didn't wake until later. Meltzer was sitting near me and he told me that I had not responded to Sarin's call, so he and Fodiev left.

I quickly got dressed; the host tried to reassure me that they had not gone far, and I could chase after them. I got on my bike and tried to follow the tracks left in the mud, but couldn't find them. I returned to the town to rejoin Meltzer, and we set off on the road to Minsk. There was little activity in the town, only a few pedestrians. The bridges had been torn down. As we approached Minsk we could see many tanks from the distance marked in front by a red insignia. At first we thought they were Russian tanks, but when we got closer, we could see that the tanks were manned by German soldiers, with black swastikas.

Peasants lined the streets, watching the tanks. We merged with them and also watched. We heard the peasants talking to each other, and one of them, pointing to some young fellows astride the tanks, remarked, "See, they are the same as we." Another said, " I remember the Germans well from the first war, and things were better for us than under the Bolsheviks. Compared to the Bolsheviks, they were good cultured men."

A cold chill ran down my back, and I knew that we had to get away from this spot. We moved off from these people and got on the road with our bikes, quite near the cheerful smiling Germans, who were driving along. When traffic was interrupted by a collapsed bridge, the tanks and other vehicles had to re-route. We were stopped by some German soldiers, who demanded our I.D.s. They were no longer smiling and now seemed hostile.

Meyer Meltzer handed over his document, and his "*Sprovka*", written in German and stamped with the German eagle, which I now saw for the first time. He had been freed by the Germans and sent home to Russia in September 1939. One of the Germans tore off our caps briefly and asked, "Soldaten?". "Nyet" I replied in Russian and shook my head. After reading his documents, the German asked Meyer, "Are you Jewish?" "Yes", he answered. "Communist? Together, we answered, "No!", and shook our heads. He returned Meyer's papers, and leafed through my documents, looked at the passport photo, returned them and ordered us to ride off.

We got to the control point, where German soldiers on all sides were leading away young men under suspicion, including soldiers and officers of the Red Army, now dressed in civilian garb, and some who had been imprisoned by the Soviets and were now liberated from their camps. It was evident that the Germans were interested only in discovering Russian soldiers, since the Control consisted mainly of a head inspection. Anyone whose head had been shaved was considered a soldier and was taken prisoner. Those with hair on their heads were freed.

We quickly pedaled away towards Minsk. In the towns that we passed, the German soldiers were dealing with the peasants, exchanging their tobacco and cigarettes for eggs and lard. The soldiers brandished three fingers, "In three days Moscow is finished".

Beginning of the German Occupation

When we got to Minsk, we were stopped and taken to a control point. On the sidewalk behind a table sat a German officer and several civilians. Near them was a long row of men, protected by German soldiers. We didn't wait to get to the control table, but when the soldiers were distracted, we raced away on our bikes and merged with the civilian pedestrians. We searched for a Jewish face, found a woman and asked where to find a Jewish neighborhood. She told us to go to the East Bridge, where there were lots of Jews.

The city was still burning, entire neighborhoods and streets were devastated, and corpses were visible in the ruins. We got to Starre Vilenska, near the East Bridge. The shops and businesses had been looted. A few people were carrying food items and household wares.

A woman looking out of her window spoke to us in Yiddish. She told us she had just returned from the town where she and her daughter had been visiting at the time of the bombing. When she got home, everything had been taken. Her husband had been drafted into the army. She said, "You see how everyone is looting the stores. I would have gone too, to get some food, but I have no more strength, and didn't want to leave my daughter. But I would let her go with you." I was willing to go with the girl. The woman went upstairs as we entered, then came down the broken wooden steps with her 14 year old daughter. We stowed our bikes and the girl and I went off to find some food. People gladly showed us the way to go, but everyone was headed that way. We came to the cookie factory, too late to find any cookies, but we got some sugar and crackers, loaded our bags and came back. We weren't worried about eating, we slept all night. Meyer had told me, as we lay down, that he intended to leave at dawn, to return to Olshan. I couldn't persuade him otherwise, and said that I was was going to stay in Minsk. At sun–rise, I accompanied him to the bridge, where we bade farewell. I never saw him again.

Getting Acquainted With Olshaners Living in Minsk

I knew that a number of Olshaners had moved to Minsk, including Bery and Tema Koslovski, our distant cousins, with two sons and a daughter, whom I knew personally. After the fall of Poland, when the Soviets took over eastern White Russia and eastern Ukraine in 1939, the mother and daughter had come to visit us in Olshan. And now I was questioning older Jews here, asking if they knew any Koslovski, who had worked at the Torarner Station.

Finally I was told of a Koslovski, a young man, a civil engineer, who might be one of the sons. I was directed to his address, and as soon as I entered the house, there was Tema Koslovski. She remembered me and welcomed me warmly. I met the lovely Miriam, a niece, 17 year old Margolia, and a granddaughter, child of her son Avrasha. An older couple also lived with them, the Ratners. He had been a teacher in Minsk, and their home had burned down.

Tema introduced me as a close cousin. Our mothers had been very close like sisters. Everyone asked about their families in Olshan. I told them all the news and about my wanderings and flight to Minsk. They listened to all this and sighed, wondering where their children were now, or if they were still living. Tema's sons, Avrasha and Elia had been drafted into the Red Army.

I became a close member of the household. Tema showed me two houses which had been her property. One house fronting on the street had been requisitioned as a government food warehouse. In the other house had dwelled her son Avrasha and his wife and child. We occupied half of the house on the hill. The other half was inhabited by a Christian, Olga, and her sister. Her husband had also been drafted.

Tema regretted that she had not taken anything away from the warehouse, like all the others. It would have been possible to obtain some supplies, but she was distracted, and the warehouse had been emptied, leaving only four walls and some stalls. There was a locked wooden shed on the hill, whose contents were unknown. We decided to open it. I procured a hatchet and furtively tore open a board and entered. There we found about 20 cartons of soap, which we unloaded at night. We hid them in the house and put 5 or 6 underground in back of the Koslovski property.

The Germans issued a decree in Minsk, directing that all men aged 16–18, and those older than 50, were to assemble at various designated points. Anyone who did not comply would be shot. We decided that I, being 19, would report to the site where those over 50 were assembled, together with the

Ratners and Koslovskis. The site was a huge plaza, next to a park and an adjacent burned neighborhood. Many thousands of men had gathered, and women too who had accompanied the elderly and the sick. We waited from 10 in the morning until 3, when a notice was posted on a tree. A truck pulled up and a German officer addressed the crowd in broken Russian to explain with gestures around his neck, that any disobedience would be punished by hanging. Then he sent everyone home.

The fate of the younger group was quite different. They were not sent home, they were surrounded by soldiers, and stayed the whole night. At dawn the Christians were released, and the Jews were roped off. The Germans selected out those who were younger or who were more educated, and sent them off to work camps. Most of them were in fact shot and a few were sent to concentration camps in Minsk, from which they never returned. The remaining Jews were beaten and flogged and were not given any food, except for some brought in by the townspeople.

Under the German Terror Regimen

I stayed with the Koslovskis. We traded soap for food, and sat in our house bewildered, not knowing what to expect. Often the houses were searched by the Germans seeking men for slave labor. Several times I avoided them by hiding. But once two soldiers entered suddenly and caught me. I was taken to a crowd of captured Jews, including children, youths, girls and elderly. We were forced into a three story building which used to be a shul, and directed to empty everything out, for this was being readied to be used as a military warehouse. At evening, everyone was released to go home. But I along with another strong youth was ordered to dig some ditches on the hill. We doubted that we'd be released so we decided to flee.

No one actually knew me in Minsk, and this was an advantage because no one in the White Russian community had identified me as Jewish. There were White Russian police on every corner, armed with clubs, and they clobbered any Jews encountered. Posters on the walls exhorted the people to report any Jews or communists. One notice announced that the people of the town of Oshman had killed all the 'damned Jews who had drunk Christian blood in the past', and asked the Christians of Minsk to follow the example of the Oshman Christians.

Dealing With the Jews of Smorgen

I knew that there were Jews from Smorgen nearby, and I knew many of them. My mother came from Smorgen, where her brothers and their families lived. I used to see them when I visited my family in Smorgen. I was told that other people from Smorgen, Oshman and even Olshan lived nearby. In particular, I was told of a Smorgen boy, Avrohom Rutchanski, who was connected with a partisan group outside of the city and that might be a possible contact for me. I remembered that he had attended my school in 1939–41, before the Soviets took over, and that he had been a militant in Smorgen. He was about 3–4 years older than me. I had also met Rivke Yacov of Oshman, who was living with Dovid Baron (Dimka Baronov) a boy from Minsk. Dimka's cousin, Chaimke Kolnitchonski, also lived with them. We were the same age and became friends. He came from a barber's family and he had worked in Olshan in 1937, later in Oshman, and was also acquainted with Rivke Yacov. He was working as a barber for the Germans.

With the people from Smorgen and another friend from Olshan, Avke Kaplan, who had originally been drafted into the Red Army, we planned to return to Olshan.

Slave Labor and Suffering

Near us lived a native German, Mishke, who worked for the Minsk police. He knew that Tema Kozlovski was trading soap for food, and at first, he got some himself. Then he sent several police the next day for more soap business. Finally he brought some Germans who demanded all of the soap. After taking the supply, they beat Tema severely. I was away, but when I returned at noon, I was arrested with other Jews, brought to the police station, and put in chains. Then the Germans beat us with heavy clubs, especially those who looked healthy. One 50 year–old man, was selected as an example. He was beaten mercilessly and collapsed. As he lay unconscious, they poured cold water on him, then beat him some more as he awakened.

These two hours seemed an eternity. We could not recognize each other because we were so bloody and swollen. The Germans also became weary, were sweating heavily, and they took frequent breaks. During one such break, I managed to sneak out, and escaped home. I would do anything to escape the Germans. I would usually run off from the work crews, to avoid the blows from behind and the other forms of murderous punishment.

Building Hide–Outs in the Minsk Ghetto

After 3 months the Minsk Jews were driven into a ghetto. We left Toprovski Street and moved to #5 Zamkove Street. We occupied the second floor of this large two story building. From our room a little window led into the corridor, which we boarded up to conceal from the Germans that there was a second entry to the room. We also created some hide–outs. Our largest hide–out was underground, under the basement. The entry was very constricted, and not everyone could fit. Above the steps were several cabinets, two of which were converted to hide–outs. These hide–outs saved us from capture by the Germans.

After a month in the ghetto, my friend Chaimke Kolnitchonski, and I had saved up some food. We went to work at the station. Chaimke had introduced me to the Germans as a barber from outer Russia. I could speak enough

Russian, and didn't look like a Jew. I gave my name as Liandov Roman Adolfowitch. The Germans gave me a pass with that name, employed as a barber. Chaimke was identified as a 'connection' and also got a pass. I pretended that I didn't understand what the Germans said to me, so Chaimke translated into Russian.

Every morning, the Germans brought in chickens, ducks, eggs and *samaganka* [home–made brandy] from outlying towns, and they spent all morning eating and drinking. Most of them then fell asleep. We had eaten and decided to get as far away from the Germans as possible.

One of them, an alcoholic, used to fall asleep, with a big bottle of brandy above his head and a smaller one next to it. With his eyes closed, he continued sipping without stop. He was a real ruffian and was always brawling with his comrades. We planned to steal the large bottle, which he would assume was taken by his comrades, and that would start a fight.

And that's what happened. We stole the bottle, emptied it, washed it and broke the bottle, so there were no traces. When the German got up and saw that his bottle was gone, he accused one of his comrades of taking his bottle. They started arguing, fighting broke out, and the others joined in, creating a bloody mess. We returned home, satisfied that we had done a great deed–we had seen the Germans fighting each other..

The First German Solution *Aktion*

After I had worked at the station for a while, I became ill with rheumatism, diagnosed by the Minsk doctor Charno, in the ghetto. I was in bed for three weeks with fever. When I was finally able to get up, the first mass killings were starting in the Minsk ghetto. At dawn, November 7, 1942, we heard the Germans shouting outside, children crying and some shooting. We looked out the window and saw that the houses on Zamkove Street were being emptied of Jews who were being stuffed into open freight trucks, festooned with red banners. The Germans prodded their victims with bayonets to make them move faster.

Our house had not been disturbed yet, so together with Tema and her daughter, we fled from the ghetto. Luckily we made it to Maprovski Street, where Tema had previously lived. We were welcomed warmly by the good Christian lady Olga who gave us shelter and breakfast, and sympathized with our plight. We hadn't had time to warm ourselves, when Olga looked outside and saw Mishke, the German policeman, whom we knew well. She turned pale and told us to hide. Tema and Manye hid under the beds, while I went into the back and waited for Mishka.

He came in and immediately asked Olga where she had hidden her guests. He soon got to the back room and pointing his gun at me, asked,"Where is the old Jewess and her daughter?" I said I didn't know. "You don't know?" and he hit me in the head with his gun. "Come on out, you'll be better off".

Tema and Manye crawled out, joined me and begged our captor not to beat me. He pushed Manye with his left hand, and pointed the way with his gun. He ordered us to walk down the middle of the street, not on the sidewalk, while he walked behind with his gun pointed. He bragged to the White Russian pedestrians, proudly proclaiming, "You see, the Jews wanted to escape from their death." Tema asked where he was taking us, and he replied, "To the Tower". She offered him money, but Mishke was not interested, and pushed her to go faster. I thought that this time I was done for. I wasn't able to run because I was so weak from my recent illness. That was the only time that I thought I would die.

We were led to Nimiger Street, on the edge of the ghetto. Suddenly a group of German soldiers shouted at us and started shooting in the air. Mishke was frightened and hid in a doorway. With all my might I ran towards the Germans, along with Tema and Manye. When we approached them they only asked where we lived. I pointed to the house near where we stood. "Quick, run into the tower". In the tower we found an exit to the next street, and so we were free from Mishke. The Germans who had freed us, were guarding the properties confiscated from the empty ghetto houses, which had not been looted by the civilians. We came home to #5 Zalkova, where nothing had been moved. The *Aktion* had targeted only part of the ghetto, up to Zamkova Street. The other side of the street had been liquidated, but not ours.

The Second *Aktion* and the Childbirth in Hiding

Several weeks later, the second *Aktion* was carried out in Minsk, including the other side of Zalkova Street. We could not escape, all the streets were guarded. I hid in our hide-out, while the others including Tema and her daughter stayed in the house. In our little dug-out, we had huddled with a 15 year old boy, and an older woman with her pregnant daughter. There was no room for any movement. Soon the Germans began to search, and then began to check the basements. But they did not find us. After the cries of those who had been captured died down, we realized that the houses were now empty. We could hear the voices of the murderers who were searching the houses.

At night, the pregnant woman started to have labor pains. She had suffered in silence, but her agonized movements had caused some noise. The men warned that they might stifle her if her movements were too noisy. In the darkness, she continued to labor, and then gave birth on the floor. Her moans quieted down, and we heard nothing of the actual birth. But the woman's mother pleaded that someone should enter the house to find a scissors, for the placenta was bleeding and she thought that might be fatal. I was chosen to do this. The door into our house was blocked, but I heard sounds within and called. Tema opened the door; everyone was there, they had not been molested. Two more neighbors had also found shelter here. I told her why I was there and what had happened. Tema gave me a scissors and some thread to tie off the umbilical cord, and additional instructions.

I returned, and the mother helped me to find the cord. I cut it with scissors and tied it off. In a little while the infant began to cry. Our survival was at stake and we grimly agreed on our only dismal option. We smothered the child, carried it outside and buried it in the sand.

All night, the Germans carried out their mission of liquidating the ghetto, using torches and probes to find the hidden Jews. About 6 AM, they left our neighborhood. We ascended from the basement and encountered others who had survived. From our house emerged the Koslovski family and their two neighbors. The Germans were in no hurry to liquidate the whole ghetto entirely, they did it by neighborhoods. Those who had successfully hidden moved to another part of the ghetto. Tema, Beryl, their daughter Margolia and I moved in with the Potashnik family.

Some days later I met the woman whose baby we had suffocated. She wept, mourning her lost child, and wanted to know the location of its burial site so that she might make a proper burial in a cemetery. She brooded that her child might have lived if we had not had to make that terrible decision. Sadly, she acknowledged that we had no other choice. This had been her first child. She had married just before the war, and her husband had been drafted into the army.

We stayed a week with the Potashniks, then moved to Tankovaya Street, where we found a hiding place under the stairs leading to a little house which had two rooms. I didn't report for the work which was being managed by the Judenrat. Whenever the Germans caught anyone hiding, they brought him to the Judenrat to torture him publicly and then shoot him. Several times when I passed the Judenrat, I saw the bodies of the executed boys and girls on the bridge. The Germans deliberately let the bodies stay for several days to frighten the people.

German Jews In The Minsk Ghetto

Half of the Minsk ghetto had been liquidated. The houses of those who had been evicted were occupied by White Russians. A few streets of the remaining ghetto were occupied by German Jews who had been brought from Berlin, Hamburg and other cities. They were jammed into the closed part of the Minsk ghetto. The German Jews were privileged; they received a normal bread ration before going out to work. While the Russian Jews got 100 grams of bread, the German Jews got 200. Their ghetto had its own Judenrat and policemen, who guarded the gate, so that no Russian Jew could deal with those Jews exiled from Germany.

Trade consisted of exchanges of materials. The German Jews had brought a lot of things with them and they were glad to exchange them for food.. The

Russian Jews used to buy clothes, watches and other valuables, and later traded them to the White Russians for food, such as flour or lard.

Often I visited Chaimke Kolnitchonski, who lived with Rivke Yakov from Oshman, with her sister's children David and Mishke Baron. Mishke had been in the army and had been released from German captivity. They all lived together and worked outside the ghetto in the laundry of the headquarters.

Rivke ran the household. Chaimke, who had been labeled by the Germans as a 'hybrid', worked as a group leader, who conducted the Jews to their various work sites. David Baron didn't look Jewish. Sometimes he didn't come home at night. He also worked in the laundry but had a connection with the Minsk underground Communist party. Chaimke told me all this and also told me that David had a connection to the partisans and really would like to join them. But we were 'zapodnikes', from the east, meaning Poland, and the partisans had no confidence in them. He advised me to speak with David, to see if I could join them.

My Relationship With the Patrols

Chaimketold me that for now he couldn't take me to a partisan connection. But at the auto repair plant he had heard that they were looking for a barber, and that I should apply for a job there with my documents as a White Russian. I took the suggestion and two days later I started my work as a barber at the auto repair shop. I had my tools and my documents and got there about noon. It was in another part of town and nearby were two–story white barracks housing German soldiers.

I spoke only Russian and they didn't ask me any questions. An officer told me to get to work, to cut his hair and shave him. Afterwards, apparently pleased, he slapped my shoulder and gave me some cigarettes. He got dressed and told me to come with him. He brought me into the workshop office and introduced me as a barber and I worked all day in the barracks. I was given a special place, but at first I went from room to room, serving only officers. Some would pay me, others would not. I went home in the evening.

I had been warned that not far from the workshop, patrols were common, and that I shouldn't go any further. I went back to the barracks, but I was uncomfortable because there were only German soldiers there. I turned to some Christians who lived nearby and asked if anyone would let me stay there for the night. One of them invited me in. A young man sitting there was unfriendly at first. He quizzed me about my identity and address. I told him I was working here for the Germans as a barber, and that I lived on Maprovski Street. I had gotten off the street because of the patrols . He invited me to take off my jacket and make myself at home.

I sat there anxiously and reflected that this was the wrong place for me to be. It got dark outside, and the family started to come home. I took note of whoever left the house, and when I noticed that the young man was drowsing,

I thought about how I might pass myself off before it was too late. At the right moment, I put on my tunic with my document and tools and slipped away. It was dark outside, and wandering around the barracks could be tricky. Then I remembered seeing a large gym, where no one lived, and I managed to get in unnoticed.

The door was very wide and opened only slightly. I lay down between the door and the wall. I finally closed the door because of the cold. I wondered what to say if I was found. Various thoughts ran through my mind. I wasn't worried if the Germans found me–I would be responsible for myself. But it would be worse if I were found by the White Russian police. I couldn't sleep at all. At dawn I heard the sound of soldiers' boots in the corridor. Two soldiers came in and lit their pocket lights after opening the door. I scrunched up my legs and pretended to be asleep and the Germans ignored me. In the morning I got up, left the gym, and worked at hair–cuts and shaving again. I asked the older German if he could get me an affidavit for my business, and he agreed. At the end of the day I returned home to the ghetto.

On the second day, going to work, I was on a quiet side–street and was suddenly halted by a German soldier and a White Russian policeman. My documents were approved after a superficial inspection. The German directed the cop to take me to an alley where a group of Russian youths and girls had been assembled. From all sides, captured Russian youths and maidens were assembling, then along with other such groups, were brought to the Surzeschke Market. All along the way we were accompanied by concerned Christians, families of the captives. The Germans assured these worried observers that they should not be concerned, that we were being taken to Germany to work, and would return when the war was over.

The Market was jammed. There were stalls which had once been stocked with merchandise. We were driven into the stalls under guard. A German gave a speech and assured us that we were being taken to Germany to do war work, and that at the end we would be well–paid and given houses with land. The Minsk people had brought food supplies and clothing in packages for their relatives and said their goodbyes. Everyone got a package except me. I stood there quietly and thought only about how to escape, before we were led into the de–lousing baths. It was rumored that the baths were the last step before being transported, and I feared that I might be trapped. When the order was given to start leaving, much weeping and clamor followed, and the soldiers started pushing us out of the stalls. In the confusion, I seized the opportunity to snatch an empty pack, sneaked out through the gate and escaped once more. When I met Chaimke again, I told him that I wouldn't go back to the car repair shop again.

At the General Commissary

Chaimke had been advised to bring me to a job at the general commissary, because his nephew Dimke Baronov wanted to talk to me. Dimke told me that at the commissary, the shoe–repair and tailor workshops were together. The job consisted of opening the door for German officers and their ladies when they came to the shops. Until now this had been done by a Jew, but now a directive had come down to replace the Jew with a Russian. I would be presented as a Christian to work at this job, so next morning I went to work at the Commissary on *Ploshtzad Svobodi* [Freedom Place].

The management of this place consisted of Lieutenant Shtamp, and Chief Engineer Hinig. Most of the workers in the shops were Jews. The head of the commissary was later blown up by a mine placed under his bed by his girlfriend, who belonged to the underground. The rumor was that she had been Jewish. Besides the German supervisor, there were also brigadiers and colonels, and also civilians. Most of these civilians were Jews using fake family names, and nationalists as well as mixed breeds.

I was paid 200 grams of bread daily and two meal vouchers [*stolova*] for lunch and dinner. Lunch consisted of a watery soup mixed with corn meal, sometimes a horse bone. The evening meal was a little tea or coffee and 100 grams of bread. This was not enough food for me, so I tried to manipulate the rations, and thought about how I could get some more food.

I had received my I.D. card as a Russian, and the document also described me as White Russian. The secretary in the chancellory of the labor division where I had gotten my documents was a young German woman who was in the military service, and was the daughter of the engineer Hinig. This office was in the vicinity of the shops where I worked.

I Become a Shopper, Get a Revolver and Prepare to Join the Partisans

Max was one of the German Jews, who spoke a little Russian. He came from Lodz and in childhood his family moved to Germany. Max was about 40 and had a 17 year old daughter. He was sort of a supervisor of the German Jews who were doing lumber work, sawing and chopping trees. I told Max that if anyone in his group would like to barter something for food, then I could handle it. He eagerly accepted the idea, and next morning he brought me a man's suit.

After work I took the suit to the market which I knew well, and traded it for 2 kilos of lard, a loaf of bread and 2 kilos of potatoes. In the morning I brought these items to Max, who was pleased with my work and I inspired his confidence. At my request he brought in gold objects and other clothing from his friends, and I again traded them successfully at the market.

We already had enough food and money, but Max asked me to go to the market daily to barter for food. I finally declined because I had enough. The only one I told about my dealing was my best friend whom I saw every day, Chaimke Kolnitchonski.

A few months passed. We really wanted to join the partisans. I couldn't find out anything more precise, because I didn't have any contacts. But I knew that you had to have a gun before you could be accepted. One day, I noticed a young Christian lad, about 17, walking near the house where I worked, as if he were seeking someone. When I asked him who he was seeking, he didn't answer, but then called me aside and told me that he had a new unused blank passport, which could be used by anyone who might fill in the blanks. He knew that the Jews needed this and would gladly buy it. If I could sell one to the Jews inside the shop, I could keep the profit over his selling price.

I agreed to this transaction and he said he would bring the document tomorrow. It was evident that he was interested only in the money. In the morning he brought this blank document, an *udostovyenye*, affirmation that served as a passport. On very close inspection the stamp might be seen as false. I gave him ten gold rubles, and asked him if he could get me a pistol. In order to get gold coins for this I had to go to the market a number of times to barter the things that Max had brought me.

One day on the way to the market with some items to sell, including a rubber coat which I was wearing, I was suddenly halted by two guards, one in front and the other in back. "Are you Jewish?", said one of them and asked to see my documents. I also showed him my work permit from the commissary. They didn't believe me and told me to take off my coat. There they found the traces of the yellow stars which had been removed. I responded that I had bought the coat from one of the Jews who worked in the commissary shop, and that the traces of the yellow letters didn't worry me, because I wasn't a Jew. I spoke all this in Russian. I told them to take me to the commissary, where I knew the head officer, and I also mentioned the chief engineer Hinig. I also said I could identify the Jew from whom I had bought the coat. I was quite calm, because even Max didn't know I was Jewish. I put up such a good front that the guards released me.

When I had accumulated sufficient gold, I acquired the pistol along with 8 bullets from the Russian boy, and I hid them in the grass near a devastated house close to the commissary. I thought it was a good spot and I checked it frequently. However, in a few days, when I checked I saw that everything looked disturbed. I searched, trying to convince myself that I had gotten mixed up, but in fact my pistol and bullets were gone. However I found a hidden grenade, wrapped in rags, like my gun, so I hid that in a different area. Again I started ruminating about how to get a gun. The grenade was useless as an entry, even if there were an opportunity. So I set about dealing at the market place, handling only small items like rings, earrings, watches.

The German Secretary and Theft of Documents for the Partisans

The secretary at the commissary, the daughter of the engineer Hinig, was 18 years old with a round face. She didn't crack a smile during work, just like her father. She prepared the orders for the labor brigade, gave out *propusken* [passes], leaves, extended leaves and prepared various documents on her typewriter. There were two typewriters in her room, one for her, the other for her father. The round rubber stamp with the 'birdie' was there too. All the documents signed and stamped by the lieutenant in charge and the head engineer were issued by this girl. She would often ask me to fetch one of the workers to come to her office. She even gave me some cigarettes, and I had gotten her to extend a pass for someone who wasn't working. As a gift, I gave her a pair of earrings

Some weeks later, Chaimke told me that a barber institute, a *parikmacherske*, was scheduled, only for the commissary workers. and that we would be working there. The session lasted a few days and was held in the reception room of the Chancellory house. There I made some contact with the underground partisan organization in Minsk, for which I had been yearning. Chaimke and I were asked to steal some of the blank documents from the desks of the secretary and her father. These blanks were inscribed in big letters, "The General Commissary of White Russia", and had the round stamp with the emblem of the German eagle.

The assignment to steal the blanks was given us by Norusevitz, who also received them from us. He was one of the first Jews in the underground and had been sent into the forest. There he was the commander of a partisan group. Before that he had worked as a manager in the commissary, and had been identified as a *mischling*, of mixed origins. In autumn 1942 Norusevitz was shot by the partisan command, because he had refused to take orders from other Russian commando groups.. He was a heroic comrade, and was probably killed because he was Jewish.

We had carried out our assignment very well without mishap. With several valuable pieces of jewelry from Max, I approached the secretary when she was alone, and offered them for sale. Chaimke stood watch to warn if anyone was coming. She spoke only German and I only Russian. We communicated by hand gestures, so I understood what she wanted. In order that I might visit more often, I would bring in slightly different items, not quite what she wanted, pretending that I hadn't understood.

The blanks lay on the desk. The stamp was locked in a cabinet on the wall. If the stamp was needed, she unlocked the cabinet, then locked it again after replacing the stamp. Often she left the key in the lock, or she went out for a few minutes. We utilized those occasions. Chaimke alerted me, I would enter, use the stamp on the blank forms on the desk, as many as I wanted, then restore the stamp and lock it back in the cabinet. Everything went smoothly.

We provided more blanks than were requested. The stamped documents were used for various purposes. With the help of these papers, cars were driven out into the woods carrying Jewish boys and girls, who had been working in our commissary. The blanks were entitled: "The work detachment of the General Commissary includes men and women, sent into the forest to do forestry work". The numbers of men and women were listed and also the director and so on. The signatures of the lieutenant and the chief engineer were forged.

At 6AM, the vehicle would enter the ghetto, just like other trucks, that were taking the Jews to work. People were already standing in place to be picked up, holding saws, axes and other tools for forest work. The driver was a Christian, Valodya, who had been driving trucks for the commissary. He was accompanied by Norusevitz, and they both had legitimate documents. Weapons were hidden under the hood.

It was about 40 km from the city to the forest. Valodya would drive the truck to a certain point for the workers. After a few trips, Norusevitz would stay in the forest, and only Valodya knew where to meet him. The partisans took away the workers, and Valodya drove back. One of these trips included: Chaimke's cousin David Baronov, who had also been a unit leader at the commissary, Rivke Yacov, Chaimke Aginski, his Christian wife, and others.

Partisan Activities and German Terror

In Minsk it was already known that the partisans were lurking in the forest, attacking the German transports. In response the Germans carried out deadly missions against the partisans, and would hang them in the public squares of Minsk. In the ghetto, the Germans intensified their terror campaign, by the 'liquidation of the Jews'. Many of the Jewish workers at the commissary were seized and shot in an *Aktion*.

Chaimke and I had carried out our assignments from the underground. In order to take care of the boys and girls, we used to steal tools from the warehouse such as saws and axes. I remember one case where we were in the process of carrying out the stolen tools, which we hid in the closet of the Chancellory, near the back door of our house. When we left, we had in error taken the lock with us. We had gotten it from engineer Hinig. We intended to retrieve the tools after work to keep on the hill, for the workers who were to be driven off by Volodya.

While I was alone in the barber shop, suddenly Hinig came in and asked me to unlock the closet. I was terrified, I was sure we were goners. I told him that Kolnitchovski had the key, and that I'd get it when he returned, and then unlock the closet. He became angry and ordered me to go find Kolnitchovski and get the door opened. He left, I quickly unlocked the door and threw the tools out onto the hill outside. By the time Hinig returned, there was no trace left in the closet. I gave him the key, and he ordered me to remove a broken stool to move into the furniture shop.

Shortly thereafter, Chaimke and I had procured pistols and bullets and were waiting for the call to go into the forest. I didn't want to chance hiding them as before, lest they be stolen, so I decided to carry them with me. I bought a pair of German military boots with wide uppers and stuffed my gun into one of them. I was on the way to the market to do some more trading, when suddenly on a side street, I encountered two German soldiers. One of them pointed to my boots, had me sit down and told me to take off my boot. He took off his own left boot, which was damaged, and pulled off my left boot, which did not contain the gun. I thought I'd have to flee barefoot if I had to take off the other boot containing the gun. The soldier started to put on my left boot, but fortunately it was too small. He gave it back to me and retrieved his own boot. And so I evaded another seemingly disastrous mishap.

On April 5, 1942, Chaimke, as a group leader from the commissary, accompanied a group of Jews into the forest. At 5:45 AM, I was picked up; Valodya was driving. Chaimke was bearing a sign identifying him as a group leader. I sat in the truck and we drove into the ghetto. After our documents were checked, we picked up the people standing ready to go. I knew most of them who had worked at the commissary. We drove out of the ghetto to the east bridge, where I said farewell to Chaimke and the group, and I returned to my work earlier than usual.

It was past the time when Valodya should have returned, and our people were getting restless, uneasily checking outside. He finally returned at 11, and reported that everything went well, but the partisans had not been there as scheduled, because they were engaged in a battle with a German unit. The newcomers had decided to wait in the forest for the partisans.

The Tragic Fate of Chaim Kolnitchovski and Our Underground Fighters

No vehicles or people showed up, and three days went by without a message. The engineer Hinig demanded to know where Kolnitchovski was. Certainly something must be amiss since he was absent from work. He directed me to check Kolnitchovski's residence. When he returned next day to demand an answer, I turned to a Jewish girl, Bronia, who worked cleaning up the shops and toilets, to explain in German my rehearsed statement, that Kolnitchovski had gone off to Ruzivevitz where his father had died. Hinig listened to me, searched deeply into my eyes and said, "He's crazy." Why didn't he tell me? I could have given him a pass. He's probably a goner now." I looked him steadily in his eyes and said nothing. He knew that I 'could not' speak German, that was always Chaimke's job.

The fate of the group was revealed on the 4th day. A young Jewish girl of 17, who had been in the group led by Chaimke, had returned to Minsk. She was short, didn't look Jewish, and appeared to be 13–14. She related that after the partisans had failed to appear, some decided to return to the city to try to re–connect with a messenger from the partisans. Chaimke, another boy and this girl set off on the trail, but were halted by a German patrol, who decided that their documents looked suspicious. So they drove them back to the Commissary, allowing the young girl to escape.

Two days later on April 9, three soldiers brought Chaimke and his comrade back to Minsk. They had first been checked at the Commissary, where their documents were identified as forged. Both of them were thrown into jail. Additional participants and ring–leaders were arrested, including Duner, who was thought to be a *mischling* and Milinke, who had passed as a Christian. On two successive days, Duner was taken to the City Garden and seated alone on a bench. Near him on another bench were sitting Germans disguised as civilians. If any of the pedestrians greeted him or stopped near him, they would be arrested afterwards.

Volodya disappeared after this disaster. After the first news from the partisans, I fled into the forest, and met up with one of the Jewish comrades from the underground, Lapidus, who arranged my connection with the partisans; he himself returned to Minsk. He told me that Chaim Kolnitchovski had not betrayed anyone, and was executed by hanging in the Minsk public square in May 1942.

In Those Days

April 15, 1942, at dawn, I went off in the forest with a partisan scout, a 17 year–old Jewish boy Mischke. He looked like a peasant from the town, wore peasant's clothes with a white pack on his back. I was also dressed as a peasant, with a knit cap, Russian soldier's pants,, stuffed into my German boots, where I still had my gun and bullets. I also had my Russian documents, which were needed if I crossed a control point. In my pack I had bread, a piece of lard, a packet of tobacco, a warm knit sweater and an old jacket.

In the outskirts, at a designated spot, we met a Christian couple in their forties, Ivan Ivanovich and his wife. Both were dressed as townspeople. They said they were messengers from the underground Minsk Communist party, and they accompanied us through side streets. We avoided the towns and anywhere there might have been German posts or police guards.

We didn't speak at all the whole day until sunset when we entered the Kolodiner Forest, in the Uzder region, and eventually came to the partisan outpost. Only Mischke was allowed in, but later a partisan led us to the partisan camp, whose commander turned out to be— Ivan Ivanovich. He was a tall Russian with a yellow beard. The group also contained Dimka Baronov, Rivka Yakov and some other acquaintances who had been in the group with Chaimke. They had connected with Ivanovich's partisans, who were one of several groups in Nikita's organization.

There were other groups in the Kolodina forest, disorganized and disinterested in any collective goal. There were also bandits, who posed as partisans, in order to rob the peasants. One gang was composed of former Soviet prisoners who only accepted ex–convicts who had been in prison for more than 10 years. The Communist commanders at the head of the groups were connected to the Minsk Underground. Commanders of other partisan groups thought that messengers from the city were German agents, on spying missions in order to send future German combat groups who would destroy the partisan camps. There were various shades of opinion among the groups, leading to propaganda battles with the goal of unifying forces under Nikita's *Otriad*. Sometimes armed clashes and bloodshed occurred between the groups, and commanders were shot down.

The partisans in this area consisted of about 50 per cent Jews, 40 percent Russians, soldiers who had escaped captivity, 10 per cent White Russians, residents of the area. Commanders known as Jews included Israel Lapidus and Elisha Norusevitz from Minsk–they belonged to Nikita's group. Nikita himself had been an officer in the Red Army. He looked Jewish, some said he was Jewish, but I never did find out.

Our camp was deep in the forest near a swamp which blocked any access and defended us against any of the frequent attacks by the Germans. Since my arrival no one had asked me who I was or where I came from. My comrades from the Minsk group were familiar with my work for the Underground. After I got settled, Rivka Yakov gave me a blanket and I fell into a deep sleep under the open sky.

In the morning Ivan Ivanovich summoned me and asked my name. I answered, "Romke". He repeated this smiling, then pulled a rusty rifle out of his box and gave it to me. He asked if I knew how to handle a rifle, and I answered,"*Da, tovarich* commander!" I knew how to take apart and re-assemble my pistol, but I had never handled a rifle before.

Ivan Ivanovich told me which squad I was to join. "You may part with this rifle only if you are dead. Meantime, go clean it up!" and I left with my hands full. That was the happiest moment of my life since I had left my home in Olshan.

I immediately got to work disassembling and cleaning my rifle. I was able to take it apart, but I was unable to put it back together. I didn't want to ask help from anyone and continued to puzzle over it for quite a while. Nearby was sitting a 13 year–old boy who noticed my problem. He hobbled over on one leg, leaned on his stick, grinned at me."You don't know how to put it together. Give it to me, I'll show you".

I was embarrassed, but handed over the gun. He sat down and put the parts together. He did this several times to show me the proper technique. I looked around to make sure that nobody saw that I had been taught by this young boy. His name was Bebe, a Jew from Audze. When the Germans were killing the Jews of his town, they had forced them into an open ditch and shot them all. Bebe lay there with all the others, but he had only been wounded in the foot. When the murderers had finished, they left the ditch open. He was able to crawl out, and eventually was found by the partisans. He was assigned to clean the rifles, while his wound was slowly healing.

Partisan Activity in 1942 and My First Battle Experience

In the evening after sunset, the partisans left their camp, to carry out their assigned duties, such as finding food from the towns. In partisan 'lingo', that was called *bombiashka*. A *rozviedka* [foray] and *svioz* [connection] with the nearby peasants were other missions. In addition, we were also sent to kill individual policemen who used to come visit their families, or any peasants who had collaborated with the Germans against the partisans.

We were also to disrupt and burn the milk stations where the peasants had been forced to deliver their milk to the Germans. This was actually a relief for the peasants who then were relieved of this milk 'tax'. In addition we had to go on raids to tear up the train tracks. At night there were only a few men in the camps. The partisans were busy all night and slept in the daytime. There was no scarcity of weapons, which had been abandoned en masse in the woods by the fleeing Red Army soldiers who were then taken prisoner.

One night the commander gave us an assignment for 8 men and a leader. Our goal was a *bombiashka* and we had to traverse a field in single file. We neared our designated town at night, and two of our men went in to see if there was any danger. We stretched out behind the town. In case our comrades encountered an enemy, we were to light a fire to guide their escape.

To complete our mission we appropriated a horse and wagon and two sheep from a peasant, whose son was a policeman. When we collected more food from the peasants, that set off a chorus of barking dogs. As they quieted down, we approached the cemetery behind the town. Suddenly we were assaulted by a burst of gunfire and flashes of rockets. We fled under a hail of bullets, leaving our booty behind, and our partisan comrades were lost. Dimke Baronov was wounded in his foot.

Subsequently our group was merged with Lapides' group. Our new camp was surrounded on all sides by swamps. At one spot we could cross over on tree branches. In our new camp, a bloody event occurred. At the order of Lapides, the partisan Mishke Baronov, a brother of David Baronov, was executed because he refused to obey an order from the commander to carry a kettle. The Jewish commander had made him a symbolic victim, to enforce discipline.

After camp had been set up and food was cooked, two of us were assigned to one of the raiding posts. We took food and water for a whole day. Our path took two hours and led us into the edge of the Kolodina forest. Across from us was the little town where we had lost our two partisans. Our objective was to observe the road into the town.

I climbed up a tree to observe any movement in the town. My comrade was guarding the trail below. At night, we switched places. Before dawn, I got up and walked back and forth to warm up. When the sun came up I noticed a man in the distance walking in my direction. Impulsively, I decided to ask him for some supplies, and approached him so that he wouldn't see our hiding place. When we got closer, my identity became obvious because of the red insignia on my cap.

I asked him where he was coming from so early. He said he had been at the mill near Kolodina to grind some corn, but didn't know how to do it at night. He had spent the night in the town, because he was afraid to be out in the dark. He named his home town, but I'm ashamed to admit that I didn't even ask him where he'd left his horse and why he was going home. I asked him for some supplies and walked back a way with him.

He gave me some food items, and I asked him to cut me a little tobacco. I walked with him a little further, actually nearing the place where my comrade was sleeping. I happened to look around behind us and to my consternation, saw groups of crouching soldiers running on the road on both sides, quite close to me. I dashed into the woods. The soldiers chased after me, shouting in Russian, *"Shtoi! Ruki vierd! Nie s'miesto!"*– "Stop, hands up, don't move!"

My buddy was already up, bewildered by the shouting. I yelled at him, "let's go—Germans!" [in fact, they were Latvians], and we ran into the forest downhill, chased by the Latvians, ordering us to stop. They didn't fire at us because they didn't want to attract more attention. With our last energy, we made it into the swamp and crawled as far as we could. Our pursuers didn't venture into the swamp. We heard some shooting in the direction of our former hide–out, and a little later, in the direction of our camp. Above the forest, an airplane droned back and forth shooting and launching grenades.

After we had rested, we left the swamp intending to unite with our comrades in the partisan group to take part in the battle. We saw only the Latvians, from whom we tried to remain hidden. Possibly we could have killed some of their scouts in the forest, but we wanted to evade them. We were unable to locate our camp, so returned to the swamp. At dusk we resumed the search, and finally found the remains of the campfire, but it had obviously been abandoned. In the distance we could hear occasional gunfire.

At the camp we found burned tents, discarded clothing, and piles of debris. We looked for something to eat in the cooking area, and saw overturned pots and a few peeled potatoes and some meat The pots and other utensils were shattered and hacked to pieces, so the Latvians must have been there. We found a little packet of coals left over by the Latvians, and we used them to cook. After eating, we decided to stay in this spot in case some lost comrades from another group might come, or perhaps our commander might send a messenger. And that's what happened. In the morning, two scouts from *Otriad* arrived, and a little later came two lost partisans. All six of us set out to find the *Otriad*. That morning we were also joined by another group of wounded partisans, and then we found our section 'hospital'.

Nikita and the *Otriad* had fled to the east, leaving their wounded behind, and a few healthy ones to care for them. We stayed with the group, and helped to care for the wounded. Every few days we'd move to another camp, and we carried along the wounded.

Traitors in the Partisan Group

After a few weeks, we were found by the partisan Mishke Kodreshov. He said he had been sent by Nikita, and he was really a lieutenant in the Red Army. His mission was to take all the wounded, whether they could walk or not, and all the other remaining loyal partisans, to re–unite with Nikita. So we all set out to try to find Nikita.

Along with me and my comrade, there were now 8 of us: Elioshka Kozotchin, a Russian who had a rifle and a pistol, Reuben, a Jew with a rifle; the wounded were: Dimke Atchminakov, a Ukrainian; Vanke Militin, a Russian–they had pistols. There were also two Jewish girls: Sara, armed with a revolver, and another unarmed girl whose name I don't recall. Kudreshov had a rifle, and I had one plus my pistol. As we moved eastward, Dimke's wound had opened so we had to go very slowly. Atchminikov was very loyal to Nikita, and encouraged us to keep moving at night and rest during the day.

One day, while I was on day watch, I observed a man, and followed him, hidden. He was alone, paused to listen, then kept going in the direction of our camp. When he heard a loud sound, he hid under a bush. I knew the noise came from our camp, so I ran up to him, pointing my gun at him. He raised his hands and I brought him into the camp. He was searched and was found to have only a small knife. He said he was a Russian who had escaped from a prison camp into the forest and had intended to join the partisans. His name was Alyoshke Alexeyev; he was tall, fair–haired and spoke perfect Russian. Our commander, Mishke, believed his story and allowed him to stay with us. A few days later, chatting with me, Alyoshke admitted to me that he had actually escaped from the police.

I told this to Mishke, and to the wounded Dimke, who, like me, had distrusted the newcomer. We both felt that we should shoot him. Mishke summoned him and we grilled him while threatening to shoot him. He maintained that he had come voluntarily, that no one had sent him. Mishke ordered me, in front of Alexeyev, to take him outside the camp and shoot him. I unleashed my rifle, and ordered Alexeyev to walk ahead and not to turn his head around. Mishke was behind me, and as I raised my rifle about to shoot, Mishke shouted, "Don't shoot!" He approached Alexeyev and urged him to confess, and we wouldn't shoot him.

After a short dialogue, Alexeyev confessed. The Uzde police had sent him to find the location of the partisan camp. The little knife was to be used to make cuts on the trees to mark the trail. He didn't have a chance to do this, because he had met us and decided to stay with us in the forest. Mishke kept his word, and let him re–join the group.

It became clear to us that Mishke had not been loyal to Nikita. He had not admitted that he wasn't leading us to the Otriad. His plan was to create his own group. I also noted that he didn't have any desire to fight the Germans, but had some other plans. It happened that I accompanied Mishke on one of the scheduled *sovchozn* in the Audzer region. Alexeyev and Ivan Miliutin also came with us. At the entry to the *sovchoz* was a little bridge, a trap for the partisans. As soon as we passed over, we were fired on, and Ivan Miliutin was killed.

Next, I was with Kudreshov in a town on a scouting mission, and he drank too much *Samogen* [home–made brandy]. One of the peasants asked him, in my presence, when he was quite drunk, "Tell me, brother, who are you fighting against?" He answered, "I'm fighting against the Jews, the *Kolchoz'n*, and against Hitler". I didn't show my dismay at my 'comrade's' answer. But I planned to leave the camp soon.

When we returned to the camp, I mulled over several possibilities. Perhaps I should just shoot him in the head. But I didn't want to waste one of my cherished bullets. I had confidence in the Ukrainian, Dimke Atchminikov, that he was loyal to Nikita. So I suggested to him that we leave Kudreshov and go search for the *Otriad*. Dimke's wound was healing, and he was able to walk better. We were joined by Reuben and Kozotchin, and left Kudreshov, Alexeyev and the two women, to depart to the east. We came to the Kapuler region, crossed Lake Nieman, in the area of Piasetzna. We learned from some peasants that there was a partisan group led by Mayer Bazianka. We were resolved to join the *Otriad* and its leader, and intended only to join this group temporarily, just to get information on how to achieve our goal.

That night we were on the road used by the partisans. We had to be especially careful that our encounter with these local partisans should not be misunderstood, and that there must be no conflict between us. After all we didn't know the lingo of these unknown partisans.

We were in the Velyeshiner Forest, in the town of Velyeshin at night. We heard some wagons arriving. The speakers' voices sounded strange, so we hid. Otherwise the town was asleep and totally silent. At Dimke's order, we stopped the next wagon to pass, hoping that it was manned by partisans. Dimke went up to the wagon, which was indeed full of partisans. When they saw this strange armed man, they quickly dismounted. Dimke introduced himself and asked for their leader. The partisans surrounded him and ordered him to stand there and wait for the next wagon, carrying their leader, Orlov. When Orlov arrived, Dimke introduced himself again as a partisan in the *Otriad*, and that he was not alone.

We approached at Dimke's call. Orlov made sure there were no others, then ordered us to lay down our weapons in the wagon. Dimke refused his order, and we didn't want to give up our weapons. Orlov explained that they were going on a mission, and would have to send us back to camp along with two guards, and it would be impossible to let us go with our weapons. So reluctantly we handed over our bullets and grenades, but kept our rifles and revolvers. Orlov agreed to this, and sent us back on the wagon with the guards, to the Storitser Forest. Until morning we were under guard, and then Mayer Kapuste showed up–he was related to one of our men.

The Partisan Brigade Clashes With a German Group

Kapuste and Natchalnik listened to our story as we told them about our past, and our intention to find *Otriad*. They praised us for our loyalty to our commander. However they assured us that Nikita and his group had gone far past our area, so we were obliged to stay in this brigade. Moreover, the directive stated that any small disaffiliated groups would be considered bandits, and would be shot by the partisans. We were told that there were already a number of other partisans from Nikita's group, just like us. At the end he told the guards that we were free, and told the cook to feed us. We weren't too happy about being obliged to stay, but we didn't have the nerve to object.

Later, three group commanders appeared, accompanied by three former Nikita partisans. One of them was Dimke Baronov, well–known to me, and we were designated as *Otriadniks*. I was to be named Tshopiev, and Baronov (Dimke Avseinikov) was now named Fartchamyenka.

Liova Hilshtik, the Jewish commander, was the first one to organize the partisans in the Kapuler sector. He had no military background. He was middle–aged, born in Kapuler. Before the war he had been a lawyer working for the Kapuler administration in the office supervising cattle production. All the original *Otriad* members were Jewish, and they were called the *Yevrieski Otriad* [*Jewish Otriad*]. Later, from Zhukov's group, Hilshtik accepted all the Jews, including elders, women and children, that the other commanders had been unwilling to accept.

Dunaiev, a bona fide lieutenant, about 30, was clad like a cossack, and was thought to be one of the better commanders in the Otriad. My group commander was Zizhkov, and his superior was Roshkov, also a real lieutenant. He was dark, didn't speak Russian well and knew about Jewish history. He never identified as such, but it was assumed that he was Jewish.

As in the other *Otriads*, there was a scarcity of rifles. After a week in the Otriad I told my commander that we had once been in a town in Auzder sector, and a peasant had offered weapons to me that had been abandoned by the Red Army, and he had buried them. He was willing to show me that hidden place. Zizhkov told his commander Roshkov and Donievin, the top commander. I was assigned to get the weapons. I took off accompanied by a comrade, Bandarenka. Before sundown we were on the main road that led from Minsk to Slotzk. We were on the edge of the forest, and had to cross 200 meters of open field to reach the road. We decided to go for it and not wait until dark.

On the road were military and civilian vehicles, and peasants were working on the field. When there was a lull in the traffic, we dashed across the field to the road. While we were running we heard the sound of an approaching vehicle. We made it across and immediately hid under some shrubs. A truck came by and then halted. The driver, a German soldier, climbed out and lifted the hood of the truck, poked around a little, then returned to his truck, took out his rifle, and crept under the truck. In the truck cabin sat a second man, wearing an officer's cap, with white officer's epaulets and a revolver. He got out of the truck too, turned his shoulder away from us and peered at the woods on the other side of the road. I ran up to him, seized his revolver and shot him. The soldier got out from under the truck and pointed his rifle at me, but Bandarenka gunned him down, hitting him in the rear. He dropped his gun, and Banderenka quickly seized it. I retrieved the officer's ID and ordered the soldier to march into the woods. He held one hand over his rear which was running blood. He could gasp only–"Kaput, kaput?", and I told him "Nisht kaput", and prodded him with my gun to make him go faster.

The sound of traffic could be heard and that led the soldier to stop, saying he couldn't go any further, he was exhausted. I tore off some material from his shirt and stuffed it into his mouth, and bound his hands behind him. He was terrified. I would have shot him, but the sound of the gun would have betrayed us. Banderenka clobbered him several times from behind, and when he was dead we pulled off his boots. A fusillade came through the woods from the road, where we had left the truck and the dead officer.

Later, we got to the town, our destination, and were told by the peasant that some other partisans had come by after I had left, and he had offered them the guns. They dug them up and departed. And so we returned to our camp. The news had already spread about the killing of the Germans on the road, only they didn't know the identity of the responsible partisans. I produced our booty, with the officer's insignia, and Banderanka brought out the boots and the rifle, so that proved that we had been the ones who had killed the officer and later, the soldier in the woods.

The Relsen War [*Relsovaya Vaina*]

After this event, my esteem rose among the partisans and the commanders. They had confidence in me. I asked that several partisans should be assigned to me so that we could go search for weapons in an area leading to Holshan. This idea came from my hope that perhaps I could save some of my family, Velvel and Rachel Liand. They were already over 50. I imagined what sort of work they could do for Otriad. I tried to imagine my 16 year–old sister Frume–Shirele, who had stayed with my parents– she could be a partisan. I was not frightened by these fantasies. They might perish here, but better to die with a gun in your hands than to be deceived into mass butchery. I tried to imagine who of my friends in Olshan would decide to unite with me? What a dangerous fantasy! My hopes dissolved into nothing. Olshan was quite far away, and my notions were rejected.

We passed through the Alexandreva Forest, and on the Saturday of the October Revolution holiday, the entire brigade gathered in the Storitzer forest in 1942. The nearest towns were Storitze, Zapolye and Schwvidizi.

On November 7, 1942, German units attacked us with tanks, starting from Storitz. We carried our defenses to the edge of the woods and took up the battle.I was in the front line with Roshkov's unit. The chief commander of Otriad, Dunaiev, was with us. We took up our defense lines toward Schwidizi and Zapolye. We fended off the German infantry, so they attacked with tanks. Our artillery unit opposed them, and smashed the first tank which approached us. But we were too weak to withstand these forces, so we retreated. On the way, Dinaiev was killed. Zhukov took over the command but he was also killed later. We had lost Storitzer forest and retreated to the Veleshiner Forest.

I was transferred on staff of Otriad, as a scout. Captain Revens had commanded our unit. With 20 partisans we were sent on a month–long mission to the railroad sector, which ran from Stolbzi, Kuidenav into the woods not far from the Neyegorelya station. Our assignment: to paralyze the rail traffic in that region.

Under Revens' direction, we set up demolition points on the rail line, to blow up the transports off the tracks. Then we would shoot down the personnel with hand guns and grenades. That wasn't an easy job because the trains proceeded very carefully, and were followed by a fortified train which could unload a hail of bullets and mines in defense. We carried out this assignment well, with very few casualties.

At the same time, other partisan units destroyed and disabled the Mitkovich station in the Kapulye sector, under Roshkov's direction. I took part in many of these so–called *Relsolvaya Vaina* [Relson Wars], which consisted of tearing up the railroad ties. Each of us carried enough material to tear up 4 ties. Every attack by us on these tracks damaged dozens of kilometers of railroad, thus stopping the German military transport system. We also engaged in a two hour battle with the Germans in Audz, stayed until dawn and afterwards destroyed the Commissary and burned down some German facilities, all without any casualties.

In the Storeh Darogi sector, partisans under Vasil Ivanovitz, were unable to destroy the German police station. Then a group of 30 partisans under Roshkov combined with local partisans to demolish and drive off the police force. We knew that in the next town, two policemen were meeting their families. At night, we entered the town, along with an informant, a peasant who showed us where one of them lived. Roshkov and I entered the house, and warned the cop's wife and father that we intended to kill him, along with them, and burn down the house. The cop came up from the basement, surrendered to us and we shot him down. The second cop was also killed as he tried to escape.

In the nearby woods we encountered a car carrying two Jews from Slotzk, who were cutting wood for the Germans. When we attacked, the driver and two guards managed to drive off and escape. But we rescued the two Jews; Herschke Krevitski, and I can't recall the other's name. Both of them were accepted into our group.

Forced Mobilization, Connection of Volunteers and Propaganda Among Police

Mobilizations were organized by the partisans, to enlist the young men and women. If they refused, they were considered deserters, and were forced to leave home. We demanded that the people not be neutral, but to join our ranks. A secret propaganda war was also waged against the police and the Ukrainian battalions who served the Germans. White Russian girls who were in contact with them, were used by us to befriend some officers among the Ukrainian draftees, to induce them to break away from their service to the Germans.

The partisan groups had increased, so that some brigades were united under command of Kapusten. The combined unit was in contact with the White Russian staff of the partisan movement, headed by Kozlov, who was in the Lvov sector. There we had an airport, where Soviet planes brought us discarded weapons, medicines and propaganda. They also took away the severely wounded. Every unit had a radio and a transmitter, and also a small printing press, to publish a little news bulletin, *Krasni* Partisan. The latest news from the front was supplied by the Soviet Information Bureau and distributed to the civilian population.

Germans and Their Helpers. The Ukrainian–*Vulasavzes*, Captivity by Partisans

I was transferred to the observer staff of the brigade. There were six of us and we each had a horse. We were assigned to a specific sector, but stayed in contact with the other units. Whenever Germans or their Ukrainian allies were captured, after evaluation, they were always executed.

Whenever we led the German captives to the execution spot, they always asked for mercy. That's how the German 'heroes' begged for their lives. They claimed that Hitler and the SS were to blame, that they were just innocent farm boys, so young, with wife and child, and we should let them live. The Ukrainians were different. They didn't beg, they looked at death calmly. When one of them was shot, the next didn't say a word as he waited for his death.

In one of the towns we captured six German soldiers and an officer, who had come into town to get supplies. After they had dined on some roast chicken, they lay down to rest in a barn. We surrounded them and took them prisoner. None of the soldiers would answer our questions–they all deferred to their officer, only he could speak for them. And when we turned to the officer, he responded arrogantly, "Who was this army which had captured them?" He would speak only with a staff person. When he was told that we were partisans, he wasn't so arrogant. He knew just like the others what was going to happen.

In winter 1942, after two months as a scout for the Otriad under Zhukov, referred to earlier as the Jewish Otriad, I joined the staff of a brigade which was 50% Christian, under command of the Jewish commander Liova Hiltchik. Our assignment was to destroy a police station near the Orlikov Forest. The preparation for the attack was done by the Otriad scouts, two 17 year–old boys, Mischke and Chanon, both from Kapuler, and two local Russians, Barbarenka and Varoboy. The leader of the group was Petrotchenka, a Russian army man, who had escaped from a German prison camp. The overall operation was led by Captain Rebus–Kuriltchik, and I was his assistant.

There were supposed to be 50 policemen in the town, protected by bunkers and in trenches. During the freezing night, our scouts had spread out along the edge of the woods, not far from the town. Then we heard the sounds of artillery and gunfire. That meant that our scouts who had been sent in to find an informer, had been detected by the police. Captain Hiltchik was upset and began to curse.

Impatiently, we waited for a message from the town, to confirm that they had been observed on entering the town. The captain ordered me to go into the town to find an informer. My companion was the scout Voroboy. In our white hoods we ran across the snow, sliding and tumbling. Any minute I expected some gunfire, just like the first scouts had encountered. I thought that the Captain had made a foolish mistake, to send us in under fire, but *frikaz* [an order] was *frikaz*.

We approached the town and heard some suspicious movements on a peasant's hill. We neared and observed that the peasant was saddling a horse. We took him prisoner, and I asked him why he was saddling the horse and where was he going. He said he was wakened by the police, and, like all the others who had horses, he was ordered to bring his horse to the police station. It was evident that the police were in a hurry to get away. That was supported by the fact that we entered the town without any resistance.

Instead of taking along the peasant, I told our second scout, Voroboy, to rush back and inform the captain. I directed the peasant to take his saddled horse down to the street and leave it tied up there. I waited on the hill to see if any of the police would come out for the horse. From another height I saw a group departing and my peasant told me that they were heading for the police station on the other side of town. He also told me a few things about their defense positions.

Then Petrashenka arrived, and said that I shouldn't move until Voraboy got there with more forces. After they came, they were to surround the station. Petroshenka and I were to pursue the departing group while Voraboy stayed with the peasant. Unopposed we reached the police station. High mounds of earth dug from trenches were piled up around the structure. We watched the door to see if anyone would come out. When an armed policeman came out, Petroshenka shot him down. Then a hail of bullets descended on the police station.

We realized that these bullets were coming from our side. We entered the police bunkers, where we found abandoned police uniforms. When the shooting subsided, we heard some cries coming from the rear. Petroshenka recognized the voice of his scout Barbarenka, one of those who had been dispatched earlier to find an informant. In a room we found Barbarenka, tied up on the floor. He was confused, his hands and face were frozen because he had been kept out in the snow too long. He was changed, unrecognizable. One policeman lay there dead, the others had fled. We set fire to the police station and returned to camp, bearing Barbarenka.

More Battles With the Germans and the Struggle With Fatigue

In winter 1942, when we were being pursued by the SS and the regular German army, we were forced to leave the Kapuler region and move east. There we continued our partisan tactics and crippled the railroad system. However a sudden attack by our enemies resulted in big losses of our men and transport. A number of wounded partisans were left behind at a so-called hospital.

The brigade reached the left side of Lake Meritchanke, which had been on the Russo–Polish border in September 1939. We checked out the main town there, Krasno–Slobode; the German garrison and police had left, and were gone also from the surrounding area. We were ordered to return to the other side of the lake, to the places where we had already fought the Germans. Our assignment was to find out where the Germans were, and to unite with our partisan hospital. We left camp before dawn.

After the night frost, the swamp was frozen, and our boots broke through the thin ice. It took some time to get to the edge of the lake which had thawed. Aided by a leaky boat, we managed to get to the other side. There we found a farmhouse owned by a Pole whom I knew, who had served in Pilsudski's army.

We were wet and chilled, our hands and feet were numb. Inside the house, we warmed ourselves at the oven. The peasant pulled off our boots and rubbed our fingers. We 'danced' around until feeling returned to our toes. We didn't get all dried out but we changed our socks, and then continued our trip.

Around noon we realized that the Germans were no longer pursuing us, and had withdrawn to the other side of the rail line. We found the partisan hospital and informed the responsible comrades about the location of the brigade which they could join when possible. Then we returned to the farmhouse and paused, deliberating if we should try to get across the lake at night with the leaky boat. We decided to go on to another farmhouse, also owned by a Pole, about 2 km away. I had never been there before. Possibly there would be a boat there, but at least we could eat and get some honey, which was plentiful at that farm. Although we got food and honey, the farmer didn't have a boat after all.

We rushed to get back to the boat that we left behind. There it stood, full of water, just as we left it. We scooped out the water and gripping the boat on one side we swam behind it. But the water quickly leaked in from the other side, and by the time we got to the middle of the lake, the boat had filled and was sinking. Fedke yelled at me, "Swim for your life!" and he dived into the lake. The boat slowly settled down while I held on until the water was up to my neck. I was almost to the shore and I swam a few meters until I could grab some reeds protruding from the lake. It was harder for me to swim to the shore, than it was in the Olshan lake, from Moshevitz to Schneider's mill, less than half a kilometer. The wet furs, the bag of coal, the flask of honey had all sunk to the bottom. Fedke was in the lake somewhere, I could see his hat floating. He surfaced briefly, then submerged. I was sure he had drowned.

I finally reached the shore. Nearby I saw a stack of hay, bound with cords. I grabbed a strand of rope and with my last strength pulled myself up on the ground. Then I saw Fedke come to the surface of the water. I threw him a rope and despite my exhaustion, I finally managed to pull him out. He could barely stand. He held on to me, but we were unable to walk. We couldn't pull our legs out of the swamp, into which we sunk knee–deep. My hands and feet became numb. Looking at the pale face and blue lips of my friend, I felt that we were doomed. We hugged together to share some warmth. In the end, miraculously, we had been seen by our partisan comrades who had been observing the lake. They ran to our help and dragged us out of the swamp. More comrades came and carried us back to camp.

Fedka needed immediate treatment. He was already unconscious. I was rubbed, my legs were massaged. I was dressed in dry clothes, wrapped in furs, and I recovered. Fedka suffered severe frost–bite injuries.

At the order of the White Russian wing of the partisan movement, Roshkov was transferred from his rank as brigade commissar, to a staff position, and he asked me to come with him. When the commander of the brigade, Shestapolov, informed me, he added that if a company leader was needed, that Roshkov should send me back.

Roshkov's aide saddled his horse 'Gniad', and I saddled my 'Strelka' and we were on our way, about 150–200 km. We had two difficult places to traverse, the Moscow–Warsaw highway, and the railroad line. We made it to staff headquarters in several days. After Roshkov got his orders, he was sent as commissar to one of the local Otriads, a small one, in which some men didn't even have rifles. Roshkov introduced me as one of his most capable and heroic 'rozviedtchikes'" (scouts). I wasn't really interested in his words of praise for me, I longed to return to Kapuler, to my brigade, which was very near and dear to me.

In a certain part of the Lyubaner–Kapatkevitzer sector, the Germans maintained their police, supported by soldiers, and they knew about the augmented partisan groups. At night they would keep watch on the places where the partisans were active. My local contacts were very helpful though it was dangerous to enter or leave the town or farm. They would inform me with certain signals, for example, opening one or both gates to the stable, adding or moving a scythe, and various other changes that could be seen from a distance.

Under Roshkov's command, the Otriad carried out important assignments, such as attacks on the German bunkers, grenade assaults, cutting wires and cables that served communications along the road, attacks on the 'somatchaves', the White Russian police stations.

Epidemics Among The Partisans

In winter 1943, the front came closer. Large units of the German regular army attacked us, and partisan resistance weakened. The Germans occupied the towns and the woods and slaughtered all those locals who were unable to hide in the forest. After killing the old men and women and the little children, the Germans took their cows and burned their houses.

The small number of locals who had survived with their families deep in the forest, were overcome by hunger and cold, and an epidemic of typhus and lice ensued, which spread to the partisans. Very little medical help was available, even for those wounded by the German mines. I'll never forget the screams of my comrade 'rozviedtchik' Michael, about 30. He had stepped on a mine, and part of his foot was torn off. He contracted blood poisoning and our doctor performed an above–the–knee amputation, using an ordinary wood saw. Michael was unable to tolerate this and he died. I remember another case of an 18 year–old partisan who had the same injury and surgery and he survived.

We didn't lose a lot of men, but our communications system was disrupted by losses of horses and wagons. My 'Strelke' was wounded, but I wasn't able to part with her. In spite of all, the Otriad survived in the forest, and I went on foot. Soon I became ill and the doctor was certain that I had contracted typhus. I was taken to an isolation ward in a town about 15 km distant from the camp. I took my weapons and my 'Strelke', special permission of Roshkov.

The town was crowded with typhus patients. Every Otriad had specific people assigned to take care of their sick partisans, who were stationed in various houses in the town. They were on guard against any attack, ready to evacuate. After two days in bed in the well–heated room, together with very sick patients with high fever and delirium, I began to doubt whether I really had typhus. I began to press for my discharge, but the doctor convinced me that I really had typhus, only a less severe form. I was transferred to a different house, where patients had already passed through their crisis, and in a few days I was discharged.

I met other partisans and learned that the Starobiner sector was nearby, commanded by Kuriltchik. I decided to visit him in order to return to the Otriad. On the way back, I encountered Roshkov. He told me that a change in staff resulted in his appointment as commissar of the brigade in Mizrach–Palesieh, on the other side of the Liuban sector. And he wanted me to go with him.

20,000 Partisans Surrounded By 60,000 Germans

After two days travel, we reached our destination in a town. After eating, I joined the rozviedtchik unit, whom I had never met. Weary, I went to sleep. I was awakened before dawn by the alarm bells, set off by a German attack. They had captured the outpost and gunned down the partisans who had been trying to escape into the forest. This was the start of the great German blockade of the partisan region which lasted for a month.

This was a battle between the regular German army of 60,000 and the partisan brigades, about 20,000, who were squeezed into one area by the Germans. Our area was the Palesyer swamp; it was closed off on two sides by the deep broad canals, dug out before the war in order to dry the swamp. On the other side of the canals, the Germans prevented any escape by the partisans. The third and only free side was heavily guarded. The Germans attacked us on the fourth side, confining us to the canals. Up until the encirclement, the brigades carried out their missions as collective actions. Now, after the blockade, each unit pursued its own goal of breaking through.

At night, Soviet planes would drop off sacks of supplies and first–aid equipment, but unfortunately most of it was captured by the Germans. Our foes advanced on the surrounded partisans and secured the high points which were dry. They lit fires in the night. The Soviet flyers thought these were fires set by partisans, and dropped their packages there. We however were trapped in the swamps, and were unable to light any fires.

Occasionally we would retrieve a Soviet package from the swamp during the night. At dawn German planes attacked us with grenade launchers and gunfire, and with propaganda telling us to surrender, before it was too late, to avoid certain death, etc. We used these papers to dry berries and tree leaves before smoking them.

The Germans flew missions over the swamp, which was still frozen in spring 1944, despite the bright sunny days. In small groups we hid in the tall grasses and avoided any conflict, hoping we wouldn't be uncovered. However, in one contact with the Germans, we opened fire at the last second, and inflicted losses. The panicked Germans fled, leaving their dead behind. We ran in the opposite direction and again hid in the tall grass until night, and again avoided the encirclement.

After these battles, we lost Roshkov. He had sent me to take a message to our commander, and when I returned, he was gone. His body was never found among the dead. Our transport and horses had been captured by the Germans. After the loss of Roshkov, I succeeded in getting out of our trap with another group. After a few days trekking through the forests and swamps, we came to the Stare–Dorogi region. In a foray into a nearby town I met three partisans from the Svorov brigade; their commander was Ivan Vasilievitz, who knew me.

I asked about some of my comrades, and decided that I would go with them to the Svorov brigade. I knew the road well on the way to the Kapuler area. I also knew that my leaving my last commander without permission, was a capital crime. However I didn't feel committed to that unit, since I was only Roshkov's messenger. My rifle and I belonged to the Tchopoyev brigade where my services would again be used.

That night we arrived at the Slutzker sector, where the Svorov brigade was camped. Several days later, a messenger came from staff and I went with him to meet with the commander Ivan Vasilievitz. I told him about Roshkov's fate, and the events in the area where I had been. Also, I told him of my hope to return to the Tchopoyev brigade in Kapuler, and asked for permission to go alone.

Though the commander knew that I was familiar with the partisan trails to the Kapuler region, he advised me not to go alone. He proposed that I stay here until either a messenger came here from Kapuler, or one was sent there from here, whom I could accompany. Meantime, I would be appointed to the rozviedke staff and would be assigned a horse and saddle. I was well acquainted with that brigade which had been one of the first in the partisan struggle. I often went scouting with Ivan Vasilievitz and met up with the otriads in the forest.

The Return From The Dead By Roshkov and the Fates of Jewish Partisans

A few weeks went by and then one evening at sunset I was summoned by the Rozviedke commander. When I arrived at his tent, I was met by three unfamiliar partisans, who were standing there expectantly. The commander informed me, "Roshkov lives! These comrades come from his group." I was left astounded and speechless.

I finally stammered, "That's impossible. Are you saying that I had deceived you?"

He interrupted, "That's possible. Roshkov has asked that you return together with these comrades. "*Yasno*?" With my head lowered, I answered, "*Yasno!*"

The three partisans shook hands with the commander and so did I.

One of the partisans was a commander Vuvoda, whose camp was near the Svorov brigade. On the road, I sensed that he didn't regard me as a criminal. I asked him to tell me how Roshkov had survived. He didn't know him personally and had not seen the new commissar Roshkov. But it was well–known that Roshkov had been lost during the encirclement and had disappeared. Apparently he had been saved by a peasant who found him lying unconscious in the swamp. He brought him home, and after he regained consciousness, he re–joined the brigade. He seemed healthy to the other two who had seen him the night before. These two were to return tomorrow, along with you, he added.

It was already dark when we arrived at Loshtshina, which used to be a big partisan camp. I crawled into an empty tent, but couldn't sleep all night. Should I let myself be taken to Roshkov against my will, or should I flee, to the Tchopiev brigade in Kapuler?

In truth, I was glad that he was alive, but I couldn't understand why he was so intent on my return, why was I that important to him? It occurred to me that possibly he needed me as a symbolic victim, to enforce more discipline in the group, as he did once before in the forest when he executed the Jewish partisan Grishke Krevitzki from Slutzk. He was not even an anti–Semite; even the Jewish commander Israel Lapides had shot a Jewish partisan, Michael Baronov from Minsk. Not to speak of the anti–Semitic commander Anantchenka, who shot the Jewish partisan Parsesaski because he was Jewish. It was rumored that Anantchenka had wanted his weapon.

I didn't know what the brigade commander had in mind, his attitude towards Jews was unclear. I didn't recognize a single Jew in this partisan group. I knew only that Roshkov was a cultured man, a doctor from Storeh–Darogi. I agonized about my fate during this sleepless night, and finally decided that I wouldn't go back with them. I thought that I could take off at any convenient point along the way. I worried also that they might have been ordered to disarm me, and I wouldn't have any way to resist them.

At dawn, I left the camp, taking the road towards Kapuler, using the partisan trails and supply points which were well–known to me. When I reached the Ouzder region, on the Slotzk–Minsk road, I encountered heavy traffic. I waited until night, and then by the next day I reached the Tchopiev brigade in the Velishiner Forest. The Otriad here was named 'Dunayeva' in honor of a dead commander. The leader was my first commander Vuvada Zizshov. He greeted me cordially and proposed that I stay with him, and he assured me that he would discuss my situation with his superior Shestapolov. I didn't agree, and let him know that I had to see the commander right away because of my history.

Along with Zizshov, I rode my horse to staff headquarters, not far from the otriad. Shestapolov greeted me with a smile, and asked me about Roshkov. I told him everything I knew, i.e. that Roshkov had arisen from the dead, and had ordered me to return to his brigade. The commander questioned me closely about the circumstances of the encirclement, then slapped my shoulder and called out. "*Provilna zdielal*" [well–done!].

Tzishov then requested from Shestapolov that I be allowed to remain in his otriad. "He'll stay on staff here and we'll see later," he responded to Tzishov, who then rode back to his otriad. A few hours later, scouts reported hearing artillery fire on the other side of the Slotzk–Minsk road. Since I had just come from that region, Shestapolov asked me what I thought was going on. I told him that two days ago, while I was at the Svorov brigade, they were getting ready to attack one of the 'sovtchozn' in order to capture the cattle that had been collected there by the Germans. Again I saddled my horse, again the 'rozviedke', the reunion and the thirst for victory, *nkoma*.

Like most partisans, I could not imagine the historic day of the partisan parade in July 1944, when the tortured city of Minsk was liberated. Sovtchoz was the site of a battle with the German forces. Shestapolov decided to join in and support the embattled partisans, so I became his assistant. We galloped off together to the new battle position. We met up with the commander of the Svorov brigade, Ivan Vasilievitz, and the commanders conferred. After, Shestapolov and I returned to our camp which now occupied a favorable position for the battle. We awaited the onslaught of the Germans, but they decided to avoid the conflict. So the fighting subsided as the Red Army began to advance toward us. The Germans retreated under the mounting threat of increasing partisan attacks. At our camp we could hear the sounds of heavy artillery.

ШТАБ
Партизанской бригады
имени Чапаева № 27
„*16*" июля 1944 г.

№ *35*

УДОСТОВЕРЕНИЕ

Настоящее дано ___*партизану*___ *Лиондову Роману Вульфовичу*

в том, что он с „*15*" ___*апреля*___ 194*2* года по „*16*" июля 1944 года

проходит службу в должности ___*разведчика*___

___*штаба партизанской*___

Бригады имени Чапаева № 27.

Представлен к награде: _____

_____

Что и удостоверяется:

„*2*" июля 1944 г.

Командир бригады   Комиссар бригады
имени Чапаева   имени Чапаева

Майор   (Шестопалов)   Бат. комиссар   (Емельянов)

Нач. штаба бригады
имени Чапаева

Лейтенант   (Рогожников)

Id

Liberation and Back to Olshan

In July 1944, after major battles, the Red Army had driven the Germans out of Minsk. All partisans were assembled in the liberated city. After the grand parade, accompanied by speeches about the heroic fighters and the party symbols, the forest brigades were mustered out. Half the brigade, including me, was immediately inducted into the Red Army. Many of these were former police, White Russians and other ethnic groups who had initially worked for the Germans and had later joined the partisan ranks. The other half was composed of Soviet personnel who had been sent to special schools for indoctrination and leadership.

I was confirmed as an inspector,"*sliedovatel*" for the Kapuler district. I was immediately intent on being allowed to go to Olshan to find out what happened to my family; permission was given. When I arrived in my home town, the huge transformation was obvious. With deep sorrow I learned about the terrible fates of my loved ones. My father Velvel and mother Rachel, together with the rest of the Jews of Olshan, Smorgen and Kreve, had all perished in Zielanka. My sister Frume had miraculously survived and now lives in Israel. After a short stay in Olshan and Oshman, I emigrated to Israel.

[Page 365]

Final Words

In concluding this Yizkor book about Olshan, certainly we have not completed the description of our vanished shtetl, where our parents, grandparents and great grandparents were rooted for centuries. Unfortunately, the greatest intellectuals of our town who would have been able to re-create the historic foundations of Olshan, are gone.

Nevertheless, blessed is that handful of dedicated Jews who have taken on this duty of describing whatever they remembered before the Holocaust, and what they themselves experienced during the Holocaust, thus creating a memorial for the remembrance of these tortured Jews of Olshan.

The most important parts of the Yizkor Book are the chapters about the fate and suffering, the sea of blood and tears. Blessed are they who were so dedicated to inscribe the days of horror and darkness, which we must never forget to our last breath. And do not forget the German Nazi murderers and their accomplices, the enemies of our people who spilled so much of our blood.

We express our deepest thanks to the Olshaners in Israel and America who provided the means and support for the publication of this book. Special thanks to our friends in America, Moshe Baron and Yakov Kaplan, who raised most of the financial support.

Special thanks and acknowledgement to our dear Shepsel Kaplan, who initiated this good deed. With persistence and patience despite his age, he took on this holy work, dedicating his energy and time so that this memorial to Olshan should be as beautiful as possible. Thanks also to our compatriot Meir Shli (Zeidl Bagdanovski) who edited the Hebrew part of this book, and who collaborated in this difficult task.

At the Annual Memorial in 1964
Upper- Jews from Olshan and Kreve at the annual memorial for the victims (Tel Aviv 1964)

At the Meeting

In Memory

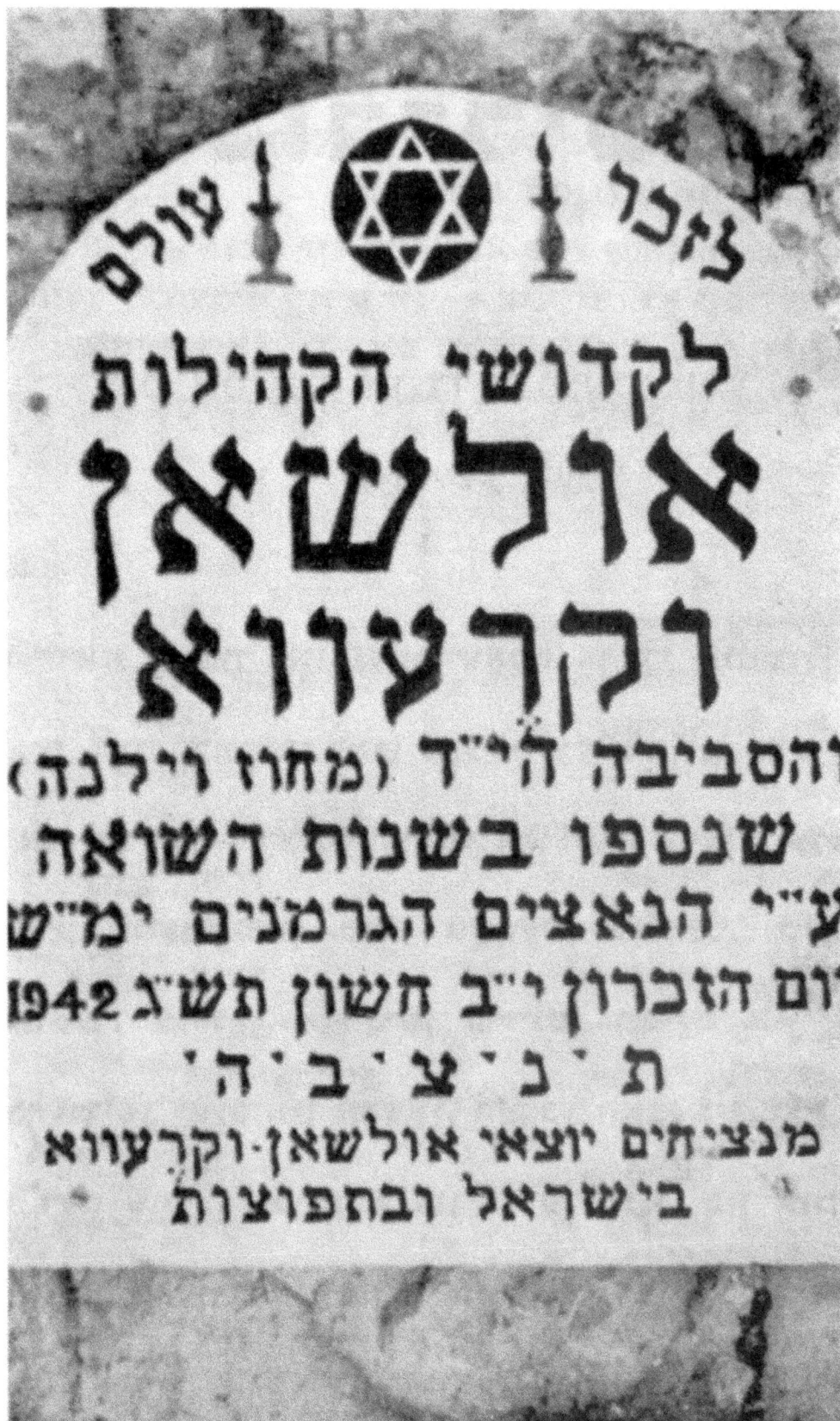

לזכר עולם

לקדושי הקהילות

אולשאן

וקרעווא

והסביבה הי״ד (מחוז וילנה)

שנספו בשנות השואה

ע״י הנאצים הגרמנים ימ״ש

יום הזכרון י״ב חשון תש״ג 1942

ת׳ נ׳ צ׳ ב׳ י׳ ה׳

מנציחים יוצאי אולשאן וקרעווא

בישראל ובחפוצות

Translation of the Plaque on previous page:

Eternal Memorial

To sanctify the victims of Olshan and Kreve
and other regions near Vilna.
They died in the Holocaust inflicted by
the Nazis after 1942

By the survivors of Olshan and Kreve
in Israel , and their families.

[Page 372]

MEMORIAL LIGHT

IN MEMORY OF THOSE KILLED
BY THE NAZIS

With honor and loyalty to the innocent victims
with deep sorrow for their suffering and pain
we will always remember our dear fathers, mothers,
children, sisters, brothers, relatives, friends,
comrades and all the Jewish community of Olshan
who were all part of the terrible fate of the
millions of our people who were murdered
at the hands of the German enemies and their
allies in **1941-1945.**

ETERNAL HONOR TO THEIR MEMORY

[Page 373]

VICTIMS OF THE HOLOCAUST IN OLSHAN

The organization of the Olshaners now in Israel has produced a list of all the victims.

The magnitude of the disaster is so great and the remains so limited, that it was impossible to note the full names of all of the victims.

Below we list the partial list of Olshan victims

A	B
Abramovitz, Bruch	Boyarski, Shmuel
Dinah (wife)	Chatye (wife)
Avroshe (son)	Israel (son)
Zeidl (son)	Baron, Shepsel
Rivka (daughter)	Dreisel (wife)
Abramovitz, Shepsel	Pesach (son)
Gutl (wife)	Zviah (daughter)
Gershon (son)	Baron, Psiah
Isaac (son)	Barman, Yosef
Shkop)Bruch (nephew)	Leah (wife)
Abramovitz, Michal	Tzipa (daughter)
Sheyna (wife)	Sheina-Beila (daughter)
Avrohom (son)	Letia (daughter)
Abramovitz, Edel	Aaron-David (son)
Mayer (son)	Zelig (son)
Abramovitz, Itkeh	Lazer (son)
Abramovitz, Shmerl	Benkel, Moshe
Avseyovitz, Shchina	Devorah (wife)
Sheina (wife)	Etel (daughter)
Milcha (daughter)	Berkman, Leah
Hirshel (son)	Reuben (son)
Aitzkovitz, Chaim	Berkman, Bluma
Pesyeh (wife)	Brudna, Leah
Leah (daughter)	Yudel (son)
Mayer (son)	
Afroimovitz, Afrim	
Arkin, Feigl	

[Page 374]

G

Golferin, Liebe
       Teibe (wife)
       Israel (son)
Golferin, Beniamin
Goldanski, Reizl
Golub, Moshe
Gurvitz, Bruch-Hirsh
       Reuben (son)
       Miriam (daughter)
       Feige (daughter)
Gurvitz, Shmeun
       Shulamit (daughter)
       Reuben (son)
Gurvitz, Abe
       Chana-Minye (wife)
       Meita (daughter)
Gurvitz, Shmeyehu
       Chaya (wife)
       David (son)
       Peretz (son)
Gurvitz, Chaim
       Tzipe (wife)
       Sheina-Beila (daughter)
       Israel (son)
       Shmeun (son)
Gurvitz, Beryl
       Feigl (daughter)
       Moshe (son)
       (son)
Gurvitz, Moshe
       Leib (son)
Gurvitz, Leib
       Asher (son)
       Basye-Ita (daughter)
Gurvitz, Dreisl
Grodner, Jacob
       Devorah (wife)
Gelgor, Joshua, Rabbi

Gershonovitz, Ben-Zion
       Henye (wife)
       (Trobski) Chana (daughter)
Gershonovitz, Motl
       Hershl (son)
Gershonovitz, Mariasha
       Breina (daughter)
       Chana (daughter)
       Gershonovitz, Shmuel

D

Don, Avrosha
       Shira-Ester (wife)
       Chaya-Sara (daughter)
Dolinski, Shmuel-Leib
       Tcherna (wife)
       Shepsel (son)
       Beniamin (son)
       Motl (son)
       Noah (son)

V

Voronovski, Reuben
       Chaim (son)
Voronovski, Hirshl
       Golde-Teibe (wife)
       Avrohom Shlomo (son)
       Aaron (son)
Veiner, Ester-Iteh
       Pesye (daughter)
       Chaya (daughter)
Viniski, Shmuel-Isaac
       Tzirl (son)
       Naftali (son
       Israel (son)
       Sara (daughter)

Z
Zusmanovitz, Freda-Gutl

[Page 375]

Zusmanovitz, Zundel
Zusmanovitz, Mariasha
Ziskand, Shmuel-Leib
  Shfira (wife)
  Saul (son)
Ziskand, Rivorah
  Nachoma (daughter)
Ziskand, Joshua
  Keila (wife)
  Binieh (daughter)
  Jacob (son)
  Beniamin (son)
Ziskand, Shmuel
  Chaya (wife)
Ziskand, Pinchas
  Leah (wife)
Ziskand, Avrohom-Shmuel
  Sara-Rivka (wife)
  Reizl (daughter)

Ch

Chodesh, Reuben, Rabbi
  Chaikha (wife)
  Avigdor (son)
  Mileh (daughter)
  Hadassah (daughter)
Chodesh, Feige
  Sara (daughter)
  Masheh-Chaya (daughter)
Chodesh, Perl
  Miriam (daughter)

T

Trobski, Reina-Beileh
Trobski, Fradl
  Ben-Ziion (son)
  Israel (son)
Trobski, Bas-Shiva (daughter)
Trobski, Ester
  Asher (son)
  Jacob (son)

Trobski, Fruma-Tzirl
Trobski, Ben-Zion
  Jacob (son)
  Devorah (daughter)
Trobski, Temeh
Trobski, Avrohom
  Perl (wife)
Trobski, Shmuel
  Reizl (wife)
  Sara (daughter)
  Reuben (son)
Tcheperinski, Aaron
  Teibl (wife)
  Isaac-Moshe (son)
Tchepelinski, Velvel
Tcherniovski, Chaim-Leib
  Temeh (wife)
  Velvel (son)
  Chana-Rachel (dtr)
Tcherniovski, Yudel
  Hallel (son)

Y

Yolk, Rachl
Yolk, Zusieh
  Sasha (wife)
  Alter (son)
  Blume-Leah (daughter)
Yudson, Shlomo
  Chasyeh (wife)
  Chaya (daughter)
  Sara (daughter)
Yirish, Isaac
  Sheina-Blumeh (wife)
  Chaya-Rachl (daughter)

[Page 376]

K

Katz, Reichl
    Chaya (daughter)
Katz, Shimon
    Malcha (wife)

L

Liand, Peretz
    Feigl (wife)
Liand, Velvel
    Rachl (wife)
Lieb, Isaac
    Tzipa (wife)
    Peretz (son)
    Shimon (son)
    Elihu (son)
Lidski, Elikim
    Liebe (wife)
    Chaya-Genesye (daughter)
    Sara-Simeh (daughter)
    Isaac (son)
Limon, Asher
    Shlomo (son)
Lapidus, Ben-Zion (children)
Lapidus, Isaac (children)
Leibman, Elihu
    Alte (wife)
Leibman, Lazar-Yudel
    Sarah (wife)
    Rivka (daughter)
    Motl (son)
Leibman, Shaia
    Chana-Leah (wife)
Leibman, Rivka-Leah
Leibman, Alte
Litkin, Peshe-Zloteh

    Simon-David (son)
Levin, Leib
    Chaya (wife)
    Moshe (son)

Levin, Dovroshe
    Leib (son)
Levin, Rachl
    Hirshl (son)
Levin, Hirshl
    Golya (wife)
    Leib (son)
    Elihu (son)
    Yirachmial (son)
    Sara-Rivka (daughter)
    Nchoma (daughter)
Levin, Jacob
    Bays-Shiva (wife)
    Leah (daughter)
Levin, Chana
Levin, Tzipeh
Levin, David
    Mariasha (wife)
Levin, Moshe (brother)
Levin, Hirshl (brother)

M

Mayerovitz, Chanon
    Leah (wife)
    Lazar-Pesah son)
    Shlomo (son)
    Shmuel (son)
Mutchnik, Dina
Milner, Ester-Iteh
    Israel (son)
Minyivitz, David
    Betya (wife)
    Chaya-Sara (daughter)
    Aaron (son)
    Yerachmiel (son)
Meltzer, Nachemiah
    Feigl (wife)
    Freda (daughter)
    Sarah (daughter)
    Samuel (son)

[Page 377]

Meltzer, Jacob
       Mayer (son)
Mirski, Pesach

S

Soloducha, Sarah-Iteh

Soloducha, Chanon
       Chaya-Sarah (wife)
       Zelda (daughter)
       Shmuel (son)
       Isaac (son)
Soloducha, Moshe
       Leah (wife)
       Etel (daughter)
       Yudl (son)
Soloducha, Reuben
       Liebe (wife)
       Chaya (daughter)
       Leah (daughter)
       Avrohom (son)
Soloducha, Jacob
       Michalya (wife)
       Isaac (son)

       Sonya (daughter)
Soloducha, Sarah-Milcha
       Miriam (daughter)
Soloducha, Liebeh-Yenteh
       Feiga-Reina (daughter)
Segalovitz, Kalman
       Roseh (wife)
       Masheh (daughter)
       Leah (sister)
Segalovitz, David
       Motl (son)
       Reuben (son)

Segalovitz, Bruch-Shmuel
Sfirah, Pesach
       Miryam (wife)
       Beryl (son)
       Yehudit (daughtrer)
Svirski, Chai
       Feigl (wife)
       Jacob-Leib(son)

E

Emilianer, Moshe
       Sarah (wife)
       Sheina-Beila (daughter)
       Miriam (daughter)

P

Pagoda, Gitl
       Sasha (daughter)
       Isaac (son)
       Joshua (son)
Pozniak, Shmuel
       Motl (son)
Potashnik, Avrohom-Elihu
       Chaya-Beile (wife)
Potashnik, Asher
       Chana-Sarah (wife)
       Yeshieyahu (son)
Potashnik, Reina
       Yoseph-Leib (son)
       Shulamit (daughter)
       Leah-Stirl (daughter)
       Avrohom-Moshe (son)
       Ester-Iteh (daughter)
Potashnik, Avrohom-Elihu
       Beryl (son)
Potashnik, Beryl
       Teibeh (wife)
       Leizer (son)
       Moshe (son)

[Page 378]

Peibushak, Malka
        Avrohom (son)
Pilnik, Goldeh
     Beryl (son)
     Don (son)
     Freida(daughter)
     Stesye (daughter)
Plotkin, Jacob
      Hodet (wife)
      Devorah (daughter)
      Sarah-Leah (daughter)
Plotkin, Banyeh
     Chaya-Sarah (wife)
     Leyser (son)
     Reshe (daughter)
     Hirshl (son)
Plotkin, Shmuel
      Devorah (wife)
      Bere-Leib (son)
Pertchik, Israel
     Risheh (wife)
     Avrohom (son)
Perski, Ziml
      Devorah (wife)
      Chaim (son)
      Avrohom-Isaac (son)
Press, Hertzl
     Chyena (wife)

K
Kagan, Beryl
      Pesyeh (wife)
      Elihu (son)
      Melekh (son)
      Chaya (daughter)
Kotler, Feiva-David
      Zelda (daughter)
Kominor, Motl
Kaplan, Mordechai-Mayor
      Chana Rachl (daughter)

Kaplan, Aaron
      Chasyeh (wife)
      Sarah-Hinde (daughter)
      Leib (son)
      Moshe (son)
Kaplan, Israel
      Zlote (wife)
      Aaron (son)
      Jacob (son)
      Devorah (daughter)
Kaplan, Moshe
      Chasye (wife)
      Maryashe (daughter)
Kaplan, Rachl-Leah
      Isaac (son)
      Pesach (son)
      Israel (son)
Kaplan, Binye
Kaplan, Sholom
      Golde (wife)
      Beile (daughter)
      Rivka (daughter)
Karbanovitz, Beryl
      Sarah (wife)
      Hirsh (brother)
Karpelevski, Isaac
      Liebe (wife)
Koslovski, Kreina
      Rivka (daughter)
Koslovski, Chana
Koslovski, Elihu
Koslovski, Isaac (brothers)

[Page 379]

Kozlovski, Yosef
    Ite (wife)
    Leib (son)
    Shmyah (son)
Kozlovski, Pinchas)
    Rachl (wife)
    Basya (daughter)
    Isaac (son)
    Fruma (daughter)
Kozlovski, Shimon
    Yare (mother)
    Beryl-Leib (son)
    Mayor (son)
Kozlovski, Shimon
    Rashe (wife)
    Beryl (son)
Kozlovski, Motl
    Chaim (son)
    Leib (son)
Kozlovski, David-Leib
    Moshe (son)
    Peshe (daughter)
Kozlovski, Shmuel
    Rachl (wife)
Kozlovski, Moshe
    Chanon (son)
    Feina-Dina (daughter)
    Ester-Chaya (daughter)
Kozlovski, Yekusial
    Feive (son)
    Genesye (daughter)
    Tzipa (sister)
Kozlovski, Note
    Basya (wife)
    Michle (daughter)
    Israel (son)
    Isaac (son)
Kozlovski, Milkha
Kozlovski, Rashe

Kozlovski, Beila
    Motl (son)
    Miriam (daughter)
Kozlovski, Shlomo
    Feiva (son)
    Avrohom (son)
Kozlovski, Shmuel-Hirsh
    Chasya (wife)
    Mates (son)
    Avrohom-Yosef (son)
    Sasha (daughter)
    Masha (daughter)
    Elke (daughter)
Kozlovski, Velvel
    Golde (wife)
    Feigl (daughter)
Kozlovski, Lipman
Kozlovski, Bruch-Yacov
    Chana-Tzipe (daughter)
    Feigl (daughter)
    Chasya-Rivka (daughter)
Kozlovski, Rivka-Yehudit
    Shimon (son)
Kosovski, Sarah-Ester

R

Rabinovitz, Mordechai
    Chaya-Liebe (wife)
    Joshua (son)
Rabinovitz, Israel
    Yacov 9son)
Rabinovitz, Pesach
    Beila (daughter)
Rabinovitz, Motl
    Chana (wife)
    Yuna (son)
    Devorah-Liebe (daughter)
    Chaya (daughter)
Rudnik, Joshua
    Frume (wife)

[Page 380]

Rudnik, Ben-Zion
    Sarah (wife)
    David (son)
Rudnik, Beniamin
    Berthe (wife)
    Chaya-Sarah (daughter)
Rudnik, Rachl
Rogovin, Motl
    Rachl (wife)
    Pesach (son)
    Moshe (son)
Rogovin, Frume
    Reuben (son)
    Elihu (son)
    Pesach (son)
Rozenzweig, Liza
    Chana (daughter)

Sh

Shafran, Sholom

Shuster, Mordechai-Note
    Rachl (wife)
    Elihu (son)
Shein, Liove
    Rachl (wife)
    Yentl (daughter)
    Yuna (son)
Shmukler, Shmuel-Elihu
    Chiyena (daughter)
    Tzivia (daughter)
Shmukler, Leah
Shneider, Aaron
    Baftshe (wife)
    Moshe (son)
    Leib (son)
Shneider, Sarah
Shneider, Shaul
    Feine-Basya (wife)
    Tilie (daughter)
Shklarevitch, Leib
    Mere (wife)
Shelubski, Elihu
    Nita (wife)

[Page 381]

Necrology

Translated by Sheldon Clare

[Page 382]

Blank

[Pages 383]

In Memory of My Little Son Mayerl-

That the Nazi murderers took away from me and murdered.

The lonely and remaining mother.

Sora Kozlovski-Baran

To the Eternal Memory

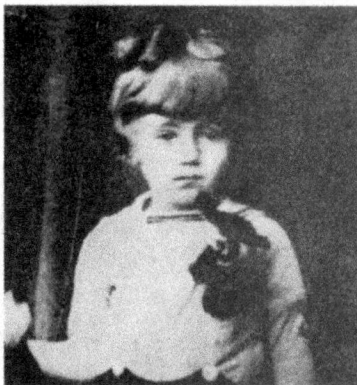

The innocent victims of the Nazi murderers. My niece Feygele

Daughter of Tzipe and Borukh
Yakav Kozlovski. Killed in the children's action in Kovno.

Yakov Kozlovski

To the illustrious memory

With great sorrow and pain in the heart,
I recall my unforgotten
Little daughter - Shulamit, little son - Reuven
(children of Esther and Shimon Gurvitz)
Who were killed during the Fascist children's assassination in Kovno.
I will eternally carry in my broken heart.

The mournful mother Esther

To the illustrious memory –

With great sorrow and pain in the heart,
I recall my unforgotten
Little daughter - Shulamit, little son - Reuven
(children of Esther and Shimon Gurvitz)
Who were killed during the Fascist children's assassination in Kovno.
I will eternally carry in my broken heart.

The mournful mother Esther

Instead of a Tombstone

On a grave that does not exist for my unforgotten little children –
Little son - Reuven,
Little daughters - Mirele and Feygele
(children of Hana and Borukh-Hirsh Gurvitz)
killed in the children's action in Kovno.

They will forever remain in my broken heart.

In grief - remaining mother Hana - From the house of Baran

Yizkor Light

We eternalize the memory of our dearest who were killed because of the Germans

Brother Yitzhok Yerush

his wife- Sheyne Blume,

their daughter - Hana-Rokhele

We will never forget you !

Binyomin Yerush and Hanniye Gurvitz (Israel)

Yizkor Light

On a grave that does not exist of my dear and close ones who were tortured by the Germans in the dark years of our peoples' calamity.

My father - Morkhe-Noson Shuster killed in (wailing??) (Estonia) 9/19/1944

My mother Rokhl shot in Zelianke, Spring 1943.

My brother Eliyahu killed in Panar (Vilna),

My sister - Bat Sheva and her little daughter Laleh killed in (wailing??) 9/19/1944,

My sister Miriam and brother-in-law Pesakh Sifia

with their little children Bereleh and Yehudis murdered in Volozhin slaughter in 1942.

I will forever remember you. In remaining sorrow.

Aharon Shuster and family

In Memory

With eternal sorrow, we recall our tortured brother and uncle

Sholem Kaplan

His wife Golde and their infants Beylke and Rivke

Shepsl, Rivke, Aharon

Instead of a Tombstone on a Grave That Does Not Exist

With loving sorrow and pain, I recall and will never forget

Bunyeh

My wife and mother of our two children

Killed on the threshold of freedom in the Kozkloverider Woods,

August 9, 1944

Shepsl, Rivke, Aharon

Yizkor Light

Our unforgotten dear parents
Mother

Gutl

Killed during the German assassination in Ponar (Vilna) in year 1942

Father

Shepsl

Killed by the Nazis in the annihilation camp in Estonia, end 1943

With great sorrow and reverential honor,
We will forever remember and carry in our broken hearts.

Rivke Shkof and family (America), Zeml Abramovitz and family (Israel)

Instead of a tombstone

Our unforgotten **2** year old little son

Borukh

Who was forever torn away from us and
Killed during the beastial children's murder in Vilna (H.K.F.) 3/27/1944

-He will constantly be with us.

In remaining sorrow

Rivkeh and Laveh Shkof

To the illustrious memory

Borukh Abramovitz
The first victim of the Nazis in Olshon
His wife
Dina
their children
Abrasha, Zeydl, Rivka, Dvora
With her husband Moshe Benkel and daughter Etel
All murdered by the Nazi beastiality.
Your images will constantly stand in front of our eyes
and we will carry you in our hearts.

The Family in Israel and America

As a memorial of my family

Murdered by the Nazi murderers in the Volozhin slaughter:

Father: Shmuel-Leyb Dolinski

Mother: Cherneh (From the house of Goldonski)

Brothers: Binyomin, Shepsl, Motl, Noak

Dr. Aron Dolinski (America)

In Memory

**With reverential honor,
We recall our unforgotten parents:**

Yona G'dalia

**And
Beyla Kozlovski**

Died with a "natural" death.

**Sister – Miriam
and
Brother - Motl
Murdered during the Nazi assassinations**

Eternal honor to their memory

Hana and Moshe Leyb

In Memory

Victorious Memories - We mourn our dearest who were murdered by the hands of the German assassins with their helpers.

Maltin and wife **Libe-Yente Solodukha** (1945)

Sister and daughter **Feygl** (1945)

Grandmother **Hana Kozlovski** (1943 Zhelianke)

Nateli Kozlovski (1944)

Batyeh Kozlovski (In Panar 1943)

Their children:

Yisrol and **Mikhle** (In Panar 1943)

Velvel and **Golde Kozlovski** (Gudegai 1943)

Their daughter **Feygl Mashe Solodukha** (1944)

Yaacov and Yitzhok Solodukha

In Memory of

I stress out my pain and sorrow for the killed, tortured, and dead.

Mother - **Esther** - Killed in Zhelianke

Father - **Mordkhe** - Died before the war

Sisters - **Shayne** and **B'tzlel Mintz**

Their children **Shimon** and **Binyomin**

Sister – **Eshke**

Aunt - **Fay Vushevitz** with a family from Oshmana

Killed by the Germans

Yokheved Gurfinkl (Abramovitz)

Yizkor

We remember our dear sainted family members:

My parents: **Asher** – died in Vilna

Marisha Gershovitz – murdered by the Nazis

My brother **Haim** – died in Golshany

My brother-in-law **Zelig Viner** – died in Israel

My sisters: **Bryna**

Esther-Ita (Viner)

Hannah Sarah (Baran)

My Brother-in-law: **Hershal (Zvi) Baran**

My sisters' daughters **Pessya** and **Haya Leah Viner**

Esther Baran

Murdered by the Nazis

Pessach Gershovitz and family

Yizkor

With reverence and pain

We remember our father

Shmuel-Elye Shmukler

Sister **Khiene Tzivieh**

Who were tortured by the beastial Germans

Honor their memory

Freyda Leyngfayn Shmukler, Ida Lipshitz Shmukler

Yizkor

We remember our dear sainted family members

Our Parents:

Yaacov and Bluma Barkman

Our Brothers and Sisters

Yitzhak, Feiga and Batya

Our sister's son

Yaakov Svirski

Sarah Barkman-Hertz
Miriam (Barkman) Kaplan
Israel Barkman

Yizkor

With eternal sorrow

I remember my husband

Shimon Gurvitz
died in Israel

Wife: Batya Gurvitz

To the Eternal Memory

My dear brother

Yisroel Trobski

**Student in the Faculty of Medicine in France
and tortured there by the Nazi murderers**

Shifra Katin-Trobski

Soul Light

To the memory of my unforgotten wife

Esther and our children **Osher** and **Yacov**

Killed by the Nazi murderers

**They were taken away Mar. 16, 1944 from the Folimon Camp near Kovno
And tortured by the beastial Nazis**

Eternal pain in heart for you.

Moshe Trobski (America)

To the Eternal Memory

With eternal pain

I recall my dear and nearest

Killed by the German murderers

Father - Eliakim Litski (1944)

Step-mother - Libeh Kozlovski (1945 in Shtuthof)

Brother - Yitzok (1944)

Sister - Simeh (1945 in Shtuthof)

Sister- Hayeh Keygen (murdered in the Kovno children's action)

Brother-in Law - Aryeh, (1941 in Oshmana)

Nephew - Shmuel (murdered in the Kovno children's action)

Honor to their memories!

Mina (Litski) Jalovski

To the Memory of Khayele Katz

Successful Educator at Olshan Kindergarten

Murdered in her "blossoming"

Organization - Yotzei Olshon B'Yisroel

To the Eternal Memory

My Parents

Bunyeh and Mikhal Yalk

Sister - Rokhl

I will never forget them

In sorrow, remain

Haya-Sorl Glukh Yalk

R' Mordkhe Leybman (May he rest in peace)

A working person

Led an honorable and just life, fulfilled the verse, "You earn your living with hard work"

Participated in all needs of the "shtetl"

Experienced the whole HELL

And with the last worn our strength saved himself from under the spikes of the Nazi beastiality.
After the liberation, went to America to be with close relatives

Died: 1st Tammuz 5723 (1963)

"May his memory live forever"

Khayim Yosef Leybman and family (America)

To holy Memory

My unforgotten parents:

Yehoshua and Fruma Rudnik

Tortured by the Germans

And my brother

Aharon
Who went through pain in the Jewish extermination and tragically murdered in Israel

Honor to their memory

In sorrow - Remaining ones - Soreh-Malke Rudnik

To the Memory

With grief and reverence

We will eternally remember our dear and loving

Mother – **Soreh**

Father - **Leyzer-Yudl**

Sister – **Rivks**

Brother – **Motl**

Who were murderously killed by the hands of the German assassins

In sorrow remaining ones

Tzipora Laybman (Vaytzman), Rokhl Laybman (Kromnitzer)

Yizkor Light

With grief and love

We recall the Family Varanovski

Who were divided by the frightening Fate of the Nazi Holocaust

Aunt - Golde-Taybe (Daughter of Yitzhok Kozlovski)

Uncle – Hirshe

Cousins - Avrohom-Shlomo and Aharon

Eternal honor to their memory

Haya-Grunyeh Katz Kzur, Frumeh Katz-Rotshteyn, Ziml Abramovitz

To Eternal Memory

For Our dear and unforgotten parent

Mother
Malke (From the house of Kozlovski)
Murdered during the 2nd action of the Oshmona Ghetto in Zelyanke
12th Heshvan 5703 (1942)

Uncle
Shimon Katz
Murdered in the Minsk Ghetto

We will always carry in our hearts the memory of them

Frume-Soreh Katz (Rotshteyn), Hana Grunyeh Katz (Kzurr)

Putschnik, Yosef

He suffered greatly in the ghettos and camps during the Nazi conquest. After liberation he came to Eretz-Yisrael in 1946. He had lost his parents, brother and other dear family members.

Unfortunately, his serene life with his wife and children did not last long. He was celebrating with his family when he fell ill and died on the way to the hospital. He was only 47 years old.

"Father, you are always with us. Your memory will not leave us."

Sons Elisha and Hanan and wife Ita

To dedicated Memory

With eternal sorrow

We remember our unforgettable nearest
who were murdered during the German assassination

Parents
Hanah Sarah and Osher Potashnik

Brother
Shayeh
Murdered in Dachau 21st Kislev 5705 (1944)
Brother

Berl, his wife Roshl, and son Khayim-Leyb

Brother
Sender
Murdered 2nd Av 5702 (1942) with two daughters

We will constantly carry them in our hearts

I. Leyb, Avrohm- Elyohu, Max, and the family in Israel and America

Yizkor

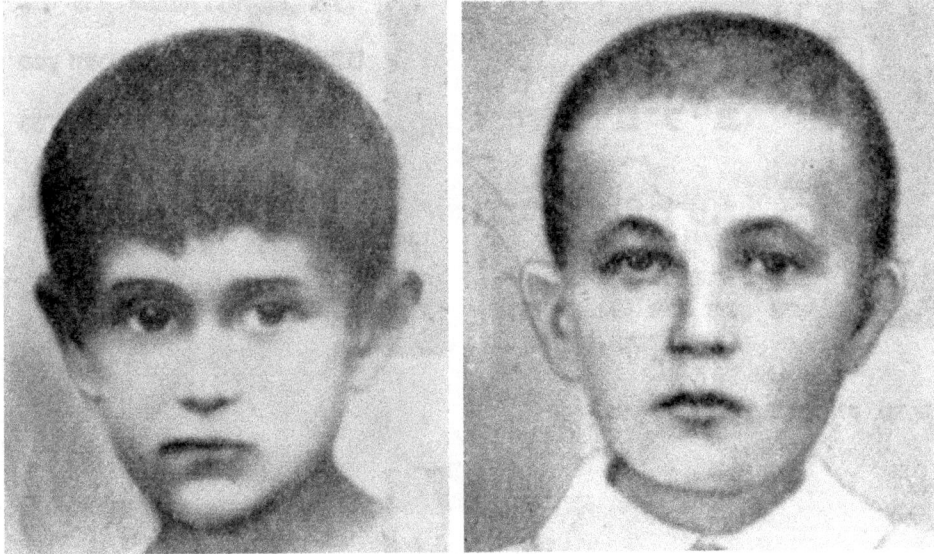

We mourn our dear two children, brother, and sister who we will never forget

Rivke Zusmonovitz, died at the age of 17 in Olshon in 1940

Marioshe Zusmonovitz, murdered in a children's action

Zundl Zusmonovitz, slaughtered in 1943 - Ponar, age 15

In sorrow, remaining mother Gitl, Brother – Yosef

Soul-Light (Candle)

We perpetuate the memory of our dear and unforgotten parents

Rokhl and Velvl Liand

**Who were murdered by the Germans
12th Heshvon 5703 (1942)
in the second action of the Oshman Ghetto in Zhelianke**

Honor to their memory Reuven, Shimon, Frumeh, Tziporeh

To the Memory

**For my grandfather
Aharon-Hirsh**

**Grandmother
Tzipeh**

**Mother
Sheyneh-Beyleh**

**Father
Fayveh-Dovid**

**Brother
Yisroel**

**Sister
Zelde**

Hayim and Tzipeh Gurvitz with their children.

Haneh Goldin-Kotler

To the Memory

With eternal love and sorrow

We remember

My Grandmother **Elke Kozlovski**
Murdered in the second action of the Oshmona Ghetto in Zelyankeh

My father - Elyahu-Yosef
Died in Olshon

My mother – Eydl
Died in Zelyankeh

My little brother Meyer
Murdered in the children's action in Kovno

In sorrow, remaining

Khayeh Altman (Abramovitz)

To the Memory

With heartfelt love

I recall my parents

Father - **Shmuel-Yitzhok Vininski**

Mother – Tzirl

Brothers - Naftali and Yisroel

Sister – Rokhl

Who were murdered during the Nazi murder in Auschwitz

Yehuda Vininski (Abishi)

To the Memory of My Wife

Kreyneh

and

Daughter Rivke

In Olshan, I lived with my family until 1938. In World War I, I was on the front in Galicia. Fell into captivity, suffered a lot of hardship, and returned home to the town of Olshon. The town was ruined. Life was not easy.

In 1938, I emigrated to America to be with my brother. I went through difficult times. But I found a way to bring the family to America. But to the great calamity, the war broke out in 1939, which brought the great catastrophe for us Jews. I read the newspaper and my pain was great. But I could do nothing to help.

My wife Kreyneh with the youngest daughter Rivke, were tortured by the murderous German hands, also my mother Elke. They were shot together with the elderly in the Zhelianke woods. A good-hearted woman was my mother Elke. She never said a bad word about people. Also my sisters Soreh-Malke and Eydl were murdered.

Pinkhas Kozlovski

Yizkor

Eternal honor to my dearest who were murdered together with the millions of our people.

Grandfather Leyzer Shindes
(the sexton of the old synagogue)

Grandmother – Esther

Uncle(and Aunt?) - Motal and Radl Gershenovitz

Niece (and husband?) - Sime and Meyer

Their children - Henye and Khaneleh

Nephew - Hirshl

Hayeh- Soreh Kozlovski (Shai)

Yizkor-Light

Our unforgotten son and brother
Moshe Rudnik who was tortured in the Nazi destruction camp of Estonia.

Honor to his memory.
The family in Israel

To the Holy Memory

My Father - Dovid-Leyb
Murdered in Zhelyanke

Mother - Miriam-Bashe - died before the war

Brothers - Yakav-Moshe
and
Shimon
His Wife- Rashe and son Berele
Murdered in different destruction camps

In sorrow, remaining

Chaya-Sarak Kozlovski (Sar)

To Holy memory

With deep sorrow and unforgotten grieving, I mention my dear parents and brothers who were murdered in agony and anguish by the bloody Nazi brutes.

My Father - **Aharon, son of Moshe Schneider**

My Mother - **Soreh-Leyeh**

My brother - **Leybe**
Murdered two days before freedom in Dachau Camp

My Brother **Moshe**
Who fell during battle against Nazi Germany
as a soldier in the Polish army in the woods of Piotrkov (1939)

Honor to their memory

Moshe Snyder and Btzalel Bergman (America)

To the memory

With sorrow and reverent honor

We recall our unforgotten

Brother
Shmuel, son of Pinkhas Ziskind

**Murdered 23rd Av 1929 during a robbery
on the way from Oshmona to Olshon**

Honor to his memory.

Esther, Henyeh, Dineh, Yitzhok, and Moshe

To the holy Memory

My brother

Shlomo, son of Avrohom

in Kloqe (Estonia). Murdered, Sept. 19, 1944.

Honor to his memory.

In sorrow, remaining brother

Yakov Kozlovski

Yizkor Light

I will never forget my unforgotten

Little children, Fayveh and Avrohom

(children of Henye and Shlomo Kozlovski)

Who were innocent victims of Nazi barbarism.

They will constantly remain in my broken heart

In sorrow, remaining mother.

Henyeh Kaganovich (From the house of Ziskond)

Yizkor light

For our unforgotten children and brothers

Eliyahu Kozlovski, Murdered on the threshold of liberation, age 21

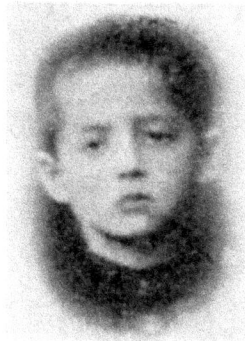

Yitzhok Kozlovski, 9 years old
Taken away from us during the children's-action in Koshintar

Moshe-Fayvl, Avrohom, Khasiye, and Yehude Kozlovski

Eternal Memory

With proud honor and sorrow

I remember my unforgettable parents

Shmuel and Khayeh Ziskand

Who were murdered by the hand of the German murderers

Eternal honor to their memory.

Abba Ziskand

To the holy memory

My father - **Lipeh Kozlovski**

Sister – **Dvoreh**

Brother-in-Law - **Shmuel Plotkin**

Nephew - **Berl-Leyb Plotkin**

All murdered during the German Extermination of Jews

Honor to their memory

Avrohom Kozlovski

Reyzele Ziskand

My girl friend Reyzl Ziskand was an only daughter of her parents Avrohom-Shmuel and Soreh-Riveh Ziskand.

Together, we played in the sand. Made "Kugelakh" and later "Bisn??". We grew up together. During my childhood and later, together we studied in Oshmona.

We lived in one room, shared the connection with her life, strolled together and found a common language. Life in that time was boring for the youth in the town Olshon. I went into their home, a pretty and well kept house, tidy in every corner. They ran a modest life.

They subsisted from their dry store. Reyzeh was a very unique child, took care "as an eye in the head". The savage German murderers killed Reyzele with her parents. The parents were murdered in the Oshmona Ghetto, Reyzele in Kovno Ghetto in July, 1944.

No sign remained of the family.

May my words be a memory for my friend Reyzele and her parents.

Shira Kutin (Trabski).

To the memory

**With love and honor
We will remember**

**Father and Grandfather
Leybe Kaplan**

Mother and Grandmother

Rivke Kaplan (Skloit)

Yitzhok, Yacov, Shepsl, Rivke, Aron

To the Memory

Rikha Abramovitz (Bogdonovski)

Died in America

Gershon

Son of Ziml Abramovitz

Died in Olshon

Their children, grandchildren, and family members in Israel and America

To the Memory

Our dear and unforgotten

Beyle and Fayveh Abramovitz (Abrams)
Emigrated from Olshon to America and died in "Friedland??" (America)

Honor their holy memory

The family in Israel and America

To the Memory

With eternal sorrow and pain
We remember our sister and aunt

Khaneh Fishkin (Kaplan)

Who was prematurely torn from us

We honor her memory

Shepsl Rivke, Aron

To the Memory

Our unforgotten husband and father

Yehuda (Yudl) Levin

Honorary president of the first Olshon Relief Committee in America

Died - Nov. 9, 1949

Honor to his memory

Mary Levin and family

Yizkor

Max Vishniak

With love and longing

I remember you

(Died Jan. 6, 1959)

Honor to his memory

Your wife
Frieda Vishniak
Los Angeles, America

Rabbi Reuben Katz

Born in Olshon 83 years ago

During his visit in Olshon, Reb Katz gratified the Olshoner countrymen with a "drosh" (Sermon), which was full of "intelligence" in "sharp sense" for small and big.

Rabbi Reuven Katz was the Rabbi and Yeshiva head in Petah-Tikva.

Until his last day, he did not stop learning during every free hour.

An author of books which were highly reviewed (judged) by rabbis.

Died in Petah-Tikva
Honor to his memory

Rabbi Reuven Khodosh

Rabbi Reuben Khodesh, son of our father, Rabbi Bruch Isaac from Mlandvruva, may he rest in peace. In his youth he studied in our cheder with all the boys from the village. He was alert and smart and beloved by all.

After cheder, father started teaching him Gomorrah at home. He was quick at understanding and remembering, and didn't need much repetition to learn the Gomorrah pages by heart. When father thought he wasn't paying attention, or thinking of his friends outside, he'd ask him to repeat, and then he could recite the whole chapter by heart.

Father recognized his talent and sent him to the yeshiva in Voloshin.

When WWI started, he and all the yeshiva students moved to Russia, and he lost touch at home. There was no contact for years. The atrocities of war and the pogroms in Russia, reinforced his religious belief. After the war, he returned as a handsome young man for a short time. Then he went to L'Kaletzk to study in the yeshiva there. There he met Deicha, daughter of Gavzi. They married, had a family, and he was appointed Rabbi in Bolshany.

He was beloved by all, and was loyal to his family, and the pride of his father.

The whole family was killed by the Nazis. Rabbi Khodesh and his son Avigdorwere tortured and murdered in Voloshin in 1942. His wife and daughter Mila died in a concentration camp in Estonia, and his five year old daughter Hadassah was killed on the way from Voloshin to Olshan.

Peace to their memory.

Ahuva and Gita, his sisters.

(this memorial was received too late to be included in the original text)

Fredl Bogdanovski

I remember you , in our youth, with your golden hair and blue eyes. I don't know where your grave is. I see you after Shabbes in the winter, in the only Jewish home in the village, with a thatched roof. The children stand next to each other, listening to their mother's song, "God of Abraham, Isaac and Jacob", and the voice of your father singing songs, next to the window. Your home was a half-hour from Olshan, on the way to Vilna. The house had its field, garden, animals, and people gathering fruit from the garden. Before holidays, everyone is working for the harvest. After Succoth comes autumn, winter, summer. The foods for winter-potatoes, carrots, beets, cabbage are kept in storage, to protect the family from hunger. Your father's sister needed care, for she was alone with her children, her husband was overseas. Her old father studied in the Bays Hamidrash. There were also an uncle and two children in the village, who study Chumash and Talmud with the father. The house was open for all, to rest or stay overnight, there was always space and no one lacked bread or wine. Your mother was a good woman, God-fearing, merciful, kind-that was her commandment from God; he made other commandments for the men. The door was open for neighbors to talk about their problems, to be consoled. The neighboring Christians got along well with them, brought items from the forest, branches, bread after Pesach. They kept watch during the High Holidays. The Jewish boys tried to teach the children the aleph, beys. The Jews seemed to be the center of the world. I remember your mother's relationship to animals, she gave them extras on holidays, spoke to them, they understood each other. To the cats, she'd say, "Don't fight! Drink your milk". She got angry at the pigs.

You created a special atmosphere for all, I remember how you at age 9, handled a 6 year old orphan with hard work and patience, you'd cry with frustration, and felt joy when she succeeded. Also, I recall the fear when the foreign peasants reached your door, when yours was the only Jewish home on the road. Your sister would help, and then sit alone and dream. Newer generations are different. I recall the goyishe holidays and processions, when we had to stay inside with the dog, and watched from the window. Also, when the young men were drafted and had to report to the city, and be separated from their families, they would get drunk, knowing that they'd be forgiven. Nothing could stop them from contacting the lone Jewish house on the way. Your sister comforted them.

In Memory of Reuben and Mordechai Segalovitz

He was from Oshman, 20 km from Olshan, and I knew him well. He spent every summer there and had many friends there, including Shia, Petchik, Hirshl and Sander Gurevitz, and the Dolinski family. He was a handsome man, outstanding and upright. He left for Israel in 1933, but came back in 1939, for a short visit. He saw the clouds gathering, but couldn't imagine what was going to happen. He loved the young people, the idealists, who joined the Khalutz. His brothers were very special for him. When I close my eyes, I can see his handsome face, and reflect on our loving friendship. He was a wonderful person.

Feigl (Trobski)

I remember you with love, and sadness, along with our mother, who was just like you. You are always in my heart and memory. I picture you at the ghetto gate, praying, terrified, waving your handkerchief, before you were killed with four children in your arms. Your father is here in Jerusalem, with good people from Kluge. Where shall I find your grave? I'd come if I knew where you were. Or your sisters? I am the only one saved, I'm an orphan, alone. You'd be a grandmother now. My daughter is now free. Our father went to the labor camp with me and our aunt and we were saved. I don't know how I survived. My daughters look like you.

Photographs of Olshany in 2016
Courtesy of Ilay Halpern

Former Jewish Homes on Castle Street

Execution site memorial, near Zhelanke, a death camp noted in the Yizkor book (pages 141 and 174). It is located approximately 10 kms northwest of Ashmiany.

On a hill overlooking the town

Headstone at the Jewish Cemetery

Headstone at the Jewish Cemetery

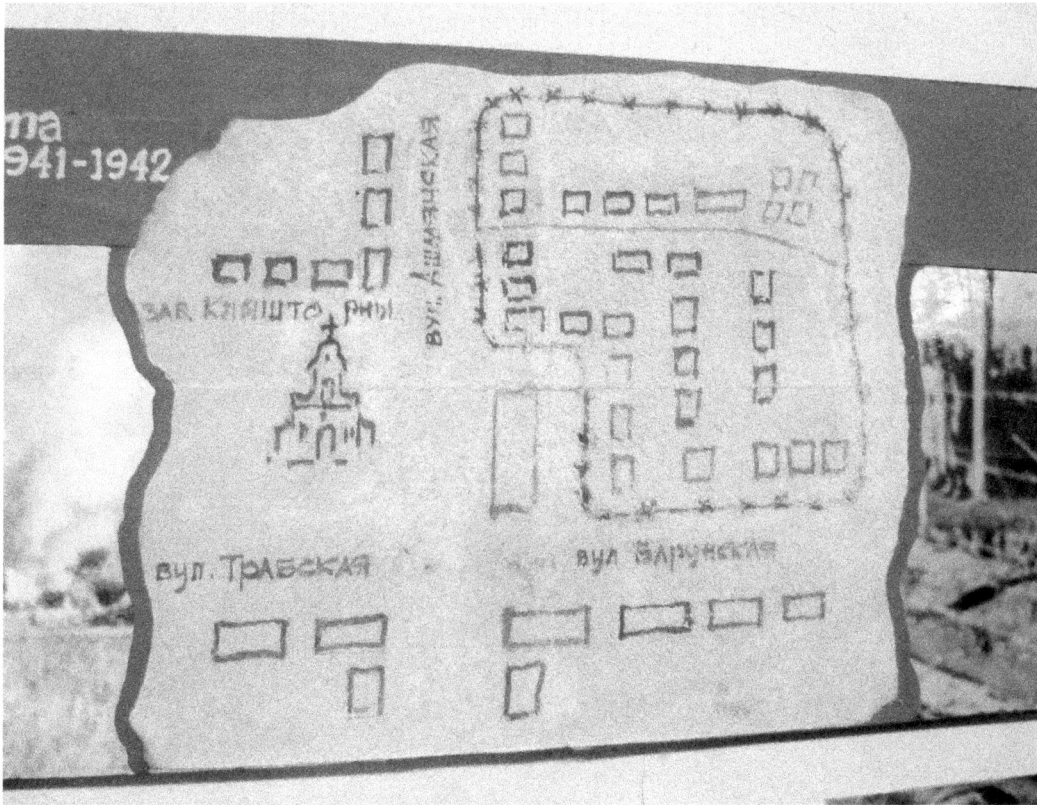

Map of the Ghetto

Outskirts of town

Old Watermill